M000117169

Wild Things

Wild Things

A TRANS-GLAM-PUNK-ROCK LOVE STORY

Lynette Reini-Grandell

MINNESOTA
HISTORICAL
SOCIETY PRESS

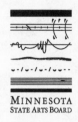

MINNESOTA
STATE ARTS BOARD

The publication of this book was supported by a generous grant
from the Elmer L. and Eleanor Andersen Publications Fund
and through a Minnesota State Arts Board Grant.

Text copyright © 2023 by Lynette Reini-Grandell. Other materials copyright © 2023 by the Minnesota Historical Society. All rights reserved. No part of this book may be used or reproduced in any manner whatsoever without written permission except in the case of brief quotations embodied in critical articles and reviews. For information, write to the Minnesota Historical Society Press, 345 Kellogg Blvd. W., St. Paul, MN 55102–1906.

Wild Thing
Words and Music by Chip Taylor
Copyright © 1965 EMI Blackwood Music Inc.
Copyright Renewed
All Rights Administered by Sony Music Publishing (US) LLC,
424 Church Street, Suite 1200, Nashville, TN 37219
International Copyright Secured. All Rights Reserved
Reprinted by Permission of Hal Leonard LLC

Unless otherwise noted, photographs are from the author's collection.

mnhspress.org

The Minnesota Historical Society Press is a member
of the Association of University Presses.

Manufactured in Canada.

10 9 8 7 6 5 4 3 2 1

∞ The paper used in this publication meets the minimum requirements of the American National Standard for Information Sciences—Permanence for Printed Library Materials, ANSI Z39.48–1984.

International Standard Book Number
ISBN: 978-1-68134-243-6 (hardcover)
ISBN: 978-1-68134-244-3 (e-book)

Library of Congress Control Number: 2022946844

This and other Minnesota Historical Society Press books
are available from popular e-book vendors.

Wild thing,
You make my heart sing.

—*Chip Taylor, channeled through Jimi Hendrix*

Contents

■✗▲✦❋■♠●✖

Author's Note

The person I married, who I am still married to and remain very much in love with, is now legally named Venus de Mars, and she uses *she* and *her* pronouns. But to get to that point was a journey of decades. At the time we didn't know where it would lead—we had no real role models and made it up as we went. Most of this story takes place at a time when the kind of knowledge and terminology we now have about being trans didn't exist. With Venus's blessing, I have used her old name and old pronouns where using them best depicts the reality of our lives at that time.

Our path was not smooth. We made mistakes, and sometimes we ended up fighting our way forward. By showing the shifts and stumbles we experienced during those years, I hope to communicate more clearly the terrain we traversed to discover ourselves. As Steve/Venus changed, so did I. And I am grateful for the changes this journey has forged in me.

Foreword

Venus de Mars

■×▴⋆✳■♠●■

I was a kid.

With a new tan-orange leather baseball mitt. And a ball. Which I threw into the air to catch. Over and over. Alone. Near the big eastern white pine that grew on the right of our front yard. In Duluth, Minnesota. That was when my sister, six years older than me, called from our porch and said it had started.

We all knew about it. The neighborhood kids. That's why I was out there alone. Everyone else was already inside tuned to the news. At 6:17 P.M., July 20, 1969.

Apollo 11, having circled a number of times already, was about to separate from the Lunar Module. The module, as we understood from news reports over the last few weeks, would then descend and land, and an astronaut would exit out a door, and step onto the moon.

For the first time. Ever.

And this all seemed normal to me.

Everything seemed possible.

Star Trek was in its third season by then. I had absorbed what seemed like a never-ending rotation of space adventures in cartoons, science fiction books, and late-afternoon television movies. Actual space flight seemed a completely expected occurrence to my nine-year-old mind. But I ran inside anyway to watch the grainy black-and-white footage as the whole event unfolded on our living room TV.

■■■

It wasn't normal. Of course. I came to understand this as I grew older. When I followed the near disaster of *Apollo 13* a year later. When I stood shocked, sixteen years later, in 1986, with everyone else at the T-shirt-printing warehouse where I worked and watched the replay footage of the *Challenger* explosion. On the boss's office TV.

I was twenty-six then. It would be two more years before I would come out to my spouse, Lynette, as a transgender individual.

The *Challenger* explosion ended NASA as we knew it. As it did our understanding of space. As it did about everything.

Nothing would ever be the same.

Something else occurred in 1969. When I was nine. Almost a month before the *Apollo 11* moon landing. The Stonewall riots happened. In New York. I recall my mom's reaction while listening to the radio in our kitchen. As news reports on those riots were presented. She wondered aloud why homosexuals in New York had to be so violent.

I didn't ask her about homosexuality.

The tree house my best friend Cory and I built in the wooded lot behind our house had graffiti all over it. The graffiti contained the painted words "Queer" and "Homo" along with additional words that suggested Cory and I were both these things.

When I saw the words, I turned to Cory and asked who might have done it. Cory didn't answer. Instead, he turned and walked quietly back to his house. Cory and I had been inseparable friends up to this point. For the rest of that summer, I hardly saw him.

■■■

I understood what the graffiti meant. In 1969. In fact, when I was four years old, in 1964, I understood I was different. But I didn't have the words. To understand. And the shame I felt after seeing that graffiti, and the shame I continued to revisit, for almost two decades, at each cruel occurrence, whenever any-one, who was different like me, was presented in the media, in the newspapers, in magazines, in TV shows, at the movies, that shame kept me closeted till I was twenty-eight. Till I had been married for five years. Till I had become suicidal. Till I knew that unless I began to untangle myself, my life would be over.

I was taught this shame.

And I still had no words.

In 1988.

Except the word transsexual. And the word transvestite. And maybe twenty or so other non-medical derogatory words used to describe anyone seen as either sexually or gender differ-ent. We were all taught, back then, to see this group of people, who I secretly understood myself to be a part of, as the same kind of people: Mentally ill. Deviant. Perverted.

■ ■

When I think about 1969, and the fearlessness of those astro-nauts, the fearlessness of the rioters at the Stonewall Inn, and the naivete of the rest of us, I realize no one had words to de-scribe our future. Let alone our present. We, those of us who felt stuck, or crushed, had only our blind courage. And a will-ingness to plunge forward into the unknown.

My spouse and I did just this. In 1988. With no knowledge. No guideposts. No language. Together and alone. We decided to remain married after I came out. We invented as we went. Improvised as the ground crew of *Apollo 13* did. We used what-ever we had at hand. We argued. We made mistakes. Hurt each other. Hurt ourselves. Misunderstood. Stumbled. Carved our own path forward. Step by step. Day by day. Month by month. We invented words where there were no words before. We in-vented concepts where there were none. We clumsily, but ul-timately, began to understand ourselves. Who we were. Who we are. After decades of trying. In lived, real time. What all of us sitting here, in the future, take for granted. As if all these things were always known.

I can assure you. They were not.

If we choose to ignore our history, close our minds to our mistakes, fear our missteps, become unwilling to acknowledge our failures, then we will have accomplished nothing.

—*Venus de Mars*

1

■×▲✦✳■人●■

1977, Duluth

Picture a girl who always behaves, who follows rules as if they were a steel rod sewn into the spine of her jacket. Picture a girl who appreciates good posture, who slouches when that jacket is taken off. Picture a girl infected with jazz, whose parents are out of town for the weekend.

I call myself a girl because I'm seventeen when this happens. At seventeen I'm still a lot more kid than woman. I've hardly ever had a drink. I've had only a couple of boyfriends, and all we ever did was kiss. But I've recently learned how to play jazz. Someone heard me sounding out songs on the piano, and the next thing I knew I was signed up for tenth-grade jazz ensemble.

I like to improvise. I stopped practicing a while ago because I never liked it, but I can play jazz just by going to class every day. I know it was a lazy, bad idea to stop practicing. Now my fingers don't always hit the right notes, but then I say I'm improvising on some weird Mixolydian scale. If I just keep my fingers moving really fast in the right general area, people seem to be impressed. And I'm, well, pretty jazzed by the sound of the rhythm, the mixture of notes that blend together, talk together, sometimes shout together, sometimes just sing, hug, throb together, all these notes that unexpectedly have something to say to each other—I love it.

But our high school band just finished a clinic with Toshiko Akiyoshi, a jazz pianist, and she was not impressed. She singled me out as someone who was not altogether there, someone who was often faking it. I was embarrassed, but it was the truth. I was covering up a lot of errors. She's a piano player, and she saw straight into the part of my brain that makes my fingers move. That critique was supposed to make me straighten up and put in long, lonely hours of practice at home, but it doesn't. I don't want to be at home, and loving the sound a piano makes is not enough. I don't want to hear just that. And I don't want to turn it into work.

I decide I'm going to be something other than a keyboard player. I don't know what I am, careening between enthusiasm and loneliness. I tell myself I'm not going to play piano the way she wants me to, but I can still be addicted to jazz. I won't realize for many years that this is a rationalization, a way to put aside the things I really fear failing at. Music is buoyant, a vessel that prevents me from drowning.

So Toshiko Akiyoshi and her saxophonist husband Lew Tabackin have done their workshop, played their gig, left town, and all that's left are some college students, jazz professors, and a handful of high school students. I'm here in the high school student category. And my parents are out of town, so no one will check to see when I get home. I follow the group. We end up at a hotel bar, Duluth's famous Black Bear Lounge. There's a jazz combo onstage playing, and everybody knows everybody, and pretty soon people start sitting in. They open their black instrument cases, and out come the horns, saxes, a flute. A bass and drum kit are already up. I won't sit in, but I'm part of the song. I feel it, sitting here so close to the stage. I'm careful to ignore the waitstaff, so no one cards me. I don't need a drink, I don't need food, I've got sound.

I sit stage left. I talk to people I know, but mostly I'm just listening, watching, being.

A boy I'm in love with—one of the many boys I'm in love

with at this time in my life, the artistic, thoughtful ones—plays alto sax, then switches to soprano sax. A high, sighing sound soars over the bed of bass and drums. Bass and sax drop back for a drum solo, sixteen bars, thirty-two bars, a little longer, the bass player watches the drummer intently, silently fingering along an imaginary line, one of many possibilities he's dreaming of, the sax player presses his lips to the reed, moves his fingers against the metal keys, eyes scanning from drummer to bass player to drummer again. Finally the drummer nods, the bass player strides in with a nice, fat, walking line, and four bars later the sax is in. They're a team, they're a chorus.

Later the bass gets his turn, then a trumpet, last call floats by, is remembered then forgotten, someone's got a flügelhorn, people leave the stage, people come back to the stage, applause after every solo. I move my hands along the table, silently fingering a line I'd like to try against that tenor sax that now has the lead. My left hand stretches into the bass clef of the table, emulating jagged rhythms and long, horizontal chords. I'm Dave Brubeck, imagining the way these notes would look on a staff of music, jagged towers of thick, black notes stomping their mad dance across the page.

People leave, more arrive, unpacking instruments, moving onto the stage, playing to the night, sitting back. So much watching and listening, like detectives following clues to a bigger pattern, then singing out their discoveries in liquid, angular notes.

And then I begin to notice the light is changing, there's a glow from the far windows.

It isn't night anymore. The morning cleaning crew stands at the back, waiting for us to recognize the cue. The music ends, the instruments get packed into their black cases, and I'm out on the street trying to remember where I parked Dad's car.

A warm, delicate light bathes the empty main street of the city, Superior Street. I've never seen it like this, so large, so calm. The sun feels like apple blossoms, cool and light on my skin. Now the light kisses me. This must be love, and it's not just affection for a boy anymore, but everything, these sounds, this angle of light, the way dawn comes to a quiet city, its sound like crystal, and every tone shines in the air.

I don't know it then, but this is how I will fall in love for real, and this is how I will marry. When that person turns out to be a shape-shifter, I will be able to reach inside myself for those dark, jagged towers of chords, because they are my inner soundtrack. They propel me forward. This is how I will remain in love with her, and this is how I will stay married.

2

■✗▲✦✦■▲●■

1973, Duluth

I first met Steve Grandell, the person I would fall in love with and marry, in eighth grade. We signed up for the same elective, a mass media class taught by Mrs. Delisle. The class wasn't quite what I wanted—I'd expected to take journalism, but the teacher who taught it previously, my English teacher in seventh grade, had left. I felt betrayed. There was something in Miss Brown's demeanor, her long brownish-blond hair and brainy, wire-rimmed glasses—a down-to-earth seriousness—that made me feel as if she understood me. Or maybe I've got that the wrong way around: I felt I could see myself in *her*. But now there was no Miss Brown, no journalism class. Mass media became the closest substitute.

I remember being fascinated by the discrepancy between the spelling and pronunciation of this new teacher's name: dee-LYLE. I loved the sounds of words and anomalies of language, how a word could be spelled one way but sound completely different, how sometimes "color" was spelled "colour." I paid attention to the unusual, the exception to the rule. Perhaps that's what made me notice someone two rows over who would later be known as Venus de Mars.

■■■

I have to pause here to say something about names. The person I married, who I am still very much in love with, is now legally named Venus de Mars. Venus now goes by *she* and *her* pronouns. But a large portion of our journey together took place at a time when she was known as Steve. Even when things began to shift, for reasons that will be explained, I continued to think of my spouse as Steve, or Sweetie, or Bug. The name *Venus* came much later, and even then, I was slow to recognize that's what she wanted me to call her. I'm not proud of myself for that. But that's what the story *is*.

■■■

In eighth grade, the person I would fall in love with had bright red hair that rounded below the ears, skimming the edge of the jaw. I saw a boy whose face glimmered with a shy smile he sometimes tucked away, as if he could make his face disappear into his hair. I thought he was cute, but what really made me notice him was his ability to draw. I watched his pencil glide across an expanse of white paper, and his drawings and cartoons looked—from my eighth-grade vantage point—like the work of a professional. A lot of kids thought *I* was a good artist, too, but my subjects were pretty much limited to horses and cats. Steve, as this person was known then, was clearly the best artist in our class.

Steve also took my breath away literally, with laughter. I cracked up when I heard him talk like Donald Duck. He could imitate a spider crawling up someone's leg, somehow playing *both* the spider and the person trying to shake the pest off their pant leg, and it made my skin itch in sympathetic horror. When Mrs. Delisle put us in small groups to create a hypothetical product and commercial to advertise it, Steve's talent for the hilarious pulled me in like a warm, bright beacon. I can't remember everyone in our group—probably another girl and a boy. Steve convinced us to create the product Bug-B-Gone, then papered over an old aerosol can and drew goofy bugs on it. For the "commercial" we performed in front of the class, I wore a mosquito-like nose cone and played the bug, slowly creeping on all fours toward everyone. Then Steve said, "No, stop! Bug, be . . . gone!" and pretended to spray me. I rolled over on my back in exaggerated insectival death throes. Our skit was a hit. Ten years later, "Bug" was one of our pet names for each other.

Our paths didn't cross again until the end of the next year, at the Ninth Grade Day talent show. That's how I discovered Steve also was an incredible musician. I thought I knew all the other music students, but Steve wasn't in any of the music classes—not orchestra, not band, not choir. I had immersed myself in music, playing violin in orchestra, and I learned to improvise when some concert-band students asked me to play the keyboard part for Dave Brubeck's "Take Five," a piece with an unusual 5/4 signature. For the talent show, I would perform with them and also play Rachmaninoff's "Prelude in C-sharp Minor," thrilling to the drama of its crashing minor chords. But first, I had to wait for Steve.

The show opened with him playing "Classical Gas" on guitar. He started slowly, just twanging a few prime notes, then slowly built to a frenzied crescendo, the melody above the descending and ascending arpeggios. I was intrigued. I had never seen anyone playing classical music on a guitar before. He attracted me from that point on. I didn't know why, but I felt a sense of unknown possibilities radiating from him, like one of those dreams where you open a door and discover an entire wing of your house exists that you never noticed before.

I continued to like him from afar throughout high school, but I didn't lust after him. I focused on poetry, orchestra, and jazz band, and our paths didn't cross. During senior year, he was on the fringes of the group I hung out with on the lawn in front of school, noodling on his acoustic guitar, now grown to a full six feet but still with that smile he often tried to hide. I admired his visual art and encouraged him to submit it for the student literary magazine I edited. We voted to put his draw-ing on the cover. When I went away to college, at Carleton in Northfield, we stayed in touch through mutual friends when I came home for summer break.

Not that I wanted to return home during the summers. It had become a lonely place. My two brothers and a sister—half siblings ten and more years older than me, from my mother's first marriage—had all gone to college and left. Carolyn, who was like a second mother to me, was the last, moving halfway across the country to Virginia just before I started seventh grade.

Perhaps because of that void I wanted my life to have big-ger vistas, more possibilities. For some reason, our high school newspaper profiled me my senior year, and I talked about all the things I looked forward to learning in college, studying po-etry and music, and all the things I loved about the arts. I had the audacity to say things like "Try to develop yourself to your fullest extent, but always realize that there is no limit," "Do as much as possible," and "Openminded people, flexible and will-ing to understand, no matter their social standard, are persons whom I enjoy."

Yes, "whom"—sometimes I talked that way. I was a gram-mar geek. I was also ambitious, without knowing exactly what I was reaching for. It didn't work out the way I expected.

3

■×▲★✦■♠●■

1980, New York City and Duluth

As an undergraduate, it didn't take me long to decide on a career where I thought I'd be able to do it all—have a job, be a poet, and participate in music or whatever else I felt drawn to on the side. It seemed that could happen if I became an English professor. But even then, there were problems with this plan. I was a good student, but nothing I learned in school covered contemporary writing. There was a tremendous gap between what I felt I knew and what I saw on bookstore shelves. I couldn't figure out how to bridge it.

Yet I tried, restless for the adventure but unsure how to begin. When Linc, one of my older college friends, got married and moved to New York with his wife, it seemed that might be the kind of adventure I wanted. He had an entry-level job at St. Martin's Press and she worked in public relations. They invited me to visit just before Christmas of my sophomore year.

I gasped with delight as they led me down the wide avenues, the bright lights and window displays gleaming in the early darkness of winter, the street food and sidewalk Christmas tree markets spicing the air. I learned how to make the tilted cube sculpture at Astor Place spin. We agreed that I would return to New York the following summer. Linc assured me that he'd line up apartment-sitting gigs so I'd have a free place to stay.

Lynette in New York City, 1979. Photo by Jonathan Stevens

My only budget concerns would be food, travel, and entertainment, which I could probably cover through temping.

I took the Greyhound bus from Duluth to New York that summer, arriving at the Port Authority in all its early eighties seediness, my feet so swollen from the ride they barely fit back into the shoes I'd removed somewhere in Pennsylvania. Linc and Marsha brought me to their small apartment in New Jersey—they were splitting their time between Hoboken and Manhattan, where Linc's grandmother had a condo. Once back in Hoboken, Linc broke the bad news: the first apartment-sitting gig had fallen through. But there were more possibilities, he reassured me. Something would come through. In the meantime, I went to the temp agency, demonstrated my typing ability, and waited for them to leave a message on Linc and Marsha's phone.

I began to explore New York. I stood in line to get tickets to Peter Gabriel in Central Park and went to see the Sun Ra Arkestra at the Squat Theatre. I watched the Fourth of July fireworks. Mostly I did a lot of walking and looking at things. But I started to worry about money. After more than a week, I'd heard nothing from the temp agency. None of the other promised apartment-sitting gigs seemed to be materializing. Linc and Marsha wanted me to leave the apartment, whether it was Hoboken or Manhattan, whenever they left, and I couldn't return until they were home. I discovered that New York was the most expensive city I'd ever encountered, and the only places I could sit down without buying something were churches. My money was running out a lot faster than I'd anticipated. Even worse, I could tell that Linc and Marsha were getting tired of seeing me sleep on their couch.

I finally gave myself an ultimatum: if I didn't hear from the temp agency or get an apartment-sit in another week, I was going to have to go back to Duluth. I felt stupid giving up the dream of a bohemian summer in New York, but it felt even worse to imagine borrowing money for the bus fare home. I was that broke. Something in me needed to stay independent. And perhaps I was afraid my friends wouldn't like me if I asked for help.

Another week went by and nothing had changed. Resigned, I took the Greyhound home to Duluth, a two-and-a-half-day ordeal. The bus's air-conditioning stopped functioning somewhere between Chicago and Minneapolis, and the windows didn't go down. When we pulled into the Minneapolis depot, the temperature on a bank marquee read 102.

It was some kind of metaphor from Dante's *Inferno*, and I was in that special circle of hell for people who bailed and fled home, roasting in a fiery lake, gored perpetually by disappointment. Throughout the whole ride I debated whether I'd given up too quickly, and it turned out I had. A few days after I got home, I opened a letter from Linc saying a temp agency had called for me, plus some other college acquaintances invited me to a party on Long Island. That probably would have led to something. I felt like an idiot for giving up so quickly. Still, I was relieved to be in a space where I didn't feel like an intruder.

I found myself back in Duluth in the middle of July feeling aimless and defeated, too late to get a seasonal job and lonely once again. I looked for friends from the previous summer and discovered Steve now played in a punk rock band. I'd already developed the habit of blasting a Patti Smith album to wake up in the morning—punk, not jazz, had taken over my inner soundtrack, and I used safety pins instead of staples to keep the pages of my term papers together. I followed Steve's band to most of their gigs, including one in a tiny township up on the Range, put together by Tanya Warwas, another local punk rocker who would later come back into our lives.

That summer I fell seriously in love with Steve. I didn't have a job and stayed out late most nights. I don't know why my parents didn't comment on this. I drove my dad's Chevy Impala everywhere (he was retired from his job as a laborer), and I think at some point after I left home for college my mother decided it wasn't worth arguing with me. Maybe it was because I was the caboose in the family, and they didn't have that kind of energy anymore. My mother was sixty-one, and my father was sixty-six. For whatever reason, as long as it looked like I was going back to college in the fall, they never asked me what I was up to.

Someone I knew through an experimental theater company lived with her mother on Park Point, a seven-mile peninsula of sandy beach on the western edge of Lake Superior, and I connected her with the band. On a typical night, after the band rehearsed, we'd meet on the beach behind her house and make a fire with driftwood. Because some of the people had been through treatment in their teen years, we weren't using booze or drugs. We just told stories and jokes until the dawn began to

Venus (as Steve), 1979

glimmer across the lake. All the things that had attracted me to Steve before amplified. I surreptitiously tried to sit next to him on one of the logs we'd dragged near the fire. If it was crowded enough, our knees might accidentally touch.

Sometimes I even trembled when I got that close to him, grateful for the darkness and firelight that cloaked my physical reactions. The shivers were in my hands, my knees, everywhere. On the shore of a lake so large we couldn't see the other side of it, with waves washing up in muffled bursts, I didn't know how to interpret the flutters inside myself. I knew I couldn't follow through with all my unruly visions of pulling Steve to myself, of gliding our two suits of skin together, unless he gave me an indication that he wanted it, too. He didn't.

I resorted to outward expressions of my infatuation, things that might pique his interest when I wasn't actually present to be rejected. I enlisted my friend Deb Hendrickson, a fellow nerd from high school who would be my roommate at Carleton in the fall. Deb helped me paste a row of gold foil stars at eye level on the wall up the stairs to Steve's second-floor apartment. Another time I left a weird, ancient puppet made to look like Jimmy Cagney (advertised as "The Man of a Thousand Faces") on Steve's door. It had been in the attic at my parents' house. It was a sacrifice to part with it, but I thought he would like it.

He seemed to appreciate it all, but he didn't make any return overtures. He didn't seem interested in dating *anyone*. He took modeling photos of the friend whose campfire we gathered around, and she told me she thought he was gay because he didn't come on to her. At this point, I knew one person who had come out as gay, and Steve didn't strike me as fitting in that category.

Somehow we became close enough to write letters back and forth when I returned to college. When he wrote that he was coming to visit, partly to see his cousin who lived in a trailer park outside of town, but also to see me, I was delirious. Yes! It was as if I grew branches and leaves. I felt one step away from becoming oxygen.

We split a pizza at Angelo's, maybe a pitcher of 3.2 beer, and at some point in the conversation, Steve began to give me the "just friends" talk. I couldn't understand why he drove four hours to give me a "just friends" talk, but I didn't want to push the point. I'd already exposed myself—it was clear he knew what my feelings were if he was explaining he didn't want to date. He got back in his car to drive to his cousin's, and I walked up the hill to my basement dorm room. I was so crushed after he left that I got drunk and passed out on the bathroom floor, leaving Deb to find me, slap me awake, and fish the shards of my broken glass out of the sink.

In the meantime, I decided it was time to lose my virginity. I began looking around for other boyfriends.

4

1982, Northfield

In my senior year, I tried to make big plans for after graduation, but I kept getting blocked. I thought maybe I could travel by signing up for the Peace Corps, but the rep at the information table said they only wanted people majoring in the sciences or engineering—not me. Although I edited the arts section for the student newspaper, I didn't think working as a journalist would be a good fit, afraid that if my day job involved writing for money, I wouldn't have energy for poetry. I liked what I saw of teaching, and teaching felt familiar—my mother and aunts had been K-12 teachers. I told my advisor that I'd like to be a professor, too, hoping he'd offer advice about graduate school. Instead, he seemed to berate me.

"Why go straight to graduate school?" he boomed. "Take a year off, see the world." I took that to mean he didn't think I could cut it in graduate school.

But perhaps it wouldn't have mattered, given what happened next. I got a letter from my mother saying my father had been in the hospital a week. I called immediately.

"What happened?" I asked.

"Oh, the doctors say he's jaundiced. They did exploratory surgery. He should be better soon."

"Surgery? Should I come home?" I checked the postmark on

the envelope. It had been mailed several days earlier. I pictured her at the dining room table writing it amid stacks of paperwork, jaw clenched with determination, her profile like a red-headed Queen Elizabeth. As far as I knew, my father didn't have a history of anything other than varicose veins. True, his skin had a yellowish tinge when I was home for Christmas break. He ascribed it to some new ointment he was using.

"No, don't interrupt your classes or anything. He's doing well. If you want, you can come up on the weekend."

This was typical of my mother—a rigid adherence to the practical. My response was also typical of me—I knew she didn't welcome questions that challenged her decisions. I always found it odd when people referred to their mothers as their best friend, someone they could confide in. I couldn't imagine being able to do that. My mother seemed to want only obedience from me. I resented it, but I played along to keep the peace. She may have developed that rigidity after her first marriage fell apart—it's what she used to hold herself together. And I didn't yet know the saying, "The apple doesn't fall far from the tree." For better or worse, I owe my spine of steel to her.

I remained in Northfield a few more days and stayed up all night Thursday to put together the Friday edition of the newspaper during a howling blizzard that swept across the entire state and closed all the highways the next day. I staggered down the hill through swirling snow to my room and went to sleep. One of my roommates woke me an hour later. My mother was on the telephone. Her usually strong voice trembled, like quivering wings, floundering in a storm. My father had died, having never recovered from the exploratory surgery.

I held the black receiver to my ear and stared out the tall windows at the still-falling snow collecting on the tree branches outside, weighing them down and bending them closer to the ground. Of course I thought only of myself. Questions raced through my mind—had he wanted me there? Had he wondered where I was? Not only would those questions never be answered, it would be another twenty-four hours before the highways reopened and I could even begin the four-hour drive north. I hung up the phone and went back to bed, not wanting anyone to see my tears.

When evening came, I realized I couldn't stay in bed any longer and decided to go with a group of newspaper friends to see a new movie, *Ordinary People*. It was playing at a theater a few blocks from campus. We'd planned to do this the night before, when everything seemed normal. As we walked along the snowy, moonlit sidewalks, I told a few people near me that my father had died that morning. A quiet sympathy settled over the group as the news made its way up the line. No, I didn't want to talk about it. I just wanted to let myself drift, to let something else occupy my mind. But that was impossible. In the dark theater, I watched Mary Tyler Moore play a mother more concerned with outward appearances than the inner emotions of her family. Watching the character's tight grimace on the screen, I wondered if that was my mother. Was that what our family had really been?

No one in our family seemed to understand anything about grief, least of all me. I finished the rest of my senior year—a little less than six months—in a distracted fog. I misread the clock while taking the GRE and had to leave the last twenty questions unanswered. I prided myself with being the second-worst player in an intramural baseball league—laughing about it meant I didn't have to try. I decided to move back home and go to the University of Minnesota's branch in Duluth for graduate school. I didn't know what else to do, and my mother liked the plan. Though she never said so, she must have been lonely, too.

Within the first weeks, she apologized for not telling me earlier about my father's health. Her dream had been to retire and then travel with him. At the time, I accepted her apology because I understood the gesture, but I still didn't understand how it had happened and was frustrated she didn't want to talk about it further. I was still angry, but of course that wasn't fair. He could have let me know as well, and he didn't.

A few years later, after Steve and I married and before Steve's name changed to Venus, we sat at my mother's dining room table for a Sunday afternoon dinner with my mother and my father's sister, Esther. Maybe we were talking about health when Esther dryly commented that when the surgeons operated on my father, "his body was riddled with cancer." I'd never heard this before and shot a look at my mother, who pursed her lips in that Mary Tyler Moore–like way, then held a napkin to her mouth as if she might choke on some gobbet of food. Steve looked across the table at me, bewildered. My aunt was genuinely surprised I didn't know about the cancer, but it was clear to all of us that any more on the subject was off-limits. People didn't like to talk about cancer then, as if the very word might summon it. Was it some stigma she felt she had to push away? Whatever the reason, she would not acknowledge what was really happening. That task would be left up to me. I stumbled a lot.

5

■×▲⋆✦■♠●■

1982, Duluth

Despite the silence between us, my mother liked having someone else in the house, and I still loved the tall sunrise windows of
my childhood bedroom. My dad's green Chevy Impala granted
me the freedom to get away from the house often, which I did,
because a gnawing emptiness made me want to go out and stay
up all night with friends talking about poetry and philosophy.
I found some of them at Sir Benedict's, a little sandwich-and-
imported-beer pub where Steve sometimes played folk guitar
with Tim Kaiser. I still liked Steve but remained wary of getting
too friendly. The "just friends" talk left a deep bruise, the kind
that turns a lot of weird colors before healing.

By now he was in a new punk band, Straight Face, doing
lead guitar and vocals. Three brothers joined him: Charlie Bailey on synthesizer, Jon Bailey on rhythm guitar, and Bill Bailey on drums. Dave Frame played bass. One day several of us
sat around the living room of the band house trying to figure
out how to better publicize the shows. I'd seen free arts-and-
entertainment newspapers like the *Village Voice*, the *Chicago
Reader*, and the *Twin Cities Reader*. I understood how they in-
formed the community about events and trends—at least that's
how it worked when I picked one up—but Duluth didn't have
anything like that. We decided to start our own.

I had $1,600 left in my college fund (a scholarship had paid for most of my education). Starting an arts newspaper seemed like a good way to spend the leftover cash. Using what I learned in college, we put the print dummy together using typed columns and rubber cement—this was before personal computers and desktop publishing. We called it the *Duluth Rag Times*.

The paper launched in early September, the same month I enrolled in graduate classes at UMD and began to teach a couple of sections of freshman composition. Pat McKinnon was the ad man for the *Rag Times* early on because he was the only one of us impervious to rejection. Tim Kaiser and I, with other band members and friends, wrote most of the stories. Steve was the photo editor. Because I was an editor and learned to develop photos in college, Steve and I spent a lot of time in the Depot darkroom together, which, given the chemical smells, was not nearly as romantic as most people imagine darkrooms to be.

The Depot darkroom was large, about the size of a classroom, with counters for several people to develop and print their work. A safety light bathed it with a warm, red glow. Steve and I fell into a pattern of working there once a week to develop and print photos for the paper. We'd spend several hours choosing and printing, then head out for dinner or a drink afterward. We still liked each other's company.

I found the velvet dark of the room and gentle swish of photograph paper in the developer bath soothing. We worked side by side for efficiency, each with a different photo.

"What do you think of this one?" I gestured at the image darkening in its liquid. It was a single, bow-backed chair on a stage, lit by a spotlight from the rigging above.

"More contrast," replied Steve. "I'll see if a different filter will bring out the dark areas."

I sighed, disappointed my work wasn't done yet, but agreeing that the thing could be made to look better. I wanted it on the cover. I thought Steve's insights often balanced out my deficiencies: I lived in a world of theory but didn't have much technical experience. I loved Richard Avedon's black-and-white portraits, the ones with the subject off-center and dark lines that created an asymmetrical balance. I tried to re-create those lines in some of my own portraits, usually with graphic design tape, not realizing until later that Avedon's lines were a product of his large-format camera.

As Steve checked the filters on my enlarger, I stepped over to swish the photo in his developer bath, then picked it up with tongs and pushed it into the stop bath.

"Did I tell you I turned in my grades?" I asked. I was relieved to have that over with, my first semester of teaching freshman comp.

"Did you give them any F's?" Steve joked. I rolled my eyes, forgetting he couldn't see me clearly.

"No, they were actually okay. But I just can't get myself motivated to write the final papers for the classes I'm taking. Latin is fun, and I'll finish that, but I think I'm going to take incompletes in the others."

"Yeah, I get it," Steve responded. He'd finished only one semester at the Minneapolis College of Art and Design before leaving due to stress, financial problems, and the sudden appearance of a bat in his apartment. We'd already talked about this and had unexpectedly bonded over how, after taking classes somewhere else, UMD was flatly uninspiring. "That looks good," he said, gesturing to the new chair print I was pushing back and forth in the developer.

"It's got a lot more contrast. Is it too high?"

"No, it'll balance out when it's printed," he reassured me. I looked at the picture. It looked great. My heart swelled like a red balloon. I squeegeed off the photos in the wash bath and hung them up to dry.

"Where do you want to go, the Hacienda?" The Hacienda del Sol was a favorite artsy restaurant for us, exotic by Duluth standards, with Mexican food made from scratch and a sort of tree house patio out back. It was winter now, late December, so we wouldn't be on the patio tonight.

"That would be great," Steve said. "I'm hungry."

The Hacienda had a counter where we often sat chatting with the waitstaff, but this time a booth was open, so we slid into that. The server was happy to see us—she was getting to know us as regulars. That made me think about what we must look like to other people: two people on a date. Except we weren't dating. We'd already had that conversation. Steve was afraid dating would destroy our friendship.

I went along with the friends-only policy because I still enjoyed his company, but by now the edict against dating felt insane and hypocritical. I felt strongly that people who were romantically interested in each other should also be friends. And I'd never felt as comfortable with previous boyfriends as I did around Steve.

Perversely, I'd relaxed more in the last month or two because a friend had asked whether I minded if she tried to date him. *Not a problem*, I said, *I've given up. Go for it*. I hadn't heard or seen anything between the two of them since.

Now I'd forgotten about that, and this night I was thinking mostly of honesty versus hypocrisy. I wanted to know what was really going on. I didn't feel I had much to lose. There were other guys I was casually dating, i.e., sleeping with—no one I saw a future with. It seemed the worst that could happen was I'd lose a photo editor. I could print the photos myself.

I dipped a tortilla chip into the salsa. I didn't expect him to say he was gay, but that would have been a reasonable explanation. The idea that he was transgender was not on my radar, though it wouldn't necessarily have diminished my interest. At that point in my life, I felt curious and empowered. I decided to broach the topic.

"So here we are," I began, gesturing around the room. "To everyone else here, it probably looks as though we're dating." I paused. "We aren't, but what are we doing, then?" Steve held a chip midair, pondering it, then me. I could tell I'd caught him off guard, but he didn't seem defensive, just thoughtful.

"You know I'm worried that if we started dating, we'd break up, and then we wouldn't be friends anymore," he said after a moment.

"I understand that, but this seems weird." I had to stop to think. What exactly felt weird about it? "It feels as if there's this artificial boundary. You know I like you, and I like being with you. And it seems as if you like being with me." Steve nodded. A little thrill vibrated through my chest. "To me," I continued, "this is what dating feels like."

"But if we dated, we'd probably break up and not be friends anymore," he reiterated. The black-hole spiral of his negativity surprised me, so I approached it from a different direction.

"Look, if we break up, I *promise* I will still remain friends with you."

Steve shook his head and laughed wryly.

"Oh no, I don't think you'd be able to do that," he said.

"Of course I could," I said, smiling back.

We continued in this vein until we were done eating. The check had been sitting on the table for some time, and we were still in a thicket of conversation.

"We should really free up this table," Steve said, seeing more people come into the restaurant. It was getting crowded. "Do you want to go somewhere else to keep talking?"

"We could try Sir Ben's." No one we knew would be playing tonight, which was maybe a good thing. We split the tab, walked out to Superior Street, and got in the green Chevy Impala. Steve once owned a Nova but had sold it and was living off what was left of that money, spending most of his time on the band and the *Rag Times*.

At Sir Ben's we found a table where we could look out the window into the blue December darkness and imagine Lake Superior out there, its frigid waves crashing against the dark rocks a few hundred feet beyond the window. By now, Steve was warming to the idea of dating but still worried an argument loomed in our future and would destroy everything.

"Sometimes I'm really difficult to be around," he said. I had trouble believing this. I felt energized and alive in his company.

"You don't *seem* difficult to be around," I countered. "I really like talking to you and being with you."

After a few more beers and splitting a piece of cheesecake for dessert, we agreed that we were dating.

"For real?" I asked, afraid the spell would break.

"For real," he reassured warmly, beaming at me.

We got up to go; I had to get up early in the morning, and I still had to drive Steve back to the band house on Fifth Street.

I parked the car in front. We got out and walked up to the door together. He invited me in, but I said no, because I really needed to get back home. We stood there, holding unmittened hands for a long moment, watching the fog-clouds from our breath drift into the icy darkness.

"Well," I said, "do I get a kiss?" Steve looked around, a little flustered and hesitant. Then he leaned down to kiss me. His lips were soft and warm. I felt the arms of his wool coat wrap me to him, at first lightly, then more firmly. I circled my arms around him, too. I felt his hips and his spine through the layers of clothing. I drew away a moment to catch my breath, then leaned in for more. As our faces tilted and met each other, he felt just the right height to me. This close, I caught a light scent of shampoo and something deeper, richer. The soft press of his arms felt exactly how I had imagined it, solid and strong. Everything about the moment felt right.

6

■ ★ ▲ ★ ✦ ■ ▲ ● ■

1982, Duluth

We'd spent so much time together that it was easy to fall into intimacy. Steve lived in the top part of a duplex with five guys, mostly band members. He'd scored his own room in the attic, and by the third date that's where we went for after-dinner kissing. Steve made a show of lighting the candles, and we sat together on the carpeted floor of his tiny, Zen-like space. Its sloping walls followed the roofline, and his homemade futon on the carpeted floor and low tables made the room feel larger than it was. We could look out the front window at the dark, snowy street below.

It wasn't long before our clothes started coming off. I don't remember who started it, but soon we were naked and giggling. Steve confessed he hadn't had sex before, and I likewise confessed that I didn't know much, but by now I'd done it more than a few times. Steve had a propitious hard-on, so I was confident that part would go well. We were rolling around together, and I guided him. Suddenly he gave a deep sigh, and there was moisture on my thighs. He was early. I didn't want him to feel discouraged, so I said something about it happening often. I had read that. Soon he was ready to go again, and the second time it worked as we both hoped. We were giddy with delight.

We saw each other as many nights as our schedules allowed, usually finishing up with sex. Within just a few evenings back at Steve's, he started exploring me in ways no one else had, lips and fingers everywhere, and thousands of tiny neurons began to firework the sky inside my closed eyelids. It became one of my favorite things—I could imagine Julie Andrews singing the song.

Steve and I would talk, cuddle, have sex, cuddle some more, and then start to fall asleep. Then it was after midnight or 1:00 A.M. or 2:00 A.M., and there was a Duluth winter outside to contend with. I still lived with my mother. We would wake up, and Steve would walk me out along the icy track of the road past waist-high snowbanks to my car, often parked a half block or more away. He'd kiss me good night, I'd get in, and he'd make sure the car started. We'd wave good-bye through the cold glass window, and I would drive away.

We joked that these were our dark little days, days that dawned and ended in the middle of the night. Each time we promised we would see each other again very soon.

■■■

But it wasn't all about sex. Steve's ability to repair things sealed the deal. The first instance took place a few weeks after we started dating. He met me at the door of the duplex.

"There's a big problem," he announced. "The landlord was late paying the oil bill, and they turned off the heat." The situation was dire. It was January in Duluth, with temperatures well below freezing, sometimes below zero. If the house froze up, all the pipes might freeze and burst, flooding the place. "He paid the bill and they delivered the oil," Steve continued, "but the heat still hasn't come on."

"Oh no. Is there someone you can call?"

"No one's answering. I think it's after work hours."

"That's bad." It was Friday night. There might not be a response until Monday.

"Yeah. You know, I think I know what the problem might be.

Can you come with me? You might be able to help." He led me to the dim basement where the oil tank and furnace were. It was cold, and we kept our coats and hats on. "I think what happened is the intake went dry, and a bubble of air got into the line. Maybe it needs to be bled." I knew about bleeding water out of radiators but never thought a furnace would need that.

"Okay, what do you want me to do?"

"Just hold this, and be ready to help me screw it all back together once the oil starts flowing." I nodded, and he started unthreading the valve. Nothing came at first, then a narrow stream of clear, ice-cold oil started gushing out.

"It's freezing!" The oil was liquid ice covering my hands.

"Quick! Have you got something to wrap this with?" I grabbed my scarf, eager to pull my hands away from the numbing cascade. I wrapped my scarf around it all, leaving just a little room for Steve to continue tightening the valve. Finally, the flow stopped. We rubbed our hands on the dry ends of the scarf and went upstairs to check for heat. Within a few minutes, we could tell it had worked. Now that I was able to catch my breath, I was amazed. We would both stink of heating oil for the next few days, and I had to throw away the scarf, but I had learned that Steve wasn't just a sexy artist, he was someone who could fix things.

I'd grown up with parents who did most of their own repairs, and when I was in fifth grade I followed instructions in a magazine to make a spotlight lamp out of a coffee can and bulb fixture. But I hadn't progressed beyond that. Steve clearly knew things I didn't, and they weren't limited to photography. I wanted to stay with him and learn.

■■■

A month later, Straight Face signed with a booking agent in Minneapolis. It meant they would move to the Twin Cities. The

Rag Times would have to end. That didn't bother me much, as we'd already started running out of energy and were publishing less often. But I wasn't sure how a long-distance relationship would work. I had to stay in Duluth until at least the end of the school year.

"Please come down to visit as often as you can," Steve said. His smile no longer disappeared into his hair.

So I visited, telling my mother I was staying with a friend but really staying at the band house. They had rented a large, drafty Victorian on Marshall Avenue in St. Paul, and Steve had again drawn the best room in the house—the entire attic, the kind with front and back stairs.

By March, I spent all of my spring break in the Cities. One night Steve made a special dinner that we ate by candlelight, perched on the edge of a futon in front of a low table. He started to say something I couldn't quite follow, something about our future together and wanting to make it official. Then he drew out a little copper ring he'd made. I looked at it, nervous about the implications.

"Are you asking me what I think you're asking?"

"Yes."

"Then you have to say it. You have to say the words."

"Lynette, will you marry me?" he asked, smiling. I kissed and hugged him. Of course I would.

■■■

A few months later, we were married in a small ceremony in the chancel of the church I grew up in. The Duluth newspaper ran engagement pictures regularly, and we wanted to be a part of that, in our own style. Steve took a picture of the two of us wearing new wave wraparound sunglasses, with him looking straight on at the camera with me sideways in profile. When I dropped off the photo at the newspaper, the page

Engagement photo, 1983

editor (Laurie Hertzel, who would go on to become books editor at the *Star Tribune*) asked if my mother knew I was doing
this. No, she didn't. She was upset when she saw it, but she
got over it.

Both of us felt a big wedding ceremony would put us too
much on display, so we put our energy into a large, informal
party in my mother's big backyard, with a wedding cake, sandwiches, and a jazz trio. The apple tree I used to climb as a child
was in full blossom, and the guests were a delightful mix of
family members, friends, neighbors, and punk rockers. A few
days later, we drove back to St. Paul, where I moved into the
third floor of the band house with Steve.

7

1973, Duluth

When I was in junior high, I bonded with a boyfriend over music. It started with a mutual love for Elton John. I credit Tom Voelk with teaching me how to play by ear, showing me how to listen to Elton John's version of "Pinball Wizard" on the radio and replicate the opening chords.

Late at night, if we weren't having a marathon conversation on the phone, both of us would sit in our separate houses writing multipage notes to each other about everything we observed and experienced, exchanging them at school the next day. One day after we exchanged our tomes, I discovered we'd both found WLS, a clear-channel radio station originating in Chicago that played all the newest music. The AM signal bounced more than four hundred miles to Duluth late at night. I listened to David Bowie's "Changes" lying in bed, blue Lloyd transistor radio pressed to my ear, and imagined the stellar space beyond the window glass.

■■■

My other passion was horses. I was unstoppable.

Lots of children love horses, girls especially. Most grow out of it, but I never did. From my first ride at the age of about five, when the horse ran away with me, I was hooked. My fifteen-year-old sister put me on the back of a neighbor's horse with a rope as a makeshift halter, and he took off in a trot. I hung on to his mane, frozen with the vision that I might break something or die if I fell off, and Carolyn tried to run after us, slowed by the swampy pasture. He stopped abruptly and I was still on. We never tried that again. But I wasn't frightened by the experience; I was exhilarated. Seeing the world from the back of a moving horse was empowering—I was taller and could move faster than I was used to. Maybe I sensed a whiff of accomplishment because I hadn't fallen off. I also formed the concept of that horse as an individual creature with his own emotions and ideas as he looked at me through his large, brown eyes.

I'd begged for years for my own horse, and in the summer of 1973 my parents finally let me lease Buttons, a Shetland pony, for a month. I was a dedicated child, where horses were concerned. It was about five miles from my house to the farm. To get there, I had to first pump my bike up Forty-Third Avenue East, then up Glenwood hill, leaving the houses behind me. Glenwood was the worst. If I shifted into the lowest gears of the yellow Schwinn, I was jogging in place, getting nowhere. If I shifted into a higher gear, my thigh muscles burned as I fought gravity up the incline. It only got better when I passed the turnoff for Skyline Parkway, a scenic drive that overlooked the neighborhood and Lake Superior beyond it.

I had loved horses for as long as I could remember, and my classmates knew me as the girl who was always drawing horses—"writing horses," as one of them used to say. I spent years galloping everywhere, instead of running, pretending to be a horse. I even whinnied.

It wasn't until fifth grade that a group of girls shamed me into stopping, but that only happened on the outside. I still felt more comfortable acting like a horse than a fifth-grade girl. My best friend from sixth and seventh grade was Mary Bradley. We spent hours galloping around her backyard, sometimes with one of us pretending to drive the other using a long piece of string for the bit and reins.

I learned about Springhill from Mary. She leased a lovely dapple-gray pony named Dynamite, and her parents eventually bought him. But my parents wouldn't budge. No, I couldn't have a horse of my own. For thirty days, at least I had Buttons.

In the horse world, Springhill was essentially a low-rent district, a Mediterranean Avenue for the budget-conscious. Formerly a dairy farm, it was now 120 acres of unmaintained pastures. In addition to horses and ponies owned by regular boarders, they also had a bunch of Shetland ponies to rent by the day or month. Included with the rental was one bridle, nothing else.

On a bright June day I got to the farm, leaned my bike against the arena fence, and walked to the tack room to get Buttons's bridle. It was typical for Springhill: western, with a curb bit, a curb strap, and another piece of leather that went around the back of the pony's head. The reins were permanently knotted together. One had been torn away from the bit and mended with orange baling twine.

I picked my way past the ankle-deep mud at the back of the barn, out the first gate, then up the hill, hoping the horses weren't too far out. At the crest, I was happy to discover they weren't. They were down in a little dip near the barbed wire fence where the grass was lush. I walked up to the herd slowly and found Buttons, offering him a carrot. He had shed most of his winter coat, and beneath the long, dull hairs that still clung, a beautiful red-chestnut color shimmered in the spring sun. But he'd been in the burdock again. His mane and tail were lumpy with burrs, and his forelock stuck out like a unicorn's horn. I watched him chew the carrot thoughtfully. Then I put the reins over his neck and pulled the bridle on. I gave him another carrot. Buttons's back came about to my sternum, so I wasn't quite too big for him, but it was close. I hopped on, clucked, and gave him a little kick to move away from the herd. We ambled back up the hill toward the barn.

I always liked to explore, a habit I developed even before riding, so once I cleaned Buttons up—removing *all* the burrs from his mane, tail, and forelock by a method I'd read about in a magazine (pull the hair away from the burr, not the opposite)—I directed him along a wide trail that followed the pasture fence line. There was a creek past the far end, and I wanted to see where the trails that ran along it led. I knew that if I crossed the creek—a branch of Amity Creek—I would end up at an old hayfield we called East End, a huge, open meadow where you could let your horse run. I didn't feel confident enough on Buttons to do much galloping, especially riding bareback, so I turned onto a trail that dipped back to the woods.

The trail wound through the trees, roughly following the curves of the stream. The leaves from the previous fall made a gray thatch that covered the forest floor. It was cooler in the woods, the sun mostly blocked by foliage. Then in front of me, I saw the narrow creek spread out into a small pond, a swimming hole, perhaps, underneath the trees.

It's impossible to describe how beautiful it looked to me. Flecks of sunlight filtered through the leafy canopy to give the pond a whisper of radiance. The tree trunks seemed to bend toward it lovingly. I petted the pony's shaggy mane and told him how wonderful he was for bringing me here. It felt as if everything I needed in the world was right here. I took a deep breath. The path led straight into the water. I urged Buttons forward. He hesitated at the water's edge, and I kicked and clucked more insistently. Then he stepped forward and into the pond.

At first, the water was just up to his knees, but it got deeper rapidly, and in a moment we were swimming. The water was at my waist, and I hung on to Buttons's mane for balance. The pond was cold, but it didn't make me feel cold. It just brought clarity. It was as if I had passed through some kind of doorway and now was where I was supposed to be. I turned Buttons back toward the trail and he stepped out of the water. I slid off to let him shake himself, then wiped more of the excess water away with my hands. Now that we were out of the pond, I was starting to feel cold, and Buttons probably was, too. I hopped on and we headed back; I let him trot a little to warm up. By the time we got back to the barn, he and I were mostly dry, except for the hem of my bell-bottom jeans.

■■■

I had forgotten all about that experience until I was in graduate school and experiencing tremendous stress. By then, we had been married about seven years. Our wedding was followed by a year or so of bliss, then increasing strains on our relationship. By the time I remembered the joy I experienced discovering the pond and riding Buttons into it, Steve had come out to me as bi and as someone who liked to dress in women's clothing. Neither of us had any kind of map for proceeding. I was trying to teach classes, finish my coursework, and write my dissertation, and he wanted to go out to clubs like the Gay 90's most nights so he could be dressed in public. He craved approval from other people for his femme self. I didn't seem to be enough for him anymore, and I didn't know where it would lead.

I was participating in a lunchtime brown bag seminar on self-hypnosis, and the facilitator led us through a guided imagery experience to go back to a time when we'd been happy. In my mind's eye, I saw myself discovering the hidden pond again in all its quiet shimmering and riding Buttons into it. I started crying. The facilitator was alarmed. No, no, I reassured him. These were happy tears. I hadn't remembered this for a long time.

8

■✗▲✦■▲●■

1984–1986, Minneapolis

The trouble that summoned my tears in the seminar room started after we'd been married a little over a year.

Until then, our lives together had gamboled forward in a rollicking blur of love and music. The attic of the band house had an unsupported turret to one side that tilted like a frail crone fighting the urge to sleep, but that didn't stop us from setting up a cast-off table and chairs in it for candlelight dinners. Nine of us lived in the house, and the band was a dynamo of rehearsal and song writing that pounded away in the basement every night.

I liked my double lifestyle. I worked by day at a small film production company and came home to supper, then read to the engine of music thrumming below. The band played gigs at the local punk bars where all the up-and-coming Twin Cities bands played, like Goofy's Upper Deck, the Seventh Street Entry, McCafferty's, and the Cabooze.

They were a little different from the other bands, appearance-wise. Charlie Bailey had introduced them to Japanese visual kei, an outgrowth of glam, and the band often wore Kabuki-style makeup for gigs. I thought it looked cool. Many people were confused that they sort of looked like Kiss, but not.

Then the band broke up.

I should have known something was up when Steve went out of his way to take me to dinner at a Mexican restaurant in a renovated warehouse, the kind with views of the Mississippi and the eastern edge of downtown Minneapolis. He waited until we left and strolled back to the car.

"*You what?*"

"I, uh, left the band. Actually, we broke up the band. First Charlie said he was quitting, then Bill said he was, then I said . . ."

I stared at him. It was insanely stupid, considering how good they were. They'd just sunk a lot of money into a four-song EP, including *our* household money. It wouldn't come back.

"You took me out to tell me this?" I looked at the Styrofoam container of leftovers in my hand, the memory of enchilada sauce suddenly like sand on my tongue, then hurled it down the street. I wanted it to sound like breaking glass. Instead, it landed with a timid, plastic thud.

We made up, and Steve vowed to do a solo album, using a few of the songs already mixed at Blackberry Way, where the Replacements would soon record *Let It Be*. In the mornings, I'd drive to work, and Steve would go to the basement to work on music. Often he'd play what he was working on when I got back home. Sometimes the two of us would try to write music together.

With the band defunct, there was no reason to renew the lease on the St. Paul house. We rented a place in Minneapolis with former bassist Dave Frame and his girlfriend, Nancy. Steve finished the solo album on a four-track in the basement, with Bill Bailey on drums and me on violin. I suggested a title he liked, *Animal Angst*, and we hand-screened the record jackets in the basement, laying everything on the floor in the unfinished space between the washtub and furnace. He sent out review copies, stocked the album at local record stores, and waited for something to happen. But nothing happened. Or more accurately, very little happened. Up to that point, local records generated local buzz, but something had changed:

Purple Rain had come out. The local press, previously lukewarm at best about Prince, finally recognized a major star in their midst. They no longer had time for a musician recording an album in the basement.

Steve didn't smile as much as he used to when I came home. He'd sit at the table or on the couch brooding, a long hank of hair obscuring his downturned face. He couldn't make eye contact with me. I thought he was depressed at the lack of attention his album was getting, but it also seemed that maybe more was wrong. It was as if my sheer presence irritated him.

"Is there something wrong? Did I do something?"

"No, it's just . . . I get like this. You know I told you when we started dating that I was difficult to live with." It confounded me. Yes, he *had* told me. I hadn't believed him then, and I couldn't see the logic in his behavior now.

"Are you depressed? Do you need to see someone?" It seemed like everyone had begun taking Prozac. It didn't seem like the best idea, but at least there were options.

"No, no, that's not it," he said more forcefully. "I don't really want to talk about it." So we didn't. Reaching out to hold his hand had once felt so natural. Now he sometimes bristled, and I was afraid to touch him.

Sometimes the arguments got so bad that we stormed away from each other, needing to cool off. But I couldn't figure out what the arguments were about. Steve would suddenly get grumpy and terse. I could tell something was wrong but couldn't get him to say what it was. One time the argument began at a shopping mall, and we had to part from each other for an hour to avoid escalating it in public. When we met again, Steve surprised me with a kitten he'd bought to apologize. I loved the kitten but kept wondering what caused these angry moods.

Still thinking Steve's depression maybe stemmed from a lack of album reviews, I joined him in a one-shot band called the Loud to perform for a festival in Duluth's Canal Park. Maybe the performance would sell some albums. I played keyboards for line-up, but the rehearsals didn't feel like the kind of collaboration I was looking for or that I'd felt when it was just the two of us a year earlier. Everyone stared at their instruments, not at each other, including Steve. I didn't have a sense of communication that signaled, *yes, I see you, yes, I like what you're doing*, or *hey, let's bring it down to something quieter*. It wasn't how this group worked. It wasn't how Steve and I worked anymore.

If I'd considered it more, I might have recognized the way he avoided eye contact, the way his face dipped. I'd seen it in eighth grade, a young Steve trying to sink into his hair as if it were a burrow, as if he wanted to disappear.

■■■

We moved again, this time to the lower part of a duplex in north Minneapolis. With the music career going nowhere, Steve returned to painting, mostly large oils on canvas, and worked in the art room at a T-shirt screen-printing company. I was back in graduate school and started teaching freshman composition at the University of Minnesota in Minneapolis.

We were at a birthday party, held in the apartment of some friends from Duluth. The music was going, and guests filled the living room. I sat on a low-slung couch with Steve to my left, balancing a beer on the armrest, Anne Hyvärinen on the other side. Somehow she found out that I had founded an arts-and-entertainment newspaper in Duluth.

"I'm the coordinator of a small press festival," she explained. "It's called the Great Midwestern Bookshow. Have you heard of it?" I hadn't. "The thing is," she continued, "we could use some new people on our board of directors. We have board members who represent different small presses—you could bring in the journalism angle."

I was flattered. I didn't think of myself as a journalist, but I was definitely a book person.

"What would you want me to do?" I worried about the time

Lynette and Venus (as Steve), summer 1987

commitment. I was taking two graduate classes a quarter, was teaching one or two sections of freshman comp, and had an incomplete in my class on Milton left over from my time at UMD. But being on a board might make my résumé look better.

"The board meetings last a couple of hours, usually once a month," she explained. "The show happens once a year, in the spring." Anne could see I was thinking. "The date and location are already set," she offered. "A lot of work for the next festival is already done. You could just see how it goes for the first year."

I said yes.

As Steve and I walked down the sidewalk back to our car, I explained what Anne and I had been talking about. I was going to be on a board of directors. I was twenty-four and felt so much like an adult. I swelled with energy and clasped his hand. He nodded, happy that I was happy.

The Bookshow board met on the second floor of the Modern Times on Chicago Avenue, behind distinctive six-foot-tall "Modern" lettering on the front of the building. The wood floors were scratched by the decades of boots and gray office furniture scuffing across the surface. Some kind of office work went on there during the day—we'd find chairs at the desks and pull them into a circle for our meetings.

There was always an agenda on Bookshow letterhead that had the board members' names and their associated presses: Bill Truesdale, New Rivers Press; Sue Ann Martinson, *Sing, Heavenly Muse*; Doris Marquit, Marxist Educational Press. They were some of the people who laid the groundwork for Minnesota becoming a literary center. John Crawford, who founded West End Press and brought Meridel Le Sueur's books back into publication, had just retired from the board. I had heard about her life as an advocate for women and the working class, although it would be years before Le Sueur's work made it into the anthologies, and years before I would see her guided through Powderhorn Park in a wheelchair, thick, dark glasses protecting her eyes, and the crowd of May Day Parade celebrants parting in deference. When my name appeared on the letterhead, it said "Journalist" beneath it.

I wasn't sure what was on the first floor of the Modern Times, if anything. I never went through the front door, but climbed to the second floor by a narrower door on the building's side. The Loft Literary Center, which was becoming a major force in the writing world, had been there six years. They moved out just a few months before I joined the board.

As Anne said, most of the work for the 1985 Bookshow had already been done and we confirmed logistics. Judith Katz replaced Anne as the coordinator, and she brought on Barrie Borich as a part-time publicist. Barrie would eventually live a few houses away from me and publish *My Lesbian Husband*, a book-length memoir about her relationship with Linnea Stenson, who was in the English grad program at the U with me. Later Alexs Pate would join the board, and Carolyn Holbrook would succeed Judith as coordinator. These people would all become pillars of the local literary community.

The first show I attended was held at Coffman Union at the University of Minnesota. Much of it was coordinated by board member Sue Grieger, who also ran an undergraduate reading series and produced *Minnesota Literature Newsletter*, a monthly calendar of literary events. It was a revelation. There must have been at least six rows of back-to-back tables for the publishers, journals, and other literary organizations. They weren't just local: some exhibitors were from several states away. The number of people I saw actively working in the small-press world amazed me. I roamed exhibitor tables, stopping at each to examine the magazines and books. I bought a small, wide, Dada-looking book with a stapled spine and mysterious blocks of words on each page.

To the people who made them, these books were beloved fledglings sent into the world in search of readers. Allan Kornblum had just moved his press from Iowa to Minneapolis because of the state's support for nonprofits. He was changing the name from Toothpaste to Coffee House Press. I bought my stapled book from a publisher even smaller than the "small presses," with editions typed on electric or manual typewriters and photocopied—zines. Around this time our friends Pat and Andrea McKinnon in Duluth created *Poetry Motel* magazine this way. Steve did the layout for their first few issues in the living room of our north Minneapolis house.

Steve's artistic career began to open up, and sinking into the work seemed to make him happy. Charlie Bailey recruited him to do music for *The Nightingale*, produced by In the Heart of the Beast Puppet Theatre. They performed in a tiny space above Roberts Shoe Store at the intersection of Chicago and Lake, a somewhat sketchy part of town we would soon call home. Charlie also introduced us to Rifle Sport Alternative Art Gallery, housed in a former arcade above Moby Dick's, a bar on Minneapolis's notorious Block E, where peep shows, hustling, and small-time drug dealing took place across Hennepin Avenue from the restaurants and retail shops that aimed to attract businesspeople and suburbanites. Steve started to create large-scale paintings—up to eight by ten feet—that he folded in half for transport to the gallery, and he focused mostly on visual and installation art, putting music aside.

Outside of peaks of creative energy, we still argued for reasons I couldn't pinpoint. I kept looking for something to fix the tension, like a nice dinner or movie. But they were temporary solutions, and the moodiness returned.

Steve confessed to Charlie that we were arguing, and Charlie recommended marriage counseling. He and his wife had gone through it, and he said it helped. That relieved some of the stigma for us.

The therapist focused on our communication styles. She had us buy a book about how to argue productively—Steve saw any kind of disagreement as destructive and went to great

Lynette with art car chained to Rifle Sport stairs, installation by Venus (as Steve), about 1987

lengths to avoid it. Her suggestions seemed to work for a while, but within a year we slid back into the inexplicable arguments again.

■ ■ ■

My favorite fairy tale is called "The Goose Girl," probably because of the prominent role of a talking horse in it. In the story, a princess must travel to another kingdom to marry the prince she is betrothed to. She rides the horse, Falada, while an accompanying waiting-woman rides a horse that doesn't talk.

Before she leaves, the princess's mother fears for her safety on the journey, so the mother pricks her finger with a needle and blots the blood on three squares of fabric. The princess must keep these three squares in her bosom. They are her protection for the journey.

After a while on a deserted road in a dense wood, the princess grows thirsty and asks her waiting-woman to take a silver cup and fill it with water from a stream.

"If you want a drink, get it yourself," says the waiting-woman.

The princess apparently isn't used to people behaving rudely toward her, because instead of arguing, she acquiesces. She gets off Falada, goes to the stream, and bends down to fill her cup. As she bends, the waiting-woman sees the squares of fabric fall from her bosom. She knows the princess no longer has her mother's protection.

As a child reading the story again and again, eventually I would see that the Goose Girl's acquiescence was her first mistake, but it didn't seem fair. I imagined her thinking, *yeah, okay, I'll get it done. I'm a capable person.* But it causes her to lose her power. As a child, I didn't understand the moral of that part of the story.

Later in the Goose Girl's journey, the waiting-woman, knowing the princess has lost her mother's strength, insists they trade clothes and horses. The waiting-woman will ride into the new kingdom as the person betrothed to the prince. The princess doesn't have the fortitude to argue. She does what she is told. She also promises not to tell a living soul what happened. And so they ride in, roles reversed. But the waiting-woman is nervous the whole thing will come out because Falada can talk, so her first request is that the horse be killed. The princess asks for one favor: that Falada's severed head be nailed to the gate that the princess, now relegated to a goose-minding girl, will walk through daily.

Nailed to the gate, Falada's head still can talk. Falada hasn't changed much, except he can't run around and carry people anymore. He sings to the princess that her mother's heart would break in two if she knew what had happened. This gives the princess enough magical power to make the wind blow to keep an unwelcome suitor (a goose boy) away from her. Eventually the strange situation reaches the king's ears, and he investigates. When he hears her pledge to never tell the tale of what happened to another living soul, he instructs her to say it into a sooty stove. He listens on the other end of the stovepipe and realizes there is a false princess and a true one. The false princess is punished, in a brutal fashion of her own making, and the true princess weds the prince. Justice is served, and even an inanimate object, a stovepipe, has a role to play.

Or maybe it's not just a stovepipe. It's a conductor of secret information, just like Falada. For many years, it often *did* feel as if some kind of secret information was being withheld from me. The story reminded me of how my mother neglected to tell me that my father had had major surgery and been hospitalized a week, how she never told me he had cancer. How could Steve run so hot and cold and not say what was really bothering him?

■■■

We were tired of our living situation in north Minneapolis—frost under the bed, a rat in the kitchen, a child living upstairs who broke our front window swinging a two-by-four around—so we decided to buy a big, cheap house and live there with two other housemates. It was in south Minneapolis and had a two-story barn/carriage house in back that seemed on the verge of collapse. The owner offered to demolish it, but we said no. Steve could paint there. He also began making experimental films, some with stop-frame animation of him jumping up and down, some with me jumping up and down. Then there were some stop-frame animation films of him in lingerie.

I saw nothing unusual in this. I was used to Steve playing with his appearance, including using makeup in Straight Face,

Tom Gensmer and Venus (as Steve), Halloween 1986

and what he wore seemed theatrical. It was 1986, and no one had added a "T" to the GLB acronym yet, not to mention a Q or a plus sign. The mainstream media mostly avoided all such topics, except to talk about AIDS. By that point, I knew four or five people who had come out as gay, but most of my friends who would later identify as gay, lesbian, or trans remained firmly in the closet. To me, what Steve was doing was art, a commentary on gender roles.

I'd had a similar reaction a few years earlier when we watched the movie *Liquid Sky*, with Anne Carlisle playing two characters, a female model and a male model. Both Steve and I were captivated by the film's style and how one actress could play characters of different genders—this was nothing like Alec Guinness in *Kind Hearts and Coronets*! I honestly liked how Carlisle looked as Jimmy. Inspired, Steve suggested we dress in drag and take artsy photos of ourselves. I dressed as "Lars" and Steve as "Sonia." But my appearance as Lars dismayed me. I'm relatively short—5'4"—and with my wide hips, a man's suitcoat made me look portly. My journey with gender fluidity might have been different if my body had been more like Carlisle's: tall, slim, fitting naturally into men's clothing. I felt shamed by the experience and refused to do it again, but I didn't see a problem with Steve doing it to create art.

He also created two large-scale paintings for a Rifle Sport group show. One caught him in a midair leap, dressed in a masculine shirt and pants; in the other, he wore a pencil-thin skirt, heels, a blazer, and a broad-brimmed 1940s-style hat and stood calmly eyeing the viewer. The hat, skirt, and blazer were mine, and both of us laughed when someone assumed the painting was of me. But Steve laughed with less warmth than I did.

9

■×▲⁴※■▲°■

1988, Minneapolis

Through Rifle Sport, we met an entirely new circle of friends. The gallery wasn't far from where I transferred between buses on my way home from the U, so on late afternoons I headed over to the space to hang out. I edited a xeroxed literary magazine for them, predictably called *Magazine*. Sometimes a group of us would go over to the New French Café and Bar, which was artist central in Minneapolis's Warehouse District. Back then, visual art culture rose like a mighty tide on the northern fringe of downtown. The more upscale galleries were located near the New French and also in the Wyman Building a few blocks away. Artists worked and lived illegally in several of the run-down warehouses in the neighborhood, like Skunk House and Berman Buckskin, hosting shows that often turned into parties. A fledgling nonprofit, Intermedia Arts, opened a gallery space on the second floor of a building near the Wyman.

We had hopes that General Mills or First Bank would purchase something of Steve's, but the art-market bubble burst before that could happen. City leaders got tired of the scruffy look of Block E and its patrons and decided to condemn the block, tear it down, and start over. Artists had made the area attractive to affluent people, causing rents to go up, and buildings got converted to more upscale housing and businesses. The galleries began to close. Intermedia started a campaign to buy their own building south of downtown, and Rifle Sport moved to a space on the edge of downtown near Loring Park. Most of the artists moved in the opposite direction, to Northeast Minneapolis, where small houses and old warehouses kept rent relatively affordable for a few more decades.

Other changes took place. Tanya Warwas had moved to Duluth with her new husband, but now they were separated, and she was back in Minneapolis. She introduced us to Michael McManus, a gay man she'd met at First Avenue. Soon we were clubbing with the two of them. Michael usually dressed as an androgynous goth dandy, in black lace, dark lipstick, and a ghostly shade of foundation. Steve had gotten more particular with his clothes, too, and I started wearing fuchsia extensions in my hair.

It must have been Michael and his circle of friends that made Steve want to tell me something. We'd been married four and a half years by now. We stood in the second-floor hallway, a glimmer of late-afternoon sun glinting through the back window. Our housemates were at work. Steve turned to me.

"You know, I've been thinking," he said. "I think I'm probably bisexual."

"What?" I was floored. I didn't know where this had come from or what it was leading to. "What are you trying to tell me?"

"It's no big deal or anything. I haven't acted on it. I won't act on it. It's just something I'm beginning to realize about myself."

"Are you sure?" I had been headed up the stairs, and now I took two steps down to sit and turn back to face him. "I mean, sure you don't want to act on it? Look, I read Dear Abby all the time, and every letter where a man tells his wife he's bi, she says he's really just testing the waters. He just isn't ready to come out as gay yet. Is that you?" If Steve was getting irritated with me so often, maybe that was the issue. And that meant the problem was not solvable. We wouldn't be able to stay married. I would

Michael McManus, about 1994

have to say good-bye to this person I felt an indescribable connection to.

"No, no," Steve insisted, smiling a little. It was infuriating. I
wanted to stand up and shake him by the shoulders. "I just realized that I like looking at both men and women. I thought you
should know. But I only want to be with you. Don't worry, I've
been faithful to you, and I plan to *keep* being faithful to you."
He sat next to me on the stairs and gave my shoulders a little
hug. I didn't know what to think. My stomach felt like a sack of
cold, wet cement.

"But you've been getting depressed and upset about things.
Is this it?"

"No." Now Steve was more serious. "No, it's not that." He
was thinking. "I don't know, it's just that these sad feelings
come over me all of a sudden. I really don't know what it is." He
looked at me. He seemed to be earnest, sad that his emotions
would mysteriously nose-dive, and that he still didn't have the
answer. Now it was my turn to put my arm around him.

"Look," I said. "I have to say I don't feel comfortable with
this." That was an understatement. I was scared shitless. I needed
answers, and I still wasn't getting any. "I need you to tell me if
you think you're gay, okay?" I looked at him, making sure our
eyes met. "I don't have anything against being gay, but if you're
gay, there's no place for me in this relationship."

"Don't worry, that's not what I was trying to tell you," Steve
said quietly. He leveled his gaze at me, then kissed me. I wished
I could understand what he *was* trying to tell me.

The revelation didn't change anything on the surface, but
it made me second-guess every isolated nuance. I can't say it
caused me to lose confidence, because that had already happened. Our sex life was still good, and we always enjoyed cuddling on the couch and watching the same shows, going to the
same restaurants, and listening to the same music. We were
up to three cats in the house now, and we would get up in the

morning singing songs about them and dancing around the kitchen, much to our housemates' embarrassment.

But the angry outbursts increased. Once or twice a year Steve lost his temper and punched a wall, sometimes breaking his hand. This had even happened in Duluth, when we were dating. I'd called my brother, a doctor, to ask if the hand might be broken.

"Did he hit a wall?" Harvey had asked. So I concluded it must be a common thing. Still, I hated it. It scared me. It didn't occur to me that I should be physically frightened of him. I was more frightened *for* him, and I worried about his self-destructiveness.

Sometimes it felt like there was no longer a place for me in his life. I had loved collaborating with him, but now there seemed to be a greater chance I'd come away feeling rejected. One night at Rifle Sport, I helped him put up an art installation, thinking we'd be there until midnight at the latest. By 3:00 or 4:00 A.M. I was so tired that I finally lay down to sleep in a corner on the cold terrazzo. Steve didn't seem to hear or notice me shivering on the floor, and I pulled my winter coat around me for warmth. In my half sleep I wondered what made me unlovable.

We needed another round of counseling. This time, the therapist split us up—a male counselor for Steve, and a woman for me. We took the Minnesota Multiphasic Personality Inventory (MMPI), a psychological inventory test. After going over the results with his therapist, Steve sat down with me on the edge of our futon, a grave expression on his face.

The MMPI profile prompted his therapist to ask if he was a crossdresser, a term commonly used at the time, or transgender. It didn't take long for Steve to recognize that yes, he was trans.

"You have to understand," he said, curling into himself. "I've had suicidal feelings for so long about this."

I don't remember if he said he felt suicidal any time before this conversation, but I had sensed that kind of ultimate stake in the arguments we'd had leading up to this point. All I could do was nod and agree.

"I'm transgender," he said, his eyes shiny. I gave him a sad, cautious hug.

For some reason, the term didn't confuse me. I'd taken Latin. Transgender: across gender.

"Transgender," Steve repeated. "It's an umbrella term. It fits everyone on the spectrum. I don't know where I am on the spectrum." He didn't offer a new name or pronoun. He didn't know where he fit given the definitions of gender we saw around us. He had no guide, no role model to help him understand who he was.

"You don't know?" I asked quietly, holding back the urge to shriek.

"Well, gender reassignment surgery is a possibility," he said.

"Oh." I was sliding down the same slippery slope I'd clawed when he said he was bi. I remembered a famous tennis player from a long time ago who'd had what was then called a sex change. And then there was the trans character Roberta in the movie *The World According to Garp*, played by John Lithgow. Steve didn't seem like a Roberta to me. Our references and language were so limited at the time that it was difficult to envision what it meant for someone to be trans.

"He wants me to think about it for a week," Steve went on, "to really explore my options."

"Oh." I couldn't cheer for this. Would we stay married if Steve chose surgery? The only women I'd ever been attracted to were a few butch lesbians, and that wasn't who Steve was. Once, in the early years of his strange moodiness, when I wondered if our marriage was a mistake, I tried making out with a female friend who also felt rejected by her husband. We both wondered if sex with each other might replace our sense of lost intimacy, our sense of no longer being cherished. But neither of us could muster enough feeling to make it work.

Much as I feared this might end our relationship, I also knew it wasn't the kind of thing I could get in the way of. He was going to move somewhere along the gender spectrum, and his resolve was a massive ship with its own momentum. I stood and looked out the window. "I can't lie, I'm not happy about it," I said. "But it's your decision." I watched the trees swaying in the wind. I felt as helpless as one of the leaves sputtering on the branches below. I was a Goose Girl, and everything had shifted around me. I faced an impossible problem. I loved Steve, and I wanted to stay with Steve, but I didn't know if he would want me in his life if he changed that much. I also didn't know if I would remain in love with him if he changed that much.

The gender issue made sense, of course. Here was the explanation for the strange anger, the art projects featuring women's clothes. I remembered how he hadn't shared my enthusiasm for *The Rocky Horror Picture Show*, with its main character, Dr. Frankenfurter, hailing from "Transsexual, Transylvania." Now I began to understand why. It made light of who he secretly was.

As an artist, Steve already dressed unconventionally. I enjoyed that and thought I could handle feminine clothing. Beyond that, I wasn't sure.

Steve felt that he didn't need surgery, but he needed to express more of his feminine side. He thought feminine clothing would work. But psychology at that time considered crossdressing and transgender identity to be mental illnesses, according to the *DSM* (*Diagnostic and Statistical Manual of Mental Disorders*). It forbade Steve's therapist from encouraging a "mental illness," so his therapy ended. Despite that, the therapist gave Steve contact information for the CLCC (City of Lakes Crossdressers Club). At the time, the term "crossdresser" was what people in the community called themselves, and it included those who identified as male outside the club, those who would later come out as trans, and anyone in between. Nowadays, the label "crossdresser" is a slur when applied to trans people; at the time, it was seen as a vast improvement over the previous term: "transvestite."

Language aside, the CLCC was a social club where people networked and sought support for possible solutions. But the word "social" doesn't convey its real role: it was a lifeline for people. Two members interviewed us, and we were in.

10

1989–1990, Minneapolis

We walked nervously in the anonymous darkness up a drive-
way to the large, suburban rambler that matched the address
the members had given us. Steve wore a leather jacket over his
short black dress, seamed stockings, and heels. I wore a longer
black dress, ordinary seamless nylons, and pumps with heels
probably two inches shorter than Steve's.

A light over the stoop was on, and below it a note with an arrow indicating we should walk around the garage to the back.
We did, following a line of low lights sunk in the earth along the
sidewalk. We found ourselves stepping up to a deck entrance.
The door slid open, and we walked in.

We were in a spacious kitchen with expansive ranks of cabi-
nets that surrounded a center island. The kitchen flowed into
a family room with a fireplace, and more living room space
stretched around the corner and toward the front of the house.
The front curtains were closed. We were used to living in and
going to parties in crumbling apartments and warehouses
in the middle of the city, and we felt out of our element. We
looked around for the only two people we'd met so far, who
went by Allison and Marsha in this space, but they had been
dressed as men when we met a month earlier at a coffee shop.
The house belonged to Marsha and her wife. They were both

older than us, and as I scanned the room, it seemed as if everyone there was older than us. Allison, the CLCC club president,
now dressed in a modest blue jersey dress and chin-length bru-
nette wig, saw us and came over to offer a warm welcome.

"You made it!"

We nodded, and Allison explained where everything was:
coats upstairs on a bed, another bedroom set up as a dressing
room if needed, and food and beverages in the kitchen.

"Nancy will be giving a short presentation on electrolysis in
about half an hour," Allison added.

CLCC was a club where crossdressers could meet socially
once a month, in secret, to dress as they preferred and feel normal. While the club was open to everyone on the spectrum,
including male-presenting people and same-sex couples, the
only people I ever met at the gatherings were female-presenting
crossdressers and their wives. Most of them lived in the sub-
urbs, had kids, and had jobs that paid more than anything Steve
and I would ever get. The female-presenting crossdressers were
generally the family breadwinners and had a lot to lose if anyone discovered they crossdressed. Marsha had a beautiful house
because of what she did wearing male clothing.

Many wives told versions of the same "discovery" story: while
putting laundry away or straightening things up, the wife came
across a stash of women's clothes that were not hers. Immediately fearing her husband was having an affair, she felt so relieved when she found out he was only crossdressing that she
helped him shop. Steve didn't want me to shop for him because
one of the few areas where our opinions diverged was fashion.

I began to read everything I could find about the community, which wasn't much. In the 1980s, saying you were a crossdresser did not mean you were necessarily at a static place on
the gender continuum. I think for many in the club, it was a
relatively safe place to pause or stop. But most of the people
I talked to were trans and wanted to go further, possibly with

HQ
77.95
.u5
L53

Volume 4 Number 5   P.O. Box 16265, Minneapolis, MN 55416   MAY 1990
                            (Club Phone: 612-476-8195)

* Priority One *   * Priority One *

* * * Priority One *   MEETING LOCATION   * Priority One * * *

* Priority One *   * Priority One *

From Karen ....

As I try to become more of a leader in the club and achieve
some measure of progress in our struggle for understanding
and acceptance, I am perplexed by one major problem and that
is a meeting place each month.

We must thank all those who let us into their homes. There
is no doubt it has been appreciated by all.

But like most out there, I am not at liberty to have the
party at my place because of concerns that I have with my
daughters at home. It is that and other concerns that make
finding a place to meet much more difficult. Add on the fact
that summer and cursed daylight add yet another complication.
We all would wish that we could be open and not concern
ourselves as to what other people think, but alas reality
sets in. The struggle will continue and unfortunately we may
not be able to reap the rewards of our efforts. It will be
the generations to come that may have the chance to live in a
freer, more compassionate world.
(see Karen on Page 2)

* *

DISCRIMINATION IS ALIVE AND WELL ....

.... EVEN IN MINNESOTA ! ! !

We often tend to get lulled into a sense of security ... of
well being ... a feeling that just maybe that "great
mainstream of our population" is gaining at least a basic
understanding of gender related issues. We read our own
literature ... we meet on a regular basis ... we begin to
feel comfortable in our feminine roles ... we become so
immersed in our "paraculture" that the concept of crossgender
life styles seems as natural ... as "normal" ... as American
as apple pie and baseball. This is great for building and
maintaining a positive self image but we are truly deceiving
ourselves if we for once think that the "mainstream" views us
in the same light.

From time to time a splash of cold water brings us back to
realities of life as seen by the "mainstream".

(see DISCRIMINATION on Page 2)

BITS & PIECES

* THANKS AGAIN ......
Mary Ann & Gladys for
hosting our April party!
You've done extra duty on
the party front ... we're
greatful and again had a
super time!

* COUPLES SUPPORT GROUP ...
met May 2 and discussed
"People in a Relationship".
Feedback from those in
attendance includes "great"
& "positive" & "we'll
definitely have more such
meetings". Thanks Lynette &
Sonia for hosting.

* OUR MAY PARTY will be
held at Lynette & Sonia's.
Please note starting time of
8:30 pm. Map on Page 10.

* NORTHLAND OUTING gets
high marks from those in
attendance.   Read full
account on Page 6.

* IFGE CONVENTION REPORT
enclosed as separate insert
with   this   newsletter.
Important info for us all !!
Also enclosed is an insert
on IFGE finances.

* WHAT A CLOSE SHAVE !! ...
Ms. Beauty Boutique reports
on "State Of The Art"
hardware in the hair removal
department ... Page 7

Page 1

CLCC News, May 1990. The "Bits and Pieces" column notes that Sonia and
Lynette are hosts for two meetings.

hormones and/or surgery. Some were already on hormones and living a good portion of their lives as women. The club acknowledged this a few years later when they changed their name to City of Lakes Crossgender Community.

Steve loved socializing and sharing tips with others in similar circumstances. I liked nearly everyone in the group, wives and trans people equally, especially Jane Fee, a retired army officer who loved to mow her suburban lawn in a bikini to give her neighbors something to talk about. She had silvery gray hair that she tousled into a rakish tomboy look, a great body, and a military ID with a picture of her femme self and name. How she finagled it, I never figured out. This was several years before "don't ask, don't tell" made it possible for LGBTQ+ people to serve openly in the military.

In the CLCC, members chose a feminine name, while their cisgender partners used their first name only. This was to preserve anonymity as well as help members feel closer to their presenting gender. We also used she/her pronouns for everyone at the meetings. Steve chose "Sonia." This was fine with me until I noticed a disturbing pattern. As Sonia, Steve seemed giddy and ditzy, dependent and irresponsible. Not only was this *not* the person I fell in love with, it also seemed to mimic every bad stereotype of female behavior. The morning after one of these episodes I pointed out the problem. We were in the kitchen on a lazy Sunday morning drinking coffee and tea. I cleared my throat.

"I want to talk to you about something." Steve looked up from the newspaper spread out on the table. I continued, "I notice that you act like a different person when you're Sonia. It scares me. You're giggly and not serious." I couldn't come up with the words to say how I really felt, that Steve, as Sonia, behaved like a promiscuous airhead. Sonia had started to seem like someone I wanted to run miles away from.

"Yes, I can see how you'd feel that way," Steve responded. I waited for more, because usually I'd get a defensive answer at a juncture like this. There wasn't any pushback, which surprised me. I continued.

"If you want to act like a woman, you shouldn't act like that. That's not what women are like." Steve nodded.

"I'm worried that you're falling into some kind of behavior where you're one type of person when you have one name and one set of clothing, and you're another type of person when you have a different name and wear different clothing." I don't know if I used the term schizophrenic, commonly used then to mean "split personality." We had a few acquaintances who had developed what we now know as bipolar disorder, but when I looked at the Sonia/Steve division, I saw a fracture. It couldn't be healthy. Steve sighed, troubled.

"Yeah, maybe you're right," he agreed haltingly. "I don't want to fall into that kind of pattern."

"Maybe a way of dealing with this," I continued, "is to express more of this in your day-to-day life, so it isn't a special occasion you saved everything up for, it's just ordinary." What I wanted to say was, *It's just you*. I wanted a return to the real, authentic person I had married, the artist I could depend on to fix the car muffler with a soup can and who also knew how to jack up a twenty-five-foot barn wall to stabilize its framing. I wanted to hang on to the person who created soulful music and knew how to make me laugh at completely unexpected things.

Steve sat across from me, forehead low, hands sweeping back his hair, masking the effects of strong emotion, then pulled his hair behind his ears.

"Yes," he affirmed. "That sounds like a good idea. I'll do that."

His quick agreement mystified me. Much later, I learned he had been reading porn magazines to understand what was happening to him as a transgender person. Overall, what he picked up from porn was that being feminine meant acting submissive.

The CLCC was crucial to our trans journey. We had honest discussions with people who planned to "fully transition"
(the way we then referred to gender-confirmation surgery)
as well as with people who didn't. I think almost all the members wanted to transition on some level, but some realized it
wouldn't work for them. Most who had surgery disappeared
from the ranks of the CLCC. They moved away to start new
lives, keeping their past a secret. That was the model recommended then—the Benjamin guidelines, developed by Harry
Benjamin in his pioneering work with trans people. I learned
about these guidelines paging through the issues of *Tapestry*
magazine that were always out for display at CLCC gatherings.
The major step that many in the group seemed focused on was
living one year as their true gender before surgery, so people
could see if it was the right thing for them to do. It seemed an
impossible barrier to some—they were afraid of being outcasts
and targets of violence during that year when their anatomy
didn't match how they presented.

Although divorce was not part of the Benjamin guidelines,
it was also part of the protocol—society wasn't ready to handle two legally married spouses of the same gender—and
most spouses in the CLCC wanted to stay married. Steve and I
wanted to stay married. I was comfortable with him dressing in
lingerie, and sex continued to be good. We still had intellectual
and philosophical conversations, still sang songs to the cats.
We shared a do-it-yourself attitude about home improvement,
working side by side on a new rehab project every year, and we
both felt sustained by art.

But Steve's terrible moodiness came back, even after I
thought we had "solved" the problem when Steve expressed
being trans. I could never predict what would bring on the suicidal moods or how they might end. I took it seriously, but I had
to learn to live with it. The emotional vagaries made me feel as
if I lacked something.

It didn't help that neither of us had any role models or

people who could give us guidance. The CLCC members provided tips, but they couldn't guide our identity as a couple. So as Steve changed his gender expression, I adjusted. We would reach a place where he was happy, and then a few years later, it would turn out to not be enough. That feeling of a mismatch between his identity and his appearance would begin to seep into his soul again.

■■■

Decades later, a therapist finally saw *beyond* Venus's transgender identity and realized she was also coping with undiagnosed ADHD. Given that information, some of the mood swings began to make more sense: Steve simply wasn't good at consciously regulating his feelings and reactions, and he had major problems in controlling attention and shifting focus. But back then it baffled me. He regularly forgot plans and promises, and I didn't know if I could trust the things he said to me.

■■■

The few friends I told about his crossdressing didn't help. They didn't understand why I wanted to stay with him, and it made me feel isolated. Steve was looking more androgynous, with shoulder-length hair, sometimes wearing women's pants and blazers for dress-up occasions. To me, the changes were gradual, and he looked like the same person I had married. Others saw a sharp difference.

And he pushed for more. We started going to the Gay 90's, a huge gay bar in downtown Minneapolis where he could dress as a woman. I liked it there because the clientele was fun and no one wanted to hit on me. My favorite place was the piano bar, where Lori Dokken sat at a grand piano, greeting everyone in a way that made them feel not just welcome, but like a cherished member of the family. I also liked the drag shows.

I'd read "Notes on 'Camp'" and viewed drag as a form of social critique. But the constant focus on how Steve grappled with expressing who he was, and the constant going out, began to feel exhausting. Worrying about his depression didn't stop my own need to breathe, and it felt like he was taking up all the available oxygen.

Here's the thing: Steve's gender issues called into question my own identity. At first, I saw it in binary terms: if he was a woman, was I not enough of a woman? Was there something deficient with me? I questioned whether I was pretty enough, sexy enough, even when I knew logically my womanhood wasn't the point. It was as if he had tipped the scale one way, and I needed to scramble to balance out the other side. I wasn't male and didn't want to look male, and the one time I'd cut my hair short (in junior high) I regretted it.

But I didn't feel comfortable being labeled female, either. It felt limiting. When I was four or five years old, my sister Carolyn asked me what I wanted to be when I grew up, and I replied without hesitation that I wanted to be a boy. I knew as I said it that I didn't *literally* want to be a boy and grow up to be a man, but I wanted to do all the adventurous things that boys could do. Peter Rabbit was the one who had the adventure, not Flopsy, Mopsy, or Cottontail. Maybe that's why I wanted to be a horse instead of a fifth-grade girl.

Soon the weekly excursions to the 90's were not enough. Mariette Pathy Allen, the photographer who had created a groundbreaking, coffee table–sized book called *Transformations: Crossdressers and Those Who Love Them*, was coming to town. One of the photo subjects was a CLCC member, and to promote the book she and any other interested members were invited to appear on local television for the noontime talk show *Good Company*. Steve wanted to participate. It would mean going public—named only as Sonia, but on camera and clearly recognizable.

I was frightened about what would happen. I anticipated prejudice, mockery, and possibly the loss of my teaching assistant job. The anonymity of the CLCC had felt safe, and running into someone at a gay bar who might create problems seemed unlikely. But television? I asked him not to do it, but even as I pleaded, I knew I wouldn't be able to stop him. He said hiding in the closet made him feel suicidal. And professional treatment was impossible. How could I argue?

We decided to tell our immediate families before the show so they wouldn't accidentally hear about it from someone else.

At the Grandells' house, we sat with Steve's parents around the heavy oak table that had belonged to his mother Lillian's parents. It nearly filled their modest knotty-pine dining room. Ade and Lillian knew we had something serious to tell them. I kept my gaze neutral, focusing on the lazy Susan that always occupied the center of the table.

"There's something we want you to know," Steve began. We'd decided Steve would introduce the discussion and do most of the talking. These were his parents, and it was his issue—at least that's how I saw it—and he was comfortable talking with his parents about feelings. I wasn't. He explained, "I'm going to be on a talk show to promote a book. The book is about crossdressers. I'm going to be on the show because I'm a crossdresser." Ade's grim countenance relaxed a little. Lillian spoke.

"You know we love both of you very much, and that we'll always love you," she said, patting Steve's hand lightly. "Don't ever worry about that." She knew we had been afraid of anger, of rejection. But there was more she wanted to know. "And you're not gay, are you?" Steve said no, and I agreed that he wasn't. That's what Ade and Lillian had been most afraid of, that Steve would turn out to be gay, and then we would get a divorce. The irony wasn't lost on us—the gay community had been our main source of support and sympathy so far, and it felt odd to deny the connection. But mostly we were overwhelmed with relief it had gone so well. For the first time I felt rock-solid in their support not just for their child, but also for me.

At my mother's house just a few miles away in the adjacent neighborhood, again we sat at a dining room table to talk. The room was bigger, and we clustered at a curve on one end of the oval. The other end was strewn with papers from my mother's correspondence, bill keeping, and leftover tax materials.

I started the conversation this time, grateful to have a model to work from.

"Mom, we came up here to let you know that Steve is going to be on a local talk show in Minneapolis." She nodded. "It's about a book on crossdressers. Steve is going to be one of the people talking about the book because he's a crossdresser." I waited for the negative response and was amazed when none came.

"Oh," she said, thinking a moment. Then she turned to Steve. "So how are you doing? Are you okay?" Steve said yes. She turned to me. "And are you okay?" I assured her I was okay. "I know it must be very hard, the way people might treat you," she continued. "I'm glad that you told me." I was floored. Given our strained relationship, this reaction seemed impossibly good. She'd come through for us.

But we still had to contend with Minneapolis. I had maxed out my graduate assistantship of six years teaching freshman comp and found another job at the U that would start in the fall, teaching study skills. It was the end of spring term, and I wanted to turn in my grades, clean out my office, and move out of Lind Hall before the show aired. I didn't want to run into anyone quizzing me about what it was like being married to "a man who dressed in women's clothing," as one of the show's co-hosts would put it. I didn't know what I could say. I hadn't found words for how I felt.

I was invited to lunch with the author and the other participants after the show aired, but my stomach rolled at the thought of it. Allen's photographs were beautiful, but I was upset with being potentially outed as a person whose spouse was transgender.

I handed my grades to the English Department secretary about fifteen minutes before the show aired and felt temporarily safe as I climbed on a bus and eased myself onto a warm vinyl seat. I watched a recording of the show at home later with Steve. He was incensed that the hosts had announced the segment was "for mature audiences only" and people were told they might want to take their children out of the audience. But overall, he felt happy about how it had gone. As I watched the interview on the screen, I was more interested in the married hosts of *Good Company*, "the husband-and-wife team, Steve and Sharon." Had they ever dealt with anything like this in *their* marriage?

"Sonia," said Sharon to Steve, "I understand you have one rule with your wife about this," prompting him for a response.

"I, ah, I'm not sure what you're talking about." A long, brass earring Steve had made with his jeweler's kit dangled from his right ear.

"The rule that you don't share clothes," Sharon filled in, obviously having discussed this before the show went live.

"Oh, well," Steve stumbled. "We're very different sizes."

At least he hadn't shamed me in that comment. The real reason was that he looked *better* in my clothes than I did. Like the actress Anne Carlisle, he had a model's slim hips and long legs. He promised not to embarrass me, and he'd kept that promise.

In the days that followed, no brigands with torches arrived. No one taunted me. No one fired me. No one even mentioned the program to me. Coming out at this level was a lot easier than I anticipated and—in the long run—the best path. But it was only one stage on a long journey.

11

1990, Washington, DC

While Steve took the first steps of openly struggling with gender, I made slow progress through graduate school. I usually taught two comp classes in the fall and winter quarters, and one in the spring. That made it easy for me to treat the classes I was taking—the ones that led to a degree—as less of a priority. They tended to be seminars, with one giant paper due at the end, which I would pull off at the last minute. That approach didn't impress my professors. I pulled mostly A's, but I was in the PhD track. I don't think the professors gave anything below an A to anyone at that point unless something was seriously wrong, or the professor was just plain mean.

I worried that I wasn't distinguishing myself, wasn't getting nominated for anything. The U's English Department had changed its admission policy sometime after I'd gotten in, and now they admitted fewer students and awarded those few with fellowships and scholarships. I recognized I was on a lower tier, grouped with the students who weren't expected to finish.

Somehow I learned there was a doctoral-dissertation travel scholarship available. It may have been the only thing I qualified for at that point, and it was only a $1,500 grant. But money was tight at home, especially in the summer when I wasn't teaching. I knew what I wanted to research—early sound recordings and their influence on poetry in the 1920s and 1930s—so I applied. I got a grant to do research at the Recorded Sound Division of the Library of Congress in Washington, DC.

August was the cheapest time to go to Washington, when Congress wasn't in session, and traveling then wouldn't conflict with my teaching schedule. But I worried about being away from Steve the entire month. As an artist, he'd already done short, weeklong residencies, and they often led to conflict. Before a trip, he'd often be moody, and then when he was away he would call, sounding jubilant. It felt like he was happier without me, and I felt deflated. A long-distance phone conversation might end with me crying, and him crying in response. (His unrecognized ADHD may have been a factor, giving him an emotional high because he was somewhere new, happily distracted by working on a project with new people.) I couldn't understand the fluctuations in how he reacted to me, but I was determined to do something for myself. I would go to Washington, and Steve would join me at the end for a Labor Day–weekend vacation.

The month was lonely yet exhilarating. Each day I walked down Second Street past the Supreme Court to the Library of Congress's Madison Building and paged through issues of *Talking Machine World* and whatever else the staff found that might be of interest. I took a bus up to Howard University in northeastern Washington to read through the archives for Langston Hughes and Sterling Brown. When I explained to the research librarian that I was from the University of Minnesota, and that John Wright was one of my advisors, she beamed and clasped her hands. "Oh, John!" she exclaimed, and welcomed me into the reading room.

By the end of the month, I looked forward to being with Steve again, but worries haunted me. I'd written him a postcard nearly every day, and he hadn't written back much. Phoning was complicated at Thompson-Markward Hall, where I lodged. There was no private phone in my room, and long-distance calls involved pushing coins into a pay phone off the lobby. We would get a note in our mailboxes if someone had called for us. The hall was an old YWCA with a strict no-male-visitors policy. We'd planned for Steve to wait for me in the lobby, and then we would shift to the Watergate Hotel, chosen for the ironic nostalgia.

I anticipated the reunion as I sat in the waiting area at Washington National Airport—the way we used to meet travelers before September 11, 2001. It was early afternoon, and the summer sun streamed through the waiting-room windows, warming the rigid back-to-back rows of chairs. It was Steve's first plane ride, and I'd coached him to expect certain sensations—the odd angles, the landing thump, and the whoosh of brakes coming on. I hoped he hadn't gotten sick and would be in a good mood. I'd told the guys at the Sound Recording Division all about him, that he was a musician and artist, that we were rehabbing a house. Pretty much everything, except that he crossdressed.

At the airport gate, passengers started coming off the ramp into the waiting area, first one or two, then some clusters, then more. Yes, this was definitely the plane disembarking. I grew more excited, ready to leap forward to hug and kiss.

It seemed like a hundred people walked by, met by the loving arms of the people around me. Finally, Steve emerged.

Instantly, I saw there was something different about him.

His clothes were fine—he was wearing his black, silky pants that I loved, and a black women's blazer over a black shirt—the moody, mysterious look. And his hair was shoulder-length, tousled and bleached to a medium blond, as it had been when I left. But his skin—his face—was different. It wasn't just the eye makeup. That I could categorize as goth or Bowie-esque, and I was used to him wearing a little of it. Here everything was too smooth, too blended. A mask. Steve's skin didn't look real to me; it looked like the skin of an imposter. It was the foundation makeup, which I must have seen already in outings to the

CLCC or the Gay 90's, but it was inexplicably jarring to see it here, in bright daylight, in an airport, beginning what was supposed to be our loving reunion and vacation together.

I moved toward him, forcing my feet forward. Steve didn't look happy, either. We gave each other a little smile, and I leaned toward him for what felt like more a gesture than a kiss. It wasn't a real kiss. It was an attempt to go through the motions.

"You're wearing foundation makeup," I blurted.

"Yes, I've been wearing it all month." There was no give in his answer, no apology. "I wear it every day," he added.

"Since when?" I was surprised. Why hadn't he told me about this?

"Well, I told you I've been going out with Michael and his friends."

Nearly every night. That fucking Michael McManus. He often met us at the gay bars where Steve could dress. I didn't think they were having an affair, but it seemed close. I was sure they'd kissed. Michael wished Steve and I would break up—he whispered that to me every time he got drunk. One winter at the Saloon, I grew so incensed by his apparent lack of respect that I poured a drink over his head and stomped outside. I sat on a mountain of snow left by a plow in the parking lot next door and waited for Steve, hoping for sympathy. I didn't get any: when he came outside, Steve insisted that since Michael had a broken leg, and we'd brought him there, we had to drive him home.

Now, we walked toward baggage claim, talking only of the simplest subjects, just to span the distance.

"The cats are okay?"

"Lisa's feeding them. I dropped off the key for her last night."

"Good."

Then I had to push it further.

"Look, I told the guys at the Sound Recording Division that we'd stop by before they close. They really want to meet you."

"Okay."

"But I need you to take the foundation off."

It was like a loading dock door being pulled down with a metal thunk. Steve shut down.

"No."

"But I can't take you to meet them like this!" I gestured at his face.

The door thunked down even harder.

"I can't change. I won't change."

"But . . . please. These guys really want to meet you. *I* want them to meet you."

There was no relenting. We found Steve's suitcase. At Thompson-Markward, I collected my baggage as quickly as possible.

We really had it out in the hotel room.

"Why won't you take off the foundation? Won't you do it, just for me?" I wasn't just worried about what other people would think. Something about his smooth, tinted face repelled me, an internal feeling I couldn't shake. My stomach hurt. It seemed I could smell the makeup when I came close to his face. I couldn't bring myself to kiss him.

"I can't. It's me. This is who I need to be," Steve pleaded.

"What do you mean? Look, maybe if it's just a little lighter, not so intense."

I realized his appearance took me back to my first funeral, my grandfather's. When my mother led me to the casket, I prepared to see someone who was dead. I was ten, and my curiosity usually overrode any potential squeamishness. I peered over the side and found Grandpa's familiar face and hands had been tinted an odd orange-pink color, his cheeks dusted with blush. He was a figure in a wax museum, an imposter. Comments about how lifelike he looked bubbled in the background. Why would people want to make a dead body look like a living person? My horror was so strong that when my own father passed away, I begged my mother to not have an open-casket funeral. She said no, so I avoided looking at my father's face in that state. Now I was married to someone whose makeup reminded me of that, a semblance of the person I loved.

He glared at me. I sat on the edge of the bed and Steve sat in a chair next to the window. The waning light in the sky told me I had really messed things up. The Sound Recording Division was closed by now. I had let my colleagues of the last month down. My dreams of future collaborations with them were probably also fucked. They'd wanted me to be a member of ARSC, the Association for Recorded Sound Collections. They'd wanted to meet my husband. Now he was in town. And I felt there was no way I could introduce him to them, no way to socialize and network, no way to develop this academic path.

"Look, maybe just for a couple of days," I said.

"I can't." Steve was crying. It wasn't the first time he had cried during our many arguments as each layer of the onion skin peeled away, each time he got a little closer to who he really was. I knew he was in trouble. "I feel as if I can't . . . "—and he broke off.

He was feeling suicidal again. I was off the bed and on the carpet, on the floor hugging his knees. I still couldn't embrace his face. His head was down, curled inward, his nose running with tears. I couldn't push him any further.

"It's okay," I mumbled. It wasn't okay.

I stopped by the library the next morning to say a hasty good-bye to the guys who had helped me do research for the last four weeks. They had started digitizing the sound from old wax cylinders and had been eager to have me listen to them. They played what might have been Walt Whitman's voice for me. I'm sure they wanted to show off the collection to my spouse. And I had wanted to show him off to them. That wasn't going to happen. I could not imagine a scenario in which they'd like him. And if they didn't like him, they wouldn't like me, either.

The next days were mostly numb. We spent four more days in the nation's capital, and all the touristy things I'd held back from doing were now our itinerary. But the days were painful. Steve dialed back the foundation and makeup but remained upset. I think the only thing we predictably enjoyed was having lunches and dinners together. And when we talked in settings that distracted us, we still got along and even laughed with each other. But in all the photographs, Steve refused to look happy. His eyes smoldered with anger at the photographer: me, holding the camera, asking him to smile.

12

1991, Minneapolis

I told myself that divorce was always an option, though the thought made me miserable.

The study-skills classes I taught were housed in the Educational Psychology Department, and most of my colleagues were professors and grad students in psychology. After I got to know some of them, I told a few that Steve was transgender, hoping for sage, quasi-professional psychological advice. They had nothing. Just sympathy. I found some do-it-yourself divorce forms at an office-supply store, next to the wills and rental contracts. For the first time in my life I had my own office with a door that locked, so I kept them in the top drawer and mentally filled in the blanks when I felt dead-ended.

Any happy interlude we felt had the potential to abruptly shift to a frightening outburst if I disagreed with anything. The arguments didn't even shock me anymore; when Steve punched a wall, I'd walk away, reminding him to patch and repaint it when he was done.

One argument did frighten me, though. It was during the day, and the slanted light of a late afternoon or early summer evening filtered through the windows. We sat in the living room, me on the couch set diagonally in front of the fireplace, Steve in a captain's chair to the right of the fireplace.

"No, I don't want to go out to the Gay 90's tonight," I might have said. "I want to have some time for just the two of us. Can we do something different, that doesn't involve . . . ?" I might have gestured at my torso, as if pulling a dress down over it.

Steve looked crestfallen. "I just need a break from all that," I added. I could see I was making it worse.

"It's just that . . ." he looked off toward some distant point through the living room window.

"Look, I know you need to do that," I countered, "but you don't act like we're a couple when we're there, when you're out and dressed." His face grew graver, but I had to stand up for myself. "I just need to feel like we're a couple," I pressed. When he went out dressed, the positive attention he got from other people, many of them strangers, made him blossom. He seemed to forget I was there. Sometimes it caused others to assume we weren't together. I'm sure his behavior also triggered a fear in me that he would rather be with a man.

"I don't know how to explain this," he said, tenting his hands over his face. His voice dwindled to a whisper: "I need to do this. I can't explain it—"

"Please," I said, "I just need to feel that we're together, I need to feel like you love me."

"Of course I love you!" he boomed. "How can you think I don't love you! Look at all the things I do for you!" I tried to stay calm. I honestly didn't understand why asking to relate as a couple would make him so angry.

"But it doesn't *feel* that way to me when you don't want to spend time with me, when you start arguing like this," I responded, gesturing at the air around us. I waited for him to say something in response. I wanted him to take me into his arms and say he loved me. Instead, there was silence. I looked at him. He glared back.

He got up from the chair and strode into the kitchen. I followed. Now I was upset, too.

"What are you doing?" I yelled. He was at the kitchen counter, his back to me. Then he turned around.

"Is this what you want?" he cried. "Because I want to die!"

He had pulled a knife—a paring knife with a blade about seven inches long—out of the butcher block. He held the point under his chin.

"*Is this what you want?*" he screamed again. I shouted something wordless, taking in at once that he might jab the blade into himself, or he might just as easily slice at me. I roared something again, and he threw it on the floor, letting it skitter to rest just between us, as if challenging me to pick it up for a duel. The knife pointed toward the corner, directed at neither of us. But Steve was still in a rage, and I was in over my head. I shrieked again and flew to the back door, unlocking it and running out of the house.

I didn't know where to go. I wanted to make sure I didn't get stabbed to death, and I didn't know what to do beyond that point. I knew Steve might hurt himself, even kill himself, but I wasn't willing to sacrifice my safety. A refrain pounded, *this is wrong, this is wrong, this is wrong.* I hid around the corner of the house for a while, waiting for him to come out the back door after me. He didn't, but I couldn't stay there. I was within full view of anyone who cared to gawk from the windows of the fourplex next door. After a few minutes, I scrambled across the yard to our two-story carriage house, then essentially a barn for squirrels. I closed the door and climbed the narrow spiral staircase Steve had made out of mismatched lumber. It vaguely resembled the one in Marcel Duchamp's *Nude Descending a Staircase*, and I had already fallen on it several times. This time I held to the stairs with my hands and didn't slip.

I sat on the second floor and tried to understand what had just happened. Pinpricks of light came through gaps in the siding and a couple of bullet holes on one end, while light from a window on the other illumined Steve's art projects stored there: the eight-by-ten-foot canvases, the tall, barbed wire–wrapped posts for the papier-mâché horse-head skulls, the stick men, and the giant canvas and wood spider. I didn't want to lose all this. I had watched all these things being created. I had helped carry them to art shows and back home again.

Eventually, the light began to dwindle. I wanted to return to the house. Would it be safe? I looked around for something to protect myself. I found a broom handle and carried it back to the house.

The kitchen was still empty, and the knife was still lying in the middle of the floor. I picked it up and put it in the sink. I looked at it, afraid it would jump to life in my hands. It seemed wrong to leave it there. I picked it up, turned on the water, and ran a soapy sponge along the blade. Then I toweled it dry and stuck it back in the butcher block.

I found Steve upstairs in our third-floor bedroom, sleeping, or trying to sleep. I went over to him and kissed him. We hugged each other and cried together.

"Do you know how frightened that made me?" I asked gently. Steve seemed puzzled. "I thought you might hurt me with the knife," I explained. "I've been hiding in the carriage house all this time."

"Oh, no, I would never hurt you!" he exclaimed. "No, that wasn't it at all!" He hugged me closer to him.

"Promise me you'll never do anything like that again," I insisted. I wasn't sure whose safety I worried about more, mine or his. It seemed like our lives together were one body, one entity. If one of us collapsed, the other would, too.

"Oh yes, of course. I'm so sorry." Now he was rubbing the sides of my head as he hugged me, trying to reassure me. I hugged him back, but it seemed there was another part of me that floated above the two of us, watchful, suspicious.

We both lay back on the bed, exhausted. I didn't understand any of this. I stared up at the angled ceiling above our bed, lost in the jangled mess of drywall and plastic that wouldn't be mudded and painted for years. I could not figure out how to fit the pieces together.

13

■⋆▲⋆✶■∧●■

1993, Paris, Berlin, Prague, Venice

Despite the crisis points, Steve never seemed to hold onto those feelings long. He became a loving partner again, and as our tenth anniversary approached, we felt like survivors. I'd finished my doctorate the previous year and bought myself a decent bookcase to mark the occasion. Then I started freaking out because I hadn't landed a teaching a job. Given Steve's evolving sense of who he was and how he needed to express that, I hesitated to apply at institutions away from the Twin Cities and the community we knew. But within a few months, I managed to piece together a good income as an adjunct at several institutions, freeway-flying from one classroom to the next.

We decided to get Eurail passes and travel in Europe for three weeks. I had been there twice, but Steve had never been out of the country. I used the Rough Guides series to set up lodging in Paris, our first stop. We planned to wander from there and use tourist-information offices in each town's center to find lodging in the other cities. This was before the internet or email, so everything was done by phone. I practiced saying and imagining all the French phrases I would need to book our hotel by international call and did fine until the proprietor asked me to spell my name. I could not for the life of me remember the

French word for "y" (*i grec*). When we checked in I found that she had spelled my name "Lunette," which means glasses.

At this point, Steve was usually dressed all in black, with skinny jeans and a black leather jacket nipped in at the waist. His hair was long—a little past his shoulders—and auburn red. I thought he looked like a rock-and-roll person, a little like Joey Ramone. But Steve's long hair and slim-fitting clothing meant that sometimes people weren't sure if he was male or female, and we didn't realize that Parisians would get mean about it.

The first time this happened, we'd bought little individual quiches and coffee at an open-air market along one side of a park and sat on a park bench. Around us, people basked in the sunshine and strolled the sidewalks; children glided briskly on the swings in a small playground maybe a hundred feet from us. People nodded and smiled as they walked by, and we did the same. We stood up and walked to the garbage can to throw away the containers and forks and began to meander, wondering what to explore next. Suddenly a short, slight man in a dark cap who had been walking on our side of the street bolted across to the other side and started shouting at us. My college French hadn't taught me the vocabulary he was using, but it was obviously negative. I turned, telling myself he must be shouting at someone or something else. Nothing like that had ever happened to me before. Steve was sure that he'd been read first as a woman and then as a man, and I didn't want to believe him. I didn't want something so jarring ruining our beautiful morning together.

Steve didn't know any French at all and became completely paralyzed by the lack of a language anchor. He compensated by shielding his face with dark sunglasses most of the time and not speaking much. He was afraid his voice would give him away. He fell into a grim silence, not wanting to talk to me, and the trip began to unravel.

The only places we felt we could be ourselves together in Paris were the cemeteries. First we went to Montparnasse, where we stumbled on Baudelaire's grave. To get to Père Lachaise, where Jim Morrison was buried, we plotted out the Metro stops and headed out for our last full day in Paris. When we emerged, I looked up for some kind of reference point and saw the sad, misshapen stumps of pollarded boulevard trees, with twiggy growth bravely trying to grow and reach again. They seemed the perfect metaphor for our trip.

We oriented ourselves, turned a few corners, and found the cemetery gates. The caretakers sold maps at a nearby shelter. I looked at one before buying it and asked in a mixture of French and English about Jim Morrison's grave. I couldn't find it on the map.

"Bah!" was the response, followed by other angry syllables I couldn't decipher. I gave the map back to the caretakers, and we proceeded, knowing that this might be a failed mission. We turned up one lane, then another, enjoying the general gothic feel of the narrow house-shaped tombs. Then Steve saw an arrow crudely painted in black on the side of a crypt. It pointed left. Underneath, it read, "Jim." We looked at each other and followed the arrow, then found another, and still another, sometimes with the words "Jim this way," and sometimes just arrows.

Jim Morrison's grave was *not* on the map of famous gravestones because the cemetery did not welcome his fans. To compensate, his admirers had painted arrows strategically on a number of tombs, thus endearing themselves all the more to cemetery staff. It was clear why my request had been met with a "Bah!"

When we got to the plot, we saw why Morrison fans were not welcome. The grave wasn't much more than a small sand pit. We knew we were in the right place because we weren't the only ones there—five or six other people stood around the sand pit, probably also trying to figure out how to react to this pilgrimage of apparent emptiness. Someone had carried away whatever headstone had marked the grave, leaving only the concrete curb that outlined a bare, sandy site where cigarettes and various small bottles of alcohol had been left in homage to the musician. One bystander gave a wry grin and shook out a cigarette to add to the offerings.

Steve had brought along our vintage Bolex 16-millimeter movie camera and started to shoot the scene, circling the space. The five or six other Morrison fans at the gravesite murmured, as if Steve were someone they should know. He continued to circle, pausing occasionally to wind the five-pound camera. Slim, tall, with the black jacket, dark glasses, and long hair, Steve looked like a somebody in rock and roll, maybe even another incarnation of Jim. We didn't say anything to the other pilgrims. We just basked in the relief of that empowering illusion.

Things got better when we traveled to Germany. In Berlin, the brother of one of my teaching colleagues showed us around, and we felt welcomed. This was more like the anniversary trip I'd imagined. We seemed to match a certain look that was accepted there, but it didn't feel completely safe. When we sat at an outdoor restaurant in the public square of what seemed like a cute, small town, a young boy kept circling the tables shouting at us. The adults all looked shocked and embarrassed. Neither of us knew German, but the adults' reaction was unmistakable. Episodes like that made both of us fear for Steve's safety, but we addressed it differently: I tried to laugh about it on the surface but stay watchful, and Steve drew inward with worry. As the trip progressed, sometimes he channeled that worry into working on pen-and-ink drawings in a sketch pad or shooting more film with the Bolex, and the silence deepened.

I didn't know what to do.

■■■

We decided to go from Berlin to Prague because Prague sounded beautiful and mysterious. Long ago, artists, composers, and writers had flocked there. The guidebook said that when we arrived at the station, we would probably be met by various agents who could find us lodgings.

"See, it's just like the book said," I pointed out as we got off the train.

"But which one?" Steve asked.

I read the signs, trying to figure out which ones looked the most legitimate.

One of the men noticed me scrutinizing the signs.

"Hey, you two need a good place to stay?" he asked. "Good location, just off Wenceslas Square. Only a few hundred meters from here."

Neither of us had a good idea of what a few hundred meters was, but we'd both heard of Wenceslas Square and were cheered by the fact that the man spoke English.

A few hundred meters turned out to be about five blocks. At first, I didn't want to relinquish my suitcase to him, but after the first three blocks or so I decided that he was going to a lot of effort just to run away with it, so I let him help. Steve kept his baggage. The man stopped in front of a door off the sidewalk, unlocked it with a large, heavy key, and led us inside to an airy, empty hall. A wide staircase went up one side of the space, and he led us up the four long flights and unlocked another door that led into a kitchen. He turned and produced a third key, which opened a much flimsier hollow-core door to our room. The room turned out to be the living room in an apartment where an old couple lived. It was clear the door and part of the wall in our room had been hastily constructed without any cosmetic finishing other than a couple of coats of white paint. Another man walked past, unlocked a door, and closed it behind him. The agent explained that he lodged in a different room. Taking our money, the agent introduced us to the old couple, then left. They didn't speak English. We didn't speak Czech. It was awkward. We all smiled and nodded.

It felt like we had invaded their home. This was probably

something they had to do to make enough money to survive, but it felt uncomfortable. The Czech Republic was moving from communism to capitalism, and it wasn't a pretty process. The menu items at restaurants were priced ridiculously low by American or European standards, but no Czech citizens could afford them. Instead, the local population lined up at lunch windows for food—that was their version of a restaurant. Salesmen hawked cheap merchandise at sidewalk tables on streets near the city center, much of it pornography. And prostitution was everywhere. I didn't recognize it at first, but learned to when Steve directed my gaze to a woman standing on a corner. She never crossed the street with the other pedestrians when the light changed.

Czechs seemed to dress the way Americans did in the 1950s and early 1960s. The men wore short hair and very traditional clothing, with fedoras and trench coats, and women seemed hypersexualized, wearing vivid lipstick and flimsy dresses. We did not fit in at all—especially Steve.

The obvious visual distinction between men and women unmoored him. His emotions seesawed. Sometimes he appeared to like exploring the city and then a moment later went cold and withdrawn. We had a few nights of tears and desperate conversations, with the absurd limit of trying to be quiet because the walls were so thin. Steve was feeling suicidal, and there was nothing I could do to help. The pressure now felt much worse because we were in a foreign country, lodging in a stranger's living room. While it was unlikely the other people in the apartment could understand what we were saying, they undoubtedly recognized the sad, desperate tone of our hushed conversations that lasted far into the night.

During the day, we searched for things to enjoy in Prague, like the cemeteries and labyrinthine streets. On a late afternoon, we stopped at a rooftop bar that overlooked the iconic Charles Bridge. We found two chairs at a large table near the railing. While the skies were perpetually cloudy, probably from

Venus (as Steve) in Prague, 1993

coal soot, it felt good to be in a spot where we could watch the river flow below us. Then two young men came up to our table. They were both extraordinarily thin.

"Hello," one said, smiling to reveal crooked, chipped teeth. "Mind if we sit here?" We were just taking up space at the edge of the table, and there were four other empty chairs. It didn't seem right to hog them all for ourselves.

While I didn't welcome the interruption, I wasn't ready to tell them to get lost. They looked vaguely artsy.

"Go ahead," I said.

Steve had his sketch pad out, and they made admiring

noises about the art. Maybe they could tell us about cool places in town to visit.

"Are you tourists?" the first one asked.

"Yes," I said. "We're really enjoying it here." I made a little nod toward Steve, hoping to include him in the conversation. "Where are you guys from?"

"Oh, we're from Bosnia," he replied and offered another broken smile. I frantically tried to remember current events in Bosnia. There had been a civil war, massacres. Were they refugees? Which side had they been on? I couldn't even remember the various sides.

"Oh. I'm sorry," I said. It was all I could think of. While I was talking, the quieter of the two had been watching Steve intently. Suddenly he got up and walked away. I looked at his friend. "Where did he go?" I asked.

"Oh, he'll be back," the young man said. But he didn't come back. After a few more minutes of innocuous conversation about Prague and the weather, he said, "I'll go see if I can find him." He didn't come back, either, which I was grateful for.

"What do you think that was all about?" I asked Steve. He shook his head. His face was pale.

"They thought we were both women. They were trying to pick us up. Then one of them read me and got angry."

I nodded. There was no other reasonable interpretation. I felt stupid for letting them sit with us, clueless about how these things worked. But I did know that if Steve got "read," he might be in danger. Steve knew that, too. That's why he had gone largely silent in their presence.

"I don't want to run into them on the way out," I said.

"I agree." We both imagined them waiting just outside the door, baseball bats in hand.

We ordered another round of drinks, buying time to relax there at least another forty-five minutes. Even if they wanted to cause trouble, they would have to be unusually determined to wait that long. When we finally left the bar, there was no sign of them.

Despite that episode, we decided to stay two more days. To do that, we would need to get to the bank the next day to change traveler's checks to currency before it closed at noon. The next morning, I was up and ready to do that, but Steve was having a terrible time, feeling suicidal again. I think of the interaction we had that morning and others like it as arguments because that's what they felt like, Steve saying he felt worthless and suicidal and me saying, *no, don't do that, I love you and you're okay*. Then Steve would disagree, I'd counter, he'd get more emphatic, and the whole thing would ratchet up from there. But how could these be arguments? What exactly were we arguing about? Those were the kinds of interactions that sometimes ended with Steve's fist hitting a wall or the floor. More often, they ended with yelling or crying and one or both of us curled up into a ball.

This was what we were engaged in now. Steve sat at one end of the couch, crying, snot and tears pouring down his face. I was crying, too, and found a roll of toilet paper to soak up the tears. Between handing Steve more tissue and blowing my own nose, I surreptitiously checked my watch. We had to make a decision. We weren't in any shape to get to the train station, and if we stayed, we didn't have the language to explain to the old couple that we would stay and pay for the room without handing them money. But if we didn't get to the bank before noon, we wouldn't have the money. I couldn't get Steve to calm down, clean up, and come with me, so at the last possible moment I decided to go to the bank by myself. I hugged him and kissed him good-bye.

I stepped out the door of the flat onto the sidewalk and was struck by how incongruously sunny the weather was. It had been cloudy the entire time up to this point. I walked quickly down the street, but each step felt spongy, as if I were walking in an unreal environment. The walk to the bank was agonizingly long—at least twenty minutes. My hand trembled as I pulled open the large, glass door to the bank lobby. There was a line in front of me where I waited, every nerve buzzing. Had I made a mistake? What was Steve doing now? Would he be looking around the room for a rope? Was there a light fixture or something strong enough to hold him? There had been a chair in the room.

I moved forward in line toward the teller. I was torn between worrying about Steve and trying to put the situation out of my head by distraction. Nothing did any good—I couldn't control my thoughts. The threat of his suicide frightened me when we were home. What would I do if he killed himself in a foreign country? I got to the head of the line and shakily signed the traveler's check, numbly putting the money into my purse. I had to plan for the worst. It's the kind of thing I constantly do, like visualizing the car crashing and where my body will go. The picture I had in my head at the bank was a drooping silhouette in front of the windows of the flat. Silent. Gone. The person that was part of me. My entity. My entirety.

Everything in my life was collapsing.

On return, I walked up the stairs of the apartment building as fast as I could, watching the level numbers as I climbed to the top of each flight. When I used my key to open the door to the apartment, I found the old woman in the kitchen. I tried to smile at her, tried to look normal so she wouldn't get worried. The core of my body ached as I drew out the key to open the door to our living room unit.

I pushed the door open and saw Steve sitting in a chair, reading something. He turned and seemed almost cheerful. He had showered and cleaned up and was ready to go out to do some sightseeing. I sank onto the couch. I should have been relieved, even happy, but I wasn't. I was something else, something I couldn't put my finger on. And then I was angry at how worked up I'd become. Was I angry at Steve? I knew I shouldn't be, but there was definitely resentment. I was also angry at myself, angry at the situation, angry at this town that made communication so difficult, angry at the decades of coal burning that blackened the buildings and made the air heavy. I was angry that I had blown so much money on a misguided attempt to celebrate a landmark anniversary that instead could have killed my spouse. I was ready to go home, but our flight back was still six days away.

We went to the kitchen to explain to the old woman that we wanted to stay longer. I used an English-German dictionary and she used a Czech-German dictionary so we could communicate. Based on what we had paid for the previous three nights, we guessed how much more would equal two nights. She was shocked by the amount we gave her. The agent who found us at the train station must have taken more than 50 percent for himself before giving her the rest.

Steve told me later that seeing things from her point of view helped him put his own emotions in perspective, and this is what calmed him enough to enjoy the rest of the trip. But I didn't have the same feeling. Something had rattled all the parts inside me. My life could fly apart at any time, with no warning, like a transmission throwing a rod and breaking the engine. Now I was the one who was unmoored.

We spent two more days in Prague. I don't remember much of what we did. We went to more cemeteries, where Steve filmed the moss-covered angels that knelt next to the markers. We tried to spend down our extra koruny, ordering champagne at a restaurant called the Mozart.

We decided to take the train to Venice next. According to my Thomas Cook guide, a train would leave the central station for Venice in the late afternoon. So the next day we packed our suitcases and headed over there. I couldn't wait to put Prague behind me. We stood in line for the tickets, and when I got to the window and explained what we wanted, showing the clerk the timetable, she just shook her head. I asked why, and she shook her head again and moved over to a different window to avoid dealing with me. I continued to ask, and finally someone who spoke English came over and explained this was the one day of the week the Venice train didn't run. We wouldn't be able to leave Prague until the next day.

Something snapped. I screamed. I cried. I became every stereotype of the ugly American. I shoved my suitcase hard across the polished tiles of the grand lobby and watched it slam into the wall on the other side of the hall. The suitcase split open and all my wrinkled, dirty clothes spilled out. I was too angry to care. I don't think Steve had ever seen me like that. I was causing a scene.

Steve came to my side and put his arm around me, led me to the suitcase and helped me put everything back in. I knelt on the floor and bent down toward the locking mechanism, crying and swearing several times as I tried unsuccessfully to align the two halves and latch the suitcase shut. We soberly walked to the front of the building and sat on the sparse lawn in front of it. The language barrier was too immense to try to find lodging, and I didn't want to sleep in someone's living room again. I was done with the city. We decided to wait there until the next morning. Strangely, we weren't the only ones—a number of people, couples and families, also camped out on the lawn in front of the station. Someone played guitar. We didn't talk with any of them, but a kind of solidarity settled over all of us as the night progressed.

I was exhausted when we got on the Venice train the next day. But Steve had new energy, a euphoria. I drifted in and out of sleep, groggily amazed at one point by the Italian Alps, the Dolomites, that loomed through the train windows. In Venice we found a cheap hotel within walking distance of most things we wanted to see. We fed the pigeons at San Marco and toured some of the Biennale, an international art show. I wanted to go on a gondola with Steve, but he said no—it made him feel too exposed. Eventually our walks through the narrow, mysterious lanes of the city, following signs to major landmarks, began to diminish my memories of Prague. Navigating the streets of Venice felt like a puzzle I could solve. Or maybe it was a healing labyrinth. I remembered that I liked this sort of thing. The Fourth of July arrived, and when we sat on the train-station steps with a few other Americans to watch sporadic fireworks in the distance, it felt like we had rejoined a secret club.

In Paris once again, in the same hotel where we started three weeks earlier, both Steve and I woke up in the middle of the night. I heard him asking how we got there and could see in the moonlight a few feet away from us a pile of stuff. I struggled in fear for a moment to understand. I could see it, too. I seemed to be looking at rubbish at the dead end of a narrow alley. Dim light glowed from somewhere—was it a window? Had we somehow fallen asleep in an alley? It looked like the kind of obscure Venetian passageway that had burned its image into my brain in the last few days. Steve tried to get up, pulling on pants and boots. Then I understood. We were both dreaming that we had fallen asleep in an alley in Venice. The rubbish was actually our luggage and clothing, piled up in the corner of the room.

"No, it's not Venice," I said. I put my hand on Steve's arm.

"What?" He was still waking up, trying to understand.

"We're in a hotel room in Paris. We're flying home in the morning. The clothes are on a chair. The light in the window just makes it look like an alley in Venice. We aren't there anymore. We're safe. We're okay." After a few moments, I got up and turned on a light to verify that we were really in a hotel room. It wasn't lost on me that we had been sharing a nightmare.

14

■★▲★❋■↑●■

1993, Minneapolis

It was an accident that Steve got back into music. He was setting up an art installation at a tiny hair salon on Franklin Avenue where Michael McManus worked when Bill Bailey walked through the door. Bill still looked fit, with a drummer's muscular torso, short, sandy hair, and a suave, almost feline manner of moving through the world. Bill had seen Steve hanging art through the salon window, and he explained that he and his brothers, along with their father, had bought a nearby house. They were turning the basement into a recording studio, Mirror Image. Would Steve like to get together and play music again? Yes, he would love to do that.

Ed Ford joined them on bass. At first it was a hobby, something they did just for the fun of it. I thought it was great that Steve reconnected with them—maybe having friends beyond those he met while crossdressing would even out his mood swings. They even scheduled a gig, and they needed a name. Steve's art was filled with horse imagery, and I had begun to lease a horse, so I suggested All the Pretty Horses. The name captured the beauty and strength Steve's androgynous look conveyed, so it stuck. A year later, Steve hinted that he'd have a wonderful surprise for Christmas. The surprise turned out to be their first album.

All the Pretty Horses with Tiffany, Venus (as Steve), and Ed Ford, about 1998. The band didn't adopt stage names until 1999

Bill's talent as a drummer matched his ability to blend backup vocals, but he had demons. He and Steve had played music together since shortly after high school. As a project verged on success, Bill would smash it all, sometimes literally. Their punk rock cover band in Duluth ended when Bill abruptly decided the music they'd been playing was Satan's music. He cracked his drumsticks in two, broke or melted all of his punk rock vinyl, and drove away to join a Christian fundamentalist camp.

It didn't take him long to reach a crisis point this time around. I awoke sometime in the middle of the night, hearing a solid strike on the third-floor window of our bedroom. I furtively looked out, hiding behind the curtain. I could see Bill and his friend Katy—also a musician—standing on the walk outside our front door, peering up where they'd seen the curtain move. I had no idea what was going on. I did not want to go downstairs and open the door. But then Steve was awake and thought it might be important, so we put on robes and shuffled downstairs.

Katy did most of the talking, saying that Bill wanted to leave the band. He was drunk or strung out on something and had zoned out of the conversation. I tried to make small talk and wondered how to get them to leave. Somewhere in the conversation I said that yes, we'd been asleep. Yes, we'd had a couple of glasses of wine before bed. Bill's whole demeanor suddenly shifted; he demanded we bring him some. Steve shot me a look. I wasn't going to give Bill anything to drink, and I'd never seen him this way. It was scary. I didn't even know he had a drinking problem—Steve had kept that from me. After a few tense minutes he calmed down again. Having decided he probably wouldn't get into a fistfight with Steve, I went back upstairs, which may have persuaded Bill that we really had nothing in the house for him. He left with Katy and was out of the band.

Bill had been the point person who organized things, knew who to talk to for bookings, and had the rehearsal space. But Steve was determined to carry on without him. His decision to be the leader and manager didn't play on his strengths, and it brought profound challenges to our relationship.

■■■

There's a song on that first CD called "Floating." It's slower and moodier than the other songs, and it describes the tension that developed as Steve expressed his female side: "You're my lover, I see that in your eyes / I love you / I am lonely, there's far too many eyes, and only / You're my lover, but I've fallen in love with something." The "something" was his desire to be seen by other people as a woman.

The problem was familiar, and it wasn't just that his appearance and behavior changed. When he dressed as a woman, people no longer saw us as a couple. He acknowledged the problem, singing, "They won't let us / be the ones we want to be." But he didn't seem to recognize when it happened in real time, when people cut him away from me, when they tried to hit on him. He just smiled and accepted the attention. His desire for other people's approval cast a spell that made me vanish.

The band amped up everything in our lives. On the song "10,000 Monsters," Steve sang, "I sleep with monsters, they move, and stumble in my head," and then everyone in the band howled a three-part harmony. I loved that chorus. We all had monsters, even me. I wanted it all: teaching career, poetry, spouse, house, art, rock and roll, all of it, even when people expected me to give up and leave my relationship with Steve. My desire to make my life with Steve work was not rational. It was a ferocious drive inside me with teeth and claws that wanted to protect, somehow, the infant spark I saw glimmering in our arms.

15

■⋆▲⋎✣■⋔●⋆

1994, Minneapolis

After two years of searching, I got a tenure-track offer at the community college in Rochester. It was a ninety-minute drive from home, and it seemed unlikely we would want to move there, given the conservative nature of Minnesota's smaller towns. But I thought I could do the commute. I told myself it would be a bonus not to run into my students while we were out clubbing. With the tenure-track job, I finally had dependable health care. It meant I could try to get pregnant.

I hadn't been that interested in kids when I was younger, but after I turned thirty and saw friends having children, it looked like a future I wanted. Steve didn't want to have children, so a new front for arguing opened. I was thirty-four. I figured I had only a year or two to try, and after that my chances would go down dramatically. But he still wouldn't budge. I'd heard of people getting divorced because they disagreed about having children. Would *this* be the issue to break us apart? One of our arguments got so bad that he drove nearly three hours to Duluth to cool off.

We finally came to an agreement of sorts. Steve wanted to take female hormones. Dressing up in a padded bra wasn't enough anymore; he wanted to feel the sensation of having breasts and softer skin. I knew a few people in the CLCC who were on hormones and didn't mind what it did to their faces, but I wasn't sure I'd be attracted to Steve if he grew breasts. I reminded myself that so many things about our bodies are out of our control, and everyone changes over time. We gain weight, and appearances are altered simply by aging. I knew I wouldn't leave Steve in those situations. Perhaps I wouldn't see the changes brought on by hormones as a problem.

In a gift-of-the-magi type of swap, I agreed that Steve could start taking a low dose of estrogen and he agreed I could try to get pregnant. Six months of charting and trying came and went, with no results. We went to a fertility specialist covered by our HMO. The doctor had short, thinning hair and seemed unusually tense around us, almost angry. He did some tests, and when he gave us the news, he bristled as if offended by something. He said that Steve didn't have enough motile sperm—that my womb had never been "challenged" with a sperm. We had no clue about how wrong his behavior was. He was the expert our health care provider had sent us to. We followed his advice.

Would anything have turned out differently if I had listened to my intuition and sought a friendlier doctor? In vitro fertilization cost about $30,000 at that time and was out of the question. A friend had adopted a child from Korea; that also cost about $30,000, and I didn't think we'd pass the home study as Steve's gender presentation evolved. It wasn't something he was going to keep a secret. On the doctor's recommendation, we decided to try a sperm bank.

For the next year and a half, I took my temperature every morning and synched it with the hours the sperm bank was open and my hour-and-a-half travel time to and from Rochester. It was hellish. Tears often ran down my face as I raced to get to the clinic before it closed. I didn't want to tell anyone I was trying to get pregnant: I couldn't bear the scrutiny. If my morning temperature indicated that I needed to go to the facility that day, I'd have to call my carpooling partner and cancel at the last minute. She must have thought I was crazy.

I was relieved the grumpy doctor was present only the first few times I went, then left everything to his assistant. She was supportive, and we had a good rapport, talking about riding horses and piloting airplanes. But I still wasn't getting pregnant. If my period was a few days late, I tried a drugstore pregnancy test. The blue line never appeared.

I gazed at each of my students and imagined their future lives, then slumped with the thought that I saw them grow for only one semester, two years at the most. Every month I shelled out $200 or more for the procedure—more than we could afford. Finally the nurse told me she thought the sperm of the donor I'd been using, the red-haired one I dreamed could be a good physical match for Steve, was maybe too old. I don't know why I didn't just switch to a new donor at that point, but I didn't. I felt defeated and humiliated. I remembered how the doctor had been so hostile and I felt I had been led on for months, spending money that should have gone to paying our other bills. So I gave up. I couldn't bring myself to throw away the sperm-donor book that I had paged through countless times, hoping something would work, but I took it and all the paperwork and slipped it behind a corner of trim in my large bookcase. No one but me would know it was there. I didn't want anyone to see how hard I had tried to do this and failed.

Riding the horse I was leasing provided some respite. His name was Prince, which struck me as unimaginative, but he answered to it, so there was no changing it. I paid only half his board bill, which in the beginning cost me $40 a month. The therapy was worth it, even as board prices began to rise. I loved the way I could depend on him to prick up his ears and nicker when I walked into the pasture and called his name. I could ride him an hour or more through densely wooded trails, and I taught him to pop over fallen logs. When his owner sent me

Lynette on Prince, mid-1990s

a letter saying she wasn't able to ride him enough and would I like to buy him, I wanted to say yes. I couldn't bear to see him go to someone else. But how could I afford him? The friend who'd gotten me back into horses suggested offering the amount of his kill weight—$500 back then. The thought was horrifying, but that's what happens to good horses who aren't particularly well trained and won't win ribbons at shows. It's not legal to slaughter them for meat in the United States, so they're shipped to Mexico.

■■■

I got my first horse nine years after my first ride on that runaway. I was fourteen, and it was the year after I rode Buttons the pony into that mysterious hidden pond. My pleas for a horse had intensified once I discovered Springhill because it had the cheapest board in town, and I knew my parents were spending more on my weekly violin and piano lessons than on Springhill's fees. I would be happy to give up either of those for a horse and said so. That enraged my mother. She saw my music lessons as a privilege, not a burden. This infuriated me. I thought having to practice on two instruments at the same time was *earning* me a horse, not canceling it out. My father just wanted peace between us.

Eventually, my mother relented. My uncle had been late getting a colt gelded and ended up with a couple of surprise foals. I could have one of them. My uncle had him gelded and sent him out for some "gentling" for a month. Then he was mine.

What does this say about me as a child—was I willful? Driven? I don't know. As an adult, I sometimes forgot I had that tenacity in me, but then it would return like spring leaves rising through snow from roots deep below. I felt in tune with horses—riding was like dancing with someone who didn't speak the same language, and having to learn a new language of motion and gesture. I sought this kind of give and take when

I played music with other people, and years later in my relationship with Steve. My mother wanted me to stop asking for a horse. But I didn't. I couldn't. I kept gravitating toward the things that made me feel alive, the things that generated that spark.

16

■★▲◆◼◆●■

1995, Minneapolis

One morning, a year after I began teaching in Rochester, I started to wake, my brain trained to the alarm that would soon command me to get out of bed. The sun cast a golden-pink glow through the curtains of our attic bedroom window. I rolled over to shield my eyes from the light. Then the phone rang.

I sat up, staring at where it lay next to Steve's side of the bed. He had also started to wake and cleared his throat. We exchanged a concerned look. People usually didn't call that early in the morning. He picked up the receiver.

"Hello?" he said, trying not to sound hoarse. He listened a moment. "It's Charlie," he mouthed to me. I relaxed. It was unlikely a family member had died. But Steve's voice grew tense. "What?" he was saying. "When?" He listened more intently. I wondered if there had been an accident. "What station?" he asked, and then, "Yeah, I was on jury duty. I was dressed like I always am."

When he got the letter summoning him to jury duty a few weeks earlier, we'd both seen it as a badge of honor. Since he worked freelance, in charge of his own time, he felt he could fit it in. The first day had been weird. All the potential jurors were in one area, milling about in some large beige and gray room in the bowels of the Hennepin County Government Center, endlessly waiting to be called to the next stage. It had all the charm of an airport waiting area, minus the windows. Steve had run into an acquaintance there, another artist, and they joked about how terminally dull the whole process was. He was glad he'd brought a book to read.

Near the end of the day, they finally called him in with a group to ask a few questions. Steve thought it was funny that when the clerk read his name aloud and he stepped forward, the judge and one of the lawyers seemed perplexed. They couldn't fathom how someone who looked like that could be named Steve. I thought it was funny, too, and rolled my eyes in response to the story. To me, Steve looked androgynous, like a lot of our friends, with his long hair and a little bit of eye makeup. He'd also been wearing black riding pants, boots, and a suitcoat—a woman's suitcoat, yes, but it was his basic formal outfit. It seemed to work for classical music concerts. The lawyers asked a few questions, and then dismissed him for the day.

After more back and forth with Charlie, Steve hung up.

"What happened?" I asked.

"You're not going to believe this," Steve responded. "Charlie called to warn me that they're making fun of me on the KQRS morning-drive show. They read something in the *Star Tribune*, and they're making it sound like I was dressed in drag, something really outrageous, like *Priscilla, Queen of the Desert*, just to get out of jury duty."

"What?" I was thunderstruck. How had this happened? I pulled on some clothes and ran down to get the newspaper.

I brought it in and unrolled it on the kitchen table, turning each page, scanning the headlines as well as the tiny stories in the margins. Steve went to the radio, turning the dial to all the stations we never listened to, hoping to get a sense of what was going on. I found the story when I got to the Metro section, and it was worse than I thought. The headline on page 3 stretched across nearly the entire width of the page: "Attorney Bars Cross-dresser from Jury." The story was about what happened *after* Steve left the room.

The attorney for the prosecution asked to have him barred from the jury with what's called a peremptory challenge. The jury would hear a case about child molesting, and the prosecutor argued a crossdresser would be sympathetic to the defendant—i.e., the possible molester. The defense argued that this *didn't* qualify as a peremptory challenge, and that Steve should be allowed to remain on the jury because he was being discriminated against due to gender. The judge had to make a decision. The judge ruled that Steve could be barred from the jury. A newspaper reporter sat in the back of the courtroom, probably thrilled that something interesting had finally happened. She had a significant story to write. And she didn't contact Steve to get his side of the story, probably thinking of the rule that reporters weren't supposed to talk to jury members.

I still had to get to school and teach three classes. I set the newspaper down, willing my fingers to stop trembling. I wasn't named in the story, but it said that Steve was married to an English professor. It wouldn't be hard for anyone who knew my name and profession to put the two things together. Steve was calmer, feeding the cats, making coffee. I had to get in the shower. I had to get dressed. I was worried about the uproar. I didn't have tenure yet.

I stood in the shower and let its hot, cleansing water run over me, trying to scrub away every minute of the last half hour. I knew it wasn't legal to discriminate against me on the basis of my marital status, who I was married to, that sort of thing. But back channels flourish in academia, and I could be denied tenure for any small detail if the administration really wanted me out. That had already happened at one of the colleges where I'd been an adjunct. After the first year, I had trouble getting more classes in the English Department and ended up teaching mostly reading and study skills. The woman who coordinated those classes told me the old guard English professors were whispering what must be an outrageous lie, that my husband was a crossdresser. I told her they were right.

Logically, I was probably also protected under Minnesota's Human Rights Amendment that had passed in 1993, two years earlier, barring discrimination against members of the LGBT community, but that seemed theoretical, not something I wanted to test. The judge's ruling had probably violated that, but I didn't have the power of a judge. I reflected on the distance between Minneapolis and Rochester. KQ probably didn't reach down there, and maybe there wouldn't be many people in Rochester who read the *Star Tribune*. It was a tense drive.

■■■

None of my students seemed to have heard about the story. After a few minutes in the first class, honors freshman composition, I fell into teaching mode and forgot to worry. After my classes ended, I went back to my office and closed the door. I needed another hour or two to grade and make a teaching plan for the next day. I was relieved no one had come up to ask what was going on with my husband.

When I finished prepping, I opened my office door and began packing to leave. Charlie O'Brien, who had the office across from me, also had his door open. I liked Charlie. He always had a quip or some pithy observation about life. He had a hobby farm and frequently joked about the frustrations of *all* the sheep getting out of the barn through one tiny opening, or what raccoons could do to a stand of corn. He came out of his office, nodding and smiling at me. I nodded and smiled back.

"Lynette, I want to let you know that I heard about Steve on the radio this morning."

I froze, trying to figure out how to respond calmly. Charlie was from an older generation, close to retirement. He loved baseball and had a tradition of traveling with his son to landmark ball fields around the country. His demeanor was more coach than college professor.

"Oh," was all I could muster.

"It was on WCCO-AM," he explained.

Of course. The AM radio station broadcast to farming communities all across Minnesota. I could imagine Charlie hearing it in his barn while he pitched hay to his sneaky sheep, between the weather reports and hog prices.

"I want you to know," he continued, "that I've been talking to other members of the department about it." He must have seen the stricken look on my face, because he quickly cut to the chase: "We all agree that this makes no difference to us. You have the support of the whole department. We are totally behind you, and if you need any help, we will be there for you." I had to blink a few times to process this. I was aware of the wooded hillside I could see through Charlie's window across the hall, still lush and green in September. This was so much better than what I had expected. Finally, I found the words.

"Thank you so much for telling me that," I said. "That's . . ." I sought the right word. I was about to burst into a geyser of tears. If I let myself do that, I wouldn't be able to stop. "That's really helpful," I said weakly. How lucky I was to land in a department where my colleagues had mentored me and now openly declared their support for me. "Thank you" was all I could say, again and again. A sense of gratitude buoyed me out of the building and back to my car.

When I got home, the issue wasn't over. Steve had been handling calls from people all day about the story. Barbara Carlson, ex-wife of the current governor, Arne Carlson, wanted to interview Steve for a WCCO radio show she broadcast live from a hot tub in her backyard. John Killacky, performing arts curator at the Walker Art Center and a friend and mentor to Steve, recommended following up with Lambda Legal to challenge the ruling. Doug Grow, a columnist for the same newspaper that had started the trouble, also wanted to interview us. The calm

I settled into after talking with Charlie O'Brien vaporized in an instant.

We both decided the Carlson interview would be a bad idea. How could sitting in a hot hub—stripped down to a bathing suit with a tech crew hovering overhead—possibly allow for a thoughtful discussion about being transgender? Although I was upset with reporters in general, I'd enjoyed Doug Grow's columns. He usually illuminated the lives of people who didn't normally make headlines, a sort of story-behind-the-story. He seemed to sympathize with the people he wrote about. Much as I didn't want more publicity, I thought he might be in the best position to set the record straight. We said he could interview us Saturday morning. I set to cleaning the house.

When he arrived the next day, we were ready with coffee, English muffins, and fruit. We lit some candles and put on a classical music CD for a relaxing morning ambience. Doug Grow seemed to be a sympathetic listener as we jointly told the story of our journeys so far. He asked questions that seemed reasonable, like how we'd met, how we'd decided to get married, and when Steve realized he was transgender. We answered honestly, and he nodded every once in a while, following up with reasonable, conversational questions. Still, I felt an electric jolt when he said the article would appear the next day, in the Sunday paper. It seemed too soon. Dazed, we both shook his hand at the door and watched him walk away down the stairs.

For the rest of the day, I did what I often do when stressed: I wandered through a thrift store and rifled through dresses, shoes, and household trinkets, wondering if any of them would make me feel better. An older man also shopping must have sensed my distress and began to talk to me. A Korean War veteran, he was filled with stories about the adjacent Lowry Hill neighborhood and a nearby Episcopal cathedral where the staff had once let him practice the organ. I had never rejected the church I grew up in, I was just too lazy to get up early on Sunday mornings. Something about the conversation led me to wonder if a place where people were exhorted to love one another might provide some bulwark against the hostility Steve and I were experiencing.

I planned to attend services the next day. But first, I had to know what Doug Grow had said in his article. Sunday morning, I crept down the cold concrete of the front steps to pick up the newspaper. It was heavy, bulging in a green plastic bag. I brought it in and flipped the pages until I found the Metro section and read the column. I finished and breathed a sigh of relief. I still felt exposed, but the article was okay, even compassionate: "Here sits a talented man with a lovely old home, decorated with artworks he has created. As he's talking, candles are flickering, coffee's brewing, classical music is playing and his spouse, a woman he loves, is adding supporting comments. It's all nice, gracious, comfortable." I knew the shock jocks were still out there, but I was consoled. Here was further evidence that some people were capable of understanding. I needed to find more of them.

17

1996–1997, Minneapolis

Steve was now doing performance art and band shows on a regular basis. One place we gravitated to was Patrick's Cabaret, created by Patrick Scully, a seven-foot-tall unapologetically gay dancer and performance artist. John Killacky had introduced us to Patrick and his space on Twenty-Fourth Street. I was writing poetry but still hadn't found my audience. Performing at the Cabaret was an option, but I worried my work would come across as dull. Who would want to listen to me? I asked Steve if he'd be willing to do a performance piece together about our relationship—we'd only have to fill fifteen minutes, the time limit at the Cabaret. I was starting to think of it as our queer marriage, in all senses of the word. He agreed. We got a date on the calendar and put together a script with several of my poems, some of his writing, and the two of us in wedding dresses.

But on the morning of the first show, Patrick phoned with unwelcome news. The fire marshal had shut down the venue. It would be months before they could make the needed changes and reopen. My performance-art debut had been squelched, and I was crestfallen. But soon we had a solution: we would do it in our living room. We called everyone we thought might have planned to attend to alert them to the change of venue, and someone put our address on the Cabaret door. One or two other artists who had also been scheduled that night came to do scaled-down versions of their performances. We did our piece in front of a packed living room, maybe thirty or forty people, with most sitting on the floor, and some peering around the corner from the front hall. Everyone applauded at the end, and my heart swelled with the sound of it.

After the show, a friend asked why Steve's wedding dress was nicer than mine. Her question caught me completely off guard. I was wearing the dress I'd gotten married in, the one I'd sewn myself from a Vogue pattern. Yes, it was nostalgic-looking, vaguely Victorian, and Steve's dress was a castoff from a bridal shop where a friend worked. That dress had a more contemporary design with satin and sheer lace, where mine was just cotton and lace, but there was a section in the back of his dress where something had obviously been hacked off. I didn't like Steve's wedding dress as much as mine—how could it be better? The question nagged and made me wonder if I saw things accurately. I could rationalize that my friend was reacting to the shine and more expensive material in Steve's dress. But I also wondered if he just *looked* better than I did in a wedding dress—tall, slim, almost gamine, with great legs. I'd never felt comfortable with the shape of my body, but having Steve fall in love with me had assuaged that insecurity. Now it flooded back, and I was again thinking of clothing as camouflage. He also did his makeup better than I did, with shading and contours. I felt that anyone looking at the two of us together would find me dumpy by comparison.

Eventually we repeated the performance for a Cabaret benefit at Bryant Lake Bowl, a bowling alley that had been turned into a trendy bar and restaurant with an eighty-five-seat theater on the side. To promote the show, we appeared on *Write On! Radio*, a community radio program that highlighted local and nationally known writers. The show was hosted by J. Otis Powell!, a Black man with a lion's mane of dreads and a voice to match. He worked at the Loft as outreach coordinator and

J. Otis Powell? at the Squid Party with John Sherrell and Kat Corrigan, late 1990s

in that capacity coordinated the radio show, but the exclamation point he added to his last name (which would later change to an interrobang) signaled that he was much more than an administrator.

J. Otis liked my poems and the sound of my voice and asked if I'd like to come back to be one of the regular volunteers for the show. It was like getting an invitation to the prom. I had worked at my college radio station deejaying a jazz program, and before that I'd read the student announcements that played in everyone's homeroom in high school. I knew how to modulate my voice for a mic. I said yes, of course.

The radio show opened a door that led me to a vast community of serious writers. Each Thursday from 11:00 A.M. to

Lynette running the board at KFAI, early 2000s. Photo by Mike Hazard

noon I would be at KFAI, first reading some of the opening and closing credits, then the calendar of literary events. I attended many of those literary events and began to invite writers I met to the show, where I would interview them about their work and creative process. Writers on national and regional book tours also would stop by the station for an interview. After each show, we continued the discussion over lunch at the Lucky Dragon, across Riverside Avenue.

I began to participate in readings at various coffee shops and art galleries, often with J. Otis's encouragement. After learning that I liked improvising with words and music, he invited me to take part in some of his larger multimedia shows that added film, music, and dance to the poetry. One of J. Otis's improvised shows had me playing violin while Patrick Scully lifted me off the floor and spun me around like a child's game of airplane.

At the same time, Steve was getting grants for performance art, including a prestigious Bush Fellowship, but rock and roll gave him a more immediate high. Yet he garnered more respect in the art world than the music world. It was easy to see why this happened: the rock-and-roll establishment was more masculine/hetero. But Steve loved being onstage. He said the stage felt like a space he could control, where he could be himself. He liked mixing the outré creativity of performance art with the gut-level intensity of rock and roll. By now, he was starting to put together what would become his signature look of corset, stockings, and heels.

The band's gigging ramped up, and Steve's drive to make it successful got more intense. For some reason, Ed Ford couldn't play bass for their Loring Block Party gig, so Steve asked Lee Ann MacDougall to substitute. We'd first met her in Duluth through Tanya Warwas. Lee Ann later moved to Minneapolis and had worked with Steve in the art room of T-Shirt Ink, usually getting a ride with him to and from work because she didn't drive. We often had her and sometimes her boyfriend over for dinner, cheering them on when they married and sympathizing with her when they divorced. It seemed a natural fit.

The Loring Bar, which hosted the block party, sat at the edge of Loring Park on the southern edge of downtown. Even on slow nights—Mondays or Tuesdays—it attracted a large bohemian crowd. The block party was a perfect blend of art, punk rock, and circus weirdness. Sometimes it included a Ferris wheel. As I stood in the warm summer rain and watched the band play underneath a narrow, striped canopy, I talked to one of my Rochester students, also a musician, who'd driven up for the event. Lee Ann was doing a good job. Moreover, she looked great: about as tall as Steve, willowy, with a pile of dyed-red dreadlocks that reached past the middle of her back. Her dark red lipstick and slight grimace conveyed the perfect combination of punk rock beauty and scorn.

Later that year, Steve used a travel/study grant to go to New York and meet other artists. Through them, he discovered an underground LGBT (no Q yet) club scene. He also began to understand how the New York rock-and-roll clubs operated. He, Matt Batchelor, Ed, and Katy had done a drive-to tour to New York a year earlier, playing some of the classic Lower East Side bars we'd heard of: CBGB's, the Spiral, and the Pyramid. They'd been thrilled to see a large audience before them at CB's, then grew mortified as they watched the audience clear out after the previous band finished. Steve ended up singing across the empty dance floor to a handful of German tourists at the upper tables. Audiences in New York didn't stay at one bar all night unless there was some kind of special theme. They bounced from one club to another, following their favorite bands. During his travel/study visit, Steve saw how the theme-night system worked and imagined a return trip. He also thought he could use the theme-night approach back in the Twin Cities.

Things between us could still be turbulent, but the issues now were more about time and money. Steve had gone freelance as a commercial artist, then that work dwindled to nothing. Though the Bush Fellowship saved us financially for a while, he hadn't put the money into an account that would allow him to stretch it out over the next few years, the kind of nest egg approach I begged him to take. He was on track to spend it all in one year and hardly brought any home, leaving me to handle most of the bills. Money was becoming an ongoing topic of stress and argument. I supported the band, but I wasn't crazy about the costs.

I also didn't like the long hours he put into rehearsals. He often left for his downtown studio after a quick supper and didn't return until after I went to bed. I had to teach the next day, and if I wanted to talk to him after rehearsal, I sacrificed hours of sleep. And I missed him. It became rare for us to cuddle on the couch as we watched something on television.

In those years we rode a repeated wave of ambition and loss—I participated in more readings, and Steve always had a new gig, a new CD, or a prospect of some kind of success. But neither of us had a big break.

Our schedules conflicted. If I went to a show, I either went home shortly after 1:00 A.M. or I stayed to help with the crew, got home by 3:00 A.M., and rose a few hours later to drive to Rochester. Sometimes Steve came in after I'd fallen asleep and roused me with a bag of White Castle gut-bomb hamburgers and onion chips, some which we'd eat, and some which we'd distribute to our cats, laughing when one got her head stuck in the cardboard box. Sometimes he didn't have any burgers but still rode a high from the show, and we'd make love. Sex often repaired the distance between us. But the two worlds didn't line up the way they had when we lived in the band house in St. Paul. I missed those days.

Steve thought the local press and booking agents would give the band more respect if they became known in New York. It seemed right: whenever a local group got signed, suddenly everyone was talking about them. There was clearly bias against Steve's gender expression in the local mainstream, but what he saw in New York led him to think there was a strong audience out there for what he and the band did. He also wanted to tour regionally, but Ed and Matt balked at going on the road. They couldn't take that much time off from their day jobs.

Steve compromised by creating a touring version of the band, inviting jazz drummer Brett Forberg to play drums when Matt couldn't make it. Lee Ann played bass when Ed couldn't. We'd gotten to know Brett as fans of his jazz band, the Wolverines, and at a certain point he confided to Steve that he wanted to dress as a woman. Steve responded with a whole list of makeup and clothing tips, which Brett loved. He began dressing in women's clothes and used the name Jendeen for Pretty Horses shows.

Steve also believed it would be better to fly to New York instead of drive. His previous experience had been nightmarish: they'd had a hard time finding parking spots and also got lost on the way back to their hotel in New Jersey after a gig. He learned from that trip that most New York clubs had backlines, speakers and a drum kit, so there was no need to bring an entire public address (P.A.) system. Flying seemed smart to me, too. Steve put together the gigs, and I started researching flights and hotels.

18

1998, New York City

Would I have chosen to get married if I'd known the difficult path ahead? I don't know. What I do know is that from the very beginning, I chose a life of art shared with a kindred soul. When the trouble started—and Steve's evolving identity was only part of the trouble—art was often what beckoned me back to our relationship, feeding my hunger for something bigger than myself, something bigger than both of us. I searched for places where we could be our authentic selves, places that rescued us like an ark in floodwaters, places that welcomed a pair of misfits who loved each other. One of those spots turned out to be a hotel in New York City.

We arrived amid a summer chorus of jackhammers. Steve and I, with three other band members—Jendeen, Lee Ann, and Tiffany, who sang backup vocals and added theatrics to the show—paused on a busy sidewalk off Third Avenue guarding a pile of amps, guitars, and suitcases, hoping the cabs had dropped us in the right place. Initially, it didn't look like they had. Construction scaffolding and a plywood fence jutted onto the sidewalk where the hotel should have been. But then I realized someone had painted the four-by-eight sections of fence with the hotel's name and large, cartoonish figures. One depicted a man with an outsized head wearing some kind of green

The fence painted by Banksy at the Carlton Arms, about 2000–2001

uniform, a cap, and a bow tie—a doorman? Next to it was a familiar green H inside a forbidding square-and-backslash "no"
symbol. A Not-the-Holiday-Inn warning. Well, the guidebook
hadn't pitched it as a standard hotel.

I felt the band members' eyes on me, ready for a screwup.
This line-up had begun to make me feel like an outsider. I
couldn't put my finger on the reason, so I usually just tried to
power through it, but in the context of the band, sometimes
even Steve made me feel like an outsider. His gender expression had been evolving for a decade now. The band gave him
more confidence, which allowed him to take it to new, much-
photographed extremes, and his usual stage look was a corset,
fishnets, and stiletto thigh-highs.

I didn't fit visually with the other band members, either.
They were all tall and gender-ambiguous, and their appearance
by day even evoked their stage look. When they walked down

the sidewalk, heads turned. In contrast, I was too short and chunky to feel attractive in goth/punk clothes. I was allergic to most makeup, and my hair needed to look reasonable for my day job. At least that was my internal script. If there had been a band called the June Cleavers, I could easily have dressed to match it, but not for a dark glam, gender-bending band.

My self-confidence, or my spirit—I don't know how to separate them—had begun to droop like a forgotten houseplant.

A red arrow to the cartoon doorman's right pointed at an entrance with a small awning overhead, with "Carlton Arms Hotel" painted in small, gold letters. We were in the right place. I walked over, motioning the band members to follow me. Several layers of paint covered the metal-grill door. I peered through its glass to a small, tiled vestibule and ascending stairs. I grasped the handle and tried the door, but it held. Locked. Shit. Steve reached past me to push a small white button. We heard a buzzer, then the click of the door unlocking. He gestured to the rest of us to follow him in and up the stairs. I exhaled with relief.

I grabbed a guitar and started up, swiveling my head as I passed the different images painted on the walls: some film noirish silhouettes of a man and a woman, another painting of a crime-scene outline, still another of a life-sized man pointing a revolver, something like Andy Warhol's *Double Elvis* picture, and more murals all the way up the stairs. I tried in vain to avoid bumping the case's splintered edges into the wall and brass railing as the narrow stairs turned and spilled into a diminutive lobby. It was also decked with murals, but the style was completely different, a rollicking hodgepodge by different artists.

An aquarium bubbled away in the empty shell of an old RCA Victor television cabinet. Near the ceiling, someone had painted a faux-medieval frieze and timbering. On an alcove to my left, a small, gold-painted Buddha sat serenely on the ledge. The narrow stairs continued their tight ascent to more floors, with what looked like graffiti art on the walls. Turning, I gazed down a long hallway with similar colors and textures. The place mesmerized me. Someone opened a door a short way down the hall, and I saw exuberant swirls of paint dripped on its surface.

Everything was art, as far as I could see. I felt a secret shudder of joy as I looked around in wonder at the avalanche of expression we had walked into, that now surrounded us. The walls were not a smooth canvas: bulges, scrapes, and damaged trim abounded, and I liked that. I already knew what art cars were—cars that had gotten so rusted and beat-up that the artists who owned them said, "Screw it," and turned them into artistic expression on wheels. We'd already done that with two of our cars. Now I was inside a hotel where the same thing had happened, large scale. I was inside an art hotel.

A gray cat curled on the only cushioned chair in the second-floor lobby—the other seat an old church pew—and now stood up, stretched, and surveyed our crew. Then he hopped down and sauntered away, rejecting our "Here, kitty-kitty" pleas. A door off the lobby was open for luggage storage, and next to the window a red-painted mannequin looked like she was materializing through a closet door. On the wall someone had painted another pulp fiction–style woman in a fedora and trench coat leaning against the side of a brick building. Above her a slogan blazed, "Live Fast, Die Young." My shiver of joy settled into something more solid. I knew immediately I was in my second home.

The hotel had no elevator, and at that time it had no air-conditioning. For about half the rooms, bathrooms and showers were shared, a short walk down the hall. The energy of the place drove me forward like a punk rock anthem. Someone from the hotel staff gave us keys to a few of the available rooms so we could choose which artworks to immerse ourselves in. We explored the three or four rooms from floors A through D to decide where to settle. I don't remember which rooms the others chose, but Steve and I decided on one off the lobby, chiefly because we wouldn't have as many stairs to climb and could put the heaviest equipment there.

Then we set about as a group to explore the neighborhood. Everything we needed was close: a grocery store just around the corner that sold creamy gelato from a stand on the sidewalk, a newsstand two blocks away where I picked up issues of *Time Out* and the *New York Times*. The Lexington Avenue subway was four blocks away, and bars and restaurants everywhere, most of them places we could afford, if we were careful. If we walked west, we found Madison Square Park, and if we walked south we found a beautiful and mysterious leafy space locked behind wrought iron fencing: Gramercy Park. I longed to encounter a little bird pulling up the key to one of its forbidding gates from a crack in the sidewalk and leaving it for me, like the robin in Frances Hodgson Burnett's *The Secret Garden*.

Tiffany wanted us to see a band she thought might be comparable to All the Pretty Horses: the Toilet Böys, fronted by Miss Guy. They were playing at Coney Island High on St. Mark's Place. And everyone wanted to go shopping for stage wear, most of it found on St. Mark's at shops like Religious Sex and Trash and Vaudeville. There were more shops over on Eighth Street, where Patricia Field had a store. Steve and I had done this kind of shopping in London a few years earlier, when he'd bought his first pair of real patent leather thigh-high stilettos, boots that I suspect were made by the company in *Kinky Boots*. I always cringed at the amount of money he spent on corsets, but we couldn't find these things back home. I balanced out Steve's spending by restricting myself to the clearance racks. At least he seemed happy. When he appreciated my exploratory spirit and map-reading skills, I felt valued.

We discovered Mother, an amazing club in the Meatpacking District, where Chi Chi Valenti curated theme nights like Click + Drag and Jackie Sixty. You had to dress the part to get in. When the velvet rope opened for us all, I was glad I'd bought something black and shiny on the shopping expedition. Of course it helped that I was with Steve, who wore impeccably pale makeup, dark lipstick, and the standard stage uniform: black corset and bra, short skirt, and the boots. The person taking our admission fee was a trans person herself dressed in a white vinyl nurse's uniform with red cross patches over her breasts. She welcomed him in.

The front door opened onto a rectangular room, elegant with gilt mirrors and buttery lighting, filled with people dressed and coifed in various versions of punk, drag, and camp. Farther down the hall a doorway opened onto a larger space that throbbed with dance music, lights washing over the undulating throng, and a few dancers grinding away on raised platforms. They were dressed in spacy silver costumes, with old computer keyboards strung across their torsos. Ah, I thought, sipping a gin and tonic that glowed whenever a black light flashed on it. The click in Click + Drag.

The band played Meow Mix, a lesbian club on East Houston made semi-famous by the movie *Chasing Amy*. When I walked in the door, I did a double take. The place looked so much bigger in the film. In reality, it was the size of most New York clubs, a small box, but I had been operating on a midwestern scale, where most buildings sprawl. The bartender wasn't working yet, so I sat at a table near the center and waited for an indication of how I might assist. Band set-up time was often awkward for me. Steve was usually frantic trying to hoist the equipment and plug everything in. I wanted to help, but he seemed to prefer to do it all himself rather than find the words to explain what needed to be done. Lee Ann was also fairly grim and terse, so I went over to see if Tiffany needed anything as she duct-taped a Teletubby, the purple Tinky-Winky, to her mic stand. She was usually calm during set-up time. Kevin Meissner and Emily Hooper, who normally go-go danced with the band in Minneapolis, appeared and went to the stage to see if there would be enough room for them. They were staying with Emily's family on Long Island. They planned to dance and play

All the Pretty Horses, 1998. Left to right: Tiffany Tieche, Ted Ammerman (holding the lights), Venus (as Steve), Matt Batchelor (hidden behind drums), and Pandora

Tiffany Tieche, late 1990s

with the lights, from either the stage or the floor. When the bartender appeared, a lithe, butch woman in a mohawk, I got everyone their drinks.

The band launched with a rousing version of "Tattoo" and kept going. The crowd, initially sparse, quickly grew and soon crowded the stage. Jendeen, in her leopard-print dress and wig of cascading blond curls, was a powerhouse drummer. Lee Ann radiated her usual snarling, chilly demeanor, and Tiffany, Emily, and Kevin provided glitz and action. But for me, Steve was the total star of the set, commanding the stage with his height, Cleopatra eyeliner, and deep, resonant voice. Near the end of the set, he sank to his knees, punching out the guitar chords, then did a backbend straight to the ground, leaning back a few moments while he raked the strings, then popped back up. Near the end of the last song, he went down on his knees again for a variation of the backbend, this time rolling onto his shoulders, guitar still across his chest, and bicycled his legs in the air. Then he rolled back up and directed the final power chords. Wild cheers burst from the audience.

Steve came up to me, smiling and sweaty, black lipstick blurred by the mic, and gave me a big, sloppy kiss. They'd done it. The bartender, now that she'd seen them perform, was eager to talk and signed to us from down the bar how much she'd liked the show. She was Barb Morrison, a multi-instrument musician who soon became a friend and would eventually be Steve's producer. Already she was helping him plan an August trip to New York. The band would return to Meow Mix and also play a cameo on the narrow stage at Mother.

I think Barb—who many years later would come out as non-binary and choose they/them pronouns—recognized us as a couple, but I know there were other people who didn't, particularly at Mother, where Steve's dramatic sexuality attracted a lot of interest. He wasn't exactly trying to pass as a woman, though he took it as a compliment when people treated him that way. He told me he was making a statement about being

Barb Morrison, the bartender at Meow Mix, about 2001

between genders, emphasizing the early stages of breast development, with feminine makeup and clothing, contrasted with the impact of his height (over six feet tall, with the heels), deep voice, and commanding energy. He also played with how he named himself, sometimes going by the genderless "S. Grandell." His appearance signaled sexual strength and otherness, and people frequently threw themselves at him. When experiencing that kind of attention, often he didn't act like we were together, and people followed his lead. Every time that happened, it felt as if a trapdoor had opened beneath my feet.

■■■

I sought other explanations for why he would suddenly seem to forget I was there, or would forget about plans we'd made. Sometimes I imagined that his shift of attention to fans and admirers was a rock-and-roll thing, that he would be more attractive to audiences, booking agents, and so on if he had an alluring air of availability. I thought the band had real potential and didn't want to jeopardize their success. I tried to turn off my emotions when the flirtations happened. The situations multiplied as he threw himself into making the band succeed. I'd been willing to intervene with people at the 90's for trying to cut him away from me, but in New York, with potential career advancement, I was less sure how or if I should get involved.

Lynette and Venus (as Steve), London 1997

I wonder now if part of the problem was that I simply didn't see Steve the way other people did. I saw him as my spouse, plain and simple, the same person he had always been. And perhaps my use of a masculine pronoun and Venus's former name when talking about those years creates the wrong picture. It's all I had at that point, and it's why I'm continuing to use it to describe these events, but the person I saw back then was someone in between, someone who hadn't yet settled. The name Venus hadn't been created, and when it was, it still wouldn't seem to adequately describe the person I loved. Venus's appearance changed over the years, but I continued to see the same person, with all the same traits I had initially been attracted to and loved.

But the dominant culture of the time was another thing, and perhaps to the typical male, heterosexual gaze, Steve looked like a hot, sexy woman or an exotic trans woman—not someone who was married, especially not to a woman. Not someone faithful to a partner.

■■■

Going to New York a second time, when we discovered the Carlton Arms, fulfilled a promise I made to my younger self. This time, I wouldn't have to go back home defeated. I knew how to find a place to stay, ATMs existed, and I had credit cards. It still felt like the right place to be, a place of creative energy. But now my life was complicated by a dual sense of self. I had an idea of what I wanted to be and what I wanted to achieve. But who was I in relation to Steve, who kept changing?

Being married to someone much of society didn't think I *should* be married to was lonely. Being married to someone whose distress about their body was so strong it led to suicidal feelings was scary. Being married to someone who, once things seemed to be going well, needed to change again and take a step further was unnerving.

Some of that hard stuff was about to ratchet up when I stood the first time in the lobby of the Carlton Arms, devouring every painted square inch of it. But as I walked to the room where Steve and I would stay, I was reminded of the kind of power and vision I had always sought. Each room and each hallway was an installation by a different artist. Even the shared bathrooms were tiny, tiled art installations. Years later I would learn that the Not-the-Holiday Inn cartoon characters on the construction fence had been painted by the infamous Banksy.

Discovering the place was like stumbling on the hidden pond I had ridden a pony into, this time obscured by a forest of skyscrapers, not trees. It was like opening a secret door to a magical kingdom, with the same rapturous gasp of discovery I would continue to experience in the unexpected geography of our lives.

19

■★◣◆■◣●■

1999, Minneapolis and New York City

Sometime after those first few trips to New York, Steve came home from rehearsal and said everyone in the band had decided to take stage names. Ed and Matt had already phased out of the band—Ed, grudgingly. He asked me once if I thought he was being pushed out because Lee Ann looked better than him, and I said no, because I didn't want to stir up trouble. But I knew he was right. She was tall, slim, with long red dreadlocks and dark lipstick, a little scary but alluring at the same time, like Poison Ivy in the Cramps. She fit perfectly.

The stage names were Tiffany's idea, Steve explained. She would be called Johnnycakes the Love Alien. Brett was already going by Jendeen when she dressed as a woman, so she chose that name. It was her grandmother's name. Lee Ann chose the name Pandora, and Steve would go by Venus.

"Okay, whatever." I found it amusing, and a bit ironic. Steve was so busy trying to promote the band, rehearse, and perform that sometimes it seemed the only time we could make love was after a show. Putting all his money into the band also didn't strike me as particularly loving. "The goddess of love, huh?" I gave him a light squeeze.

"Well, you know," Steve smiled.

"It does seem a little weird. Why not Aphrodite? That's a nicer sounding name."

"I like Venus."

"Yeah, and you know what it rhymes with. I don't have to call you that, do I?"

"No, of course not."

This response would prove to be an error.

It made sense to call Jendeen by that name because she presented as femme most of the time now and preferred it. She dressed as a man only once or twice a week to lead the Wolverines Classic Jazz Orchestra, which she and her parents had founded. Also, the name didn't have any stagy pretensions. To me, the other names were completely theatrical, something to put on a marquee, devoid of intimacy. Steve started to come home after rehearsals telling me what everyone had done that night, using the names Pandora and Jendeen, so within a couple of weeks I got used to thinking of them by those names. But he rarely called Tiffany Johnnycakes, so no one got in the habit of using it. When talking with new fans, sometimes I used the name Venus to avoid confusion. All non-band friends and relatives, including myself, still used the name Steve.

I was free to go to New York during spring break, so Steve booked gigs for a week in March. Everyone wanted to go to New York now. A new drummer named Terrica and go-go dancers Emily Hooper and Sttaci Goodman (who went by the name Sterling Kitty) joined Steve, Pandora, Tiffany, and me. Jeff Sherman and Larry Ravenswood (Danielson) came along to operate the handheld lights, and Matthew Hopping ran sound. I felt I had returned to Oz. I bought a little pot of blooming daffodils from the Union Square Green Market for our hotel room. Back home in Minneapolis, it would be weeks before anything blossomed.

I don't recall who suggested going to the Limelight on a Thursday night—probably Matthew, because he seemed to know a fair amount about the New York club scene. The rest of

Matthew Hopping with Lynette and Venus at Limelight's Giger Room, 2000

us had never heard of it, but we wanted to publicize the gigs at Don Hill's and Meow Mix. So we all put on our best club/fetish wear and piled into cabs outside the Carlton Arms.

The venue was an old, deconsecrated church. We stood in the entrance line in the cold March darkness, staring at the floodlit stone walls. The doors opened onto a high-ceilinged corridor that flickered with video monitors along the walls. We walked forward to find the bar, the bass beat booming and drowning out all non-shouted conversation. The bar counter was tall, almost to my shoulders. Steve said something about fish in the bar that I didn't quite follow as he handed me a gin and tonic. If I'd heard him properly, I would have stood on the bar rail to see the spectacle myself: there were fish in a sort of glassed-in river inside the bar.

I couldn't stop seeing the footprint of the church layout, with nave, choir, and transepts. I wondered what it had been like when it was an actual church. To the right was an over-sized black-and-white checkerboard dance floor that would have been the seating area for the congregation. A wide stage sat where the altar or chancel would have been. A deejay was on the stage, playing the thump-thump-thump of high-energy dance music for the crowd of dancers that began to increase in size. The dance floor was open to the top of the vaulted ceiling, and stained-glass windows looked down on it all. To me, the room lost none of its awe-inspiring power in the shift from church to nightclub. It felt solid and electrifying.

I stood with Steve at the edge of the dance floor, watching, enthralled by the surroundings. Matthew disappeared back into the crowd. Emily, Sttaci, Jeff, and Larry jumped in to dance.

Steve almost never wanted to dance, but I thought I'd ask. "Want to join them?"

"No, not really," Steve said apologetically, a little sheepish.

"That's okay." I looked around for something else to occupy our attention. I wanted to explore.

"Want to go upstairs?"

"Yeah!"

The first set of stairs was wide, incongruously metal and in-dustrial, leading up to a sort of gallery level where you could lean over the railing and peer down on the dance floor. We me-andered around the perimeter of the second level, found drinks at another bar, and viewed the architecture from our higher vantage point. Now I could get a better look at the stained-glass windows, a round rose window at the top. I leaned in to talk to Steve.

"This is amazing."

Steve nodded and smiled at me.

The music was hard to talk over, and I gave Steve's arm a gentle squeeze to express my delight at being together in this place. Then we noticed another set of stairs to the third level and still another short set of metal stairs, the kind you might find next to a loading dock. They led to a door. At the bottom of the stairs, a man guarded a velvet rope, keeping the area off-limits. As we watched, the door at the top of the stairs opened, and two people came out, light and thrumming music behind their silhouettes. The rope opened as they came down the stairs. I got curious and walked over to the bouncer, Steve silent and beautiful by my side.

"What's up there?" I asked.

"The VIP room," he responded, scrutinizing us. I was pretty sure I wouldn't pass that scrutiny if I'd been alone. But Steve, in the wasp-waisted corset and strappy boots, stood there patiently. I started talking to him about finding the other band members downstairs. Then the bouncer surprised us. He swung the velvet rope open.

It was like discovering a secret corner of the world. The door led to another lounge, but unlike the lower levels, this space rivaled the Carlton Arms. The walls were art—sensuous murals, paintings, and sculptures of naked bodies that transitioned into angel and reptile forms. The style was similar to artworks by Giger I'd seen on album covers, like Emerson, Lake, and Palmer's *Brain Salad Surgery*. He also created the famous monster in *Alien*. It was such a recognizable style, the images sinuous and jagged, full of vertebrae and serpentine smoothness interspersed with vulnerable bodies. It was not what one would expect in a nightclub with drunk people milling around, ready to break things. I decided that these must be copies. Really good copies.

We walked over to the bar and ordered another round of drinks. I wanted to wander around and look at the art.

"Let's go over there," I said, gesturing toward a glass display case with some kind of troll-like sculpture inside.

"I don't know," said Steve. "They probably don't want us over there."

"Please?"

"Okay." Steve smiled and kissed me. Heads turned. There. We'd gotten their attention. More important, I had Steve's attention.

We walked around, looked at the art, and eventually found a cozy banquette. It still felt as if we'd sneaked into a secret club. We *had* sneaked into a secret club. It was called the Giger Room. We leaned into each other, and Steve glowed every time someone passed by with an appreciative nod to his appearance. I knew he was feeling validated, and, as long as I still had his attention, it felt good to be a part of that. On some level, I suppose it validated me as well. We were in sync with each other.

20

1999, Minneapolis

After the band members adopted stage names, their performance schedule accelerated. They played a show every week or two and rehearsed twice a week in the basement of the Colonial Warehouse. Also housed in the Colonial's basement was Allen Christian's House of Balls. Allen was a sculptor who worked with cast-off materials—old bowling balls, for example. His art had a fair amount of visibility because his space included a street-level front door and gallery area. One of his friends, documentary filmmaker Emily Goldberg, stopped by to catch up and heard the band practice. When she asked Allen who it was, she decided to pay Steve a visit.

Emily had met Steve a few years earlier when they both attended a filmmaker's forum sponsored by Twin Cities Public Television. Steve had come out as transgender to the hundred-plus attendees at that event, and Emily had subsequently borrowed a pair of large-size pumps from him for a friend's Halloween costume. She knocked on the studio door, and when Steve opened it, she noticed something new: he had breasts. She had the subject for her next documentary.

"We have to talk," she said.

Steve came home elated.

"Hey, guess what! A documentary filmmaker wants to make a movie about the band!"

"Wow. Who is it? What kind of documentary?" We were in the kitchen, trying to figure out what to make for supper.

"I don't know yet, but it's Emily Goldberg. You know her." He pulled out a wooden chair from the table and sat down. I sat down, too.

"No, I don't think I know her," I said. "Her name doesn't sound familiar."

"You remember, I lent her some heels for a friend of hers. For a Halloween party a few years ago."

"Hmm . . ." I squinted. I could picture the black pumps but wasn't sure if that was a memory or something I had conjured up. "I don't think I met her."

"Maybe you didn't. Anyway, she works at KTCA."

"Oh, that's good!" I wanted to make sure she wasn't some crazy person who would create a lot of drama—with Steve's hypersexualized appearance, I could see this happening. If she worked at KTCA, the local public television affiliate, she was probably legitimate. "But it'll just be about the band, right?" *Survivor* and other reality TV shows were a new popular trend, and our personal life together was messy enough without camerapeople ambushing us for the sake of a trashy story. Steve repeated that it was just about him and the band.

I still wanted more reassurance about Emily. She had another project to finish up, a documentary on Jane Goodall. That was a huge point in her favor. When the film was about to air, she threw a little launch party in a side room at Memory Lanes, a bowling alley in south Minneapolis, and invited us. Steve would be out of town, performing at the Whiplash Bash in San Diego, and I was reluctant to go without him. But I needed to get a sense of Emily, her friends, and the film, so I asked a girlfriend, Alex, to come with me. We stopped at the Memory Lanes bar to get some drinks before heading to the party room. I could see a few people milling near windows still lit by the early evening light. They looked harmless enough.

I stepped into the room and saw Emily, a slim woman with sparkling brown eyes and dark, curly hair that fell to her shoulders. She stood with a small knot of friends near a television monitor, stopped talking, and looked at me quizzically. Then she walked across the carpet to say hello.

"Hi. And you're . . . ?"

"I'm Lynette."

She looked confused, unable to place me. Did she know Steve was married? She must have known. They'd already had a few meetings to start looking at schedules. And I know he told her that he couldn't make it to this party. He must have said I'd attend without him. He wouldn't have forgotten, would he?

"This is Steve's wife," Alex interceded, knowing how troubled I was when people didn't recognize Steve and I were married. "This is the wife of the subject of your next documentary," she added, drawing out each word to make sure Emily heard.

"Oh, of course!" Emily smiled now. "My brain is still on this project. Come in and meet everybody." I silently thanked Alex for pulling me back from a cliff.

The other people were mostly filmmakers and co-workers from KTCA. When the light in the sky dimmed, we all set up chairs to watch *Jane Goodall: Reason for Hope*. I loved the film's artistry and message. Emily had taken a camera crew to Africa, then followed Goodall on the lecture circuit where she spoke about protecting the environment and animals, particularly her beloved chimpanzees. Emily had used photographs and footage of Goodall as a young woman and echoed some of those images in new footage. The visuals were like rhyming couplets, visually demonstrating the continuity of Goodall's life and mission. I told her how much I admired the film as I was leaving, and she thanked me. Steve was in good hands.

21

■✗▲✦✲▦♠●▨

2000, New York City

A year or so after their adoption of stage names, my concern about the amount of time Steve was spending on the band versus our relationship intensified. I noticed my interactions with Pandora had grown increasingly uncomfortable. In all the years I'd known her, she never warmed to me. I don't think she ever smiled at me. When she worked with Steve in the art room, he would tell me what she was up to as part of our evening conversation over dinner, so I felt like I knew and liked her. We'd gone to her first gig playing bass at a block party in Uptown, and now she was in All the Pretty Horses. None of this had felt like a problem.

But the two of them had developed a habit of going out for a drink after rehearsal to a bar across the street. Since my hour-and-a-half commute to Rochester already limited our time together, Steve invited me to join them. I would leave the house at ten or eleven to meet them at the Monte Carlo and at first enjoyed the novelty of it. When we were done drinking and talking, I drove home in my own car, and, because Pandora still didn't drive, Steve gave her a ride to her apartment before coming home. Loneliness clawed at me as I drove myself home with no one to talk to but the radio. Eventually, the foul breath of repressed jealousy hovered in the air. I felt the surrounding darkness seep through my skin.

Conventional boundaries had also been crossed: after the first few New York shows, Pandora didn't want to room with Tiffany anymore, so now at the Carlton Arms she usually stayed in the room with Steve and me. When I couldn't travel because of my teaching schedule, she and Steve shared a room. And they'd gone to the top of the Empire State Building, just the two of them.

I didn't think they were having sex, but something seemed off. Pandora had always been more Steve's friend than mine, and now, as I spent time with her, her chilliness toward me got worse. If I took the front passenger seat in our van, where I normally sat, she would give me a frozen-eyed stare and grimace. I repeatedly asked Steve if she was angry with me or if I'd done something to upset her. That's what her reactions seemed to say. His reply was always, "Oh, she's just like that. Don't worry." But I did.

In addition, Steve now often focused solely on the band members in social situations, and not just her. He said he had to make sure they were okay, as if they weren't able to take care of themselves emotionally. This extended beyond the gigs. It was troubling that he didn't show the same level of concern about *my* feelings. Perhaps the allure of a potential new crisis distracted him from unresolved feelings about how to express who he was. Or maybe it was his rigid focus on making the band successful—the ADHD term for it is hyperfocus. This was different from what I'd experienced at the Gay 90's. When I brought it up to him privately, he got angry and defensive, saying he needed to watch out for them to make the band successful. Then he'd turn the conversation back on me: if I wanted him to bring home more money, I had to let him do it *his* way.

The trips to New York began to feel tainted. When we walked around with the other band members, Steve and Pandora strode ahead together, both close to six feet tall and taking long-legged steps. I was left walking in the second or third tier, often doing a running walk to keep up with them. When catching cabs to haul equipment to gigs, I'd stand on the corner to hail them (I was blond and not holding any equipment), and Steve and Pandora would usually jump into the back seat together with their instrument cases. If I got to ride in their cab at all, I'd be left to the front seat, next to the driver.

I repeatedly brought these problems up to Steve, and sometimes he apologized, but the apology usually came with a lengthy explanation of what he was doing to make the band successful. Moreover, he asked me to not do anything to make the band members feel uncomfortable on tours. They needed to be focusing on doing the best possible performances, he said, and if I felt slighted by something that happened during the downtime, I had to keep it to myself.

I felt trapped. I wanted the band to succeed, too, and I felt that if I didn't travel this journey with Steve, he would completely grow away from me. I had learned my lesson from that month spent in Washington. I reluctantly decided to ignore my instincts and do as he said. Was this turning me into the Goose Girl? Had I spilled my power into a river, where it floated far away from me? That's what it felt like. But I stayed by his side, so I could make the journey *with* him.

Before we left for the October 2000 trip to New York, Steve and I made a pact: in social, non-work situations on the road, he would try to let me know in little ways that he loved me and was thinking of me, like walking by my side when we were going to the same place, getting into the same cab together, making sure we sat together at social functions. I was relieved that we had a plan.

■■■

Emily Goldberg with Adrian Dançiu, CBGB, October 2000

Emily Goldberg and a cameraman, Adrian Dançiu, had also flown to New York to shoot footage for the documentary. Mike Ryan, who had started doing author interviews with me for *Write On! Radio*, joined us to help with equipment and lights. Walking along Gramercy Park trailed by a filmmaker with a large camera and boom microphone was an amusing novelty. Throngs of pedestrians parted for us, trying to figure out who we were. It felt like it was going to be a good trip.

We had a free day because the Meow Mix gig had been canceled, so Steve and I went to the Museum of Modern Art, at Fifty-Third Street, with Pandora and Emily Hooper joining us. When we exhausted ourselves with art, we wanted to stop somewhere for a drink, but the museum café was closing. I had the perfect solution. I'd found an item in the *New Yorker* that said a bar on Ninth Avenue called the Swine on Nine was handing out free piggy banks to all the women who came in. I'd even torn a page from the magazine so I would have the address. There was some skepticism, but the consensus was to go, so we headed west on Fifty-Third.

The weather was raw, windy, and drizzling. We had to lean into the squalls and walk fast to keep warm. I was unhappy to see we'd fallen back into the walking formation I'd grown to hate: Steve and Pandora together on the sidewalk ahead, Emily Hooper and I behind them. I was upset Steve had forgotten his promise to walk next to me but felt I'd look pathetic if I yelled ahead to him over the gusting wind. It might also violate that rule about me not making people in the band feel uncomfortable. Emily Hooper was also tall, so I walked as fast as I could, my head tucked into my collar to avoid the wind. Suddenly Steve and Pandora slowed in front of me. I didn't see them in time, and the toe of my right foot came down on the heel of Pandora's combat boot.

"Oh, no! Are you okay?" I asked. Pandora leaned against a sign to examine the heel of the boot. She pulled at it and demonstrated how the heel, still part of the sole, flapped away. "Oh, I'm so sorry!" I exclaimed.

"These are really expensive," she muttered. "I can't afford to replace them."

"I think you might be able to fix them with Barge cement, you know, that flexible stuff?" I'd often had to glue shoes back together.

She didn't seem interested in that idea.

"Can you walk in it?" I continued. "If we can just get to the bar or another warm place, maybe you can tape it up for now and glue it later." Steve liked this idea.

"Let's get somewhere out of this cold weather," he added.

Pandora put her foot back down and experimentally took a couple of steps. "I think I can do it if we go slow," she said.

We continued a few more blocks and found the bar. Not only did they provide tape for Pandora's boot, but also free ham and egg salad sandwiches and the promised piggy banks. Steve got one, too. Then we all shared a cab back to the hotel.

The next day, Sunday, started off well enough, but by the afternoon my stomach hurt, maybe from something I'd eaten. Emily Goldberg was filming interviews with the band members, one by one, in a different room, so everyone who wasn't being interviewed was crammed into Steve's and my room—which we shared with Pandora—while they waited their turn.

All the rooms at the hotel were tiny, not much bigger than a dorm room, with two double beds taking up most of the space. I decided to lie down on the bed nearest the window. Jendeen stretched out on the narrow strip of floor between the two beds. Pandora sat on the edge of the other bed, and Mike Ryan sat on the floor near the door. I lightly listened as Mike conversed with Pandora. Steve and I had talked about how cool it would be if they started dating.

We were all waiting for Steve to finish his interview with Emily Goldberg so we could get on to something else, but it was taking longer than expected. Worse, it seemed a kind of positive energy had left the room with him. Pandora and Mike were doing most of the talking, with Jendeen and I occasionally chipping in innocuous comments. After a while, it seemed to me that every time I said something, Pandora would turn and glare at me. She was a formidable sight, the fierceness amplified by vampiric makeup and bright, magenta-red dreadlocks that billowed and reached the middle of her back.

As usual, I couldn't think of anything I'd said to make her angry, so I decided to shake the feeling that there was something wrong and concentrated on trying to settle my stomach. I just wanted to be ready to go somewhere when Steve's interview

Pandora with her boyfriend Stefan Olson at the Loring Bar, about 2000

was done. I overhead Pandora say something to Mike about someone making her feel not intellectual enough. Was she referring to me? I had never thought of her as unintelligent. Was there anything I had done that might have implied that?

"And look," Pandora said to Mike, pointing to the heel on her boot, "she stepped on this and broke it. I'm probably going to have to get a new pair."

I went cold. She wasn't telling this as a funny story; she was resentful, blaming me for the whole thing and deliberately talking about this right in front of me. Did she think I was asleep and unable to hear? Or did she want me to hear her? I had no idea what to do. My promise to Steve to not upset band members on tour was foremost in my mind, and there'd been no clause that allowed confronting patently rude behavior. Pandora, Mike, and Jendeen shifted to coming up with a plan for what to do next. If my eyes weren't closed before, they were now, and I remained silent. I just wanted them out of there.

"Hey," said Pandora, "let's go rescue Venus from the interview so we can all get some coffee before dinner."

They stood up and then were gone. Some detached part of myself floated above the scene and observed that no one had asked if *I* wanted to go out for coffee or run upstairs to the other room to "rescue" Steve.

Steve came into our room a few minutes later, smiling. I got up from the bed. I was finally feeling better.

"Look, let's just do something on our own for now," I said. "Maybe we can meet up with everyone later at Avenue A Sushi. I'm just feeling . . ."

Someone knocked on the door, and Steve opened it.

"Hey, we're all going out for coffee before dinner. Want to come along?" It was Pandora.

"Uh . . ." he started. I stepped back behind the door to shield myself from view. If Steve was serious that I not do anything to upset band members on tour, I knew I shouldn't disagree with her openly. It might've started a fight. From behind the door, I vigorously shook my head, mouthing the word *no*. Steve looked puzzled and turned back to her. "No, not right now," he said. "Maybe we'll catch up with you later."

I breathed a sigh of relief as he pushed the door shut.

"What was *that* all about?"

"I don't know, she seems really hostile and angry with me," I explained. "I just can't spend any more time with her right now."

"But that doesn't make sense," he countered. "Did you do something to make her upset?"

"No, I didn't do anything. She was complaining to Mike about my stepping on her heel, maybe she's still mad about that."

"No, it couldn't be that," he said. "She's fine with that now. She told me so. You must have done or said something to upset her. What did you say to her?" I couldn't believe his words.

"I told you, nothing! I haven't done *anything* to her. She's just acting angry and grumpy with me, like she always does." Things had been good between us only moments earlier, and now everything seemed warped and wrong. I wondered if it would have gone better if I'd just said I wanted to do something different without giving a reason. Nothing in what I'd experienced, witnessed, or read bore any resemblance to the kind of argument we were having, and everything I said seemed to make it worse.

"You must have done something to upset her. And I can't have my band members stressed out when we're on tour. I need them to be focused, so we can do good shows. You must have said something." He pronounced it like a judicial decision, like a wigged judge proclaiming a grim sentence.

We continued like this for the next three hours, sometimes crying, then finally started to settle down. Steve decided it would be a mystery as to why Pandora was acting like that. It seemed like a supremely wrong conclusion to me, but clearly the argument wasn't productive. I wanted to have my happy husband back, and I also wanted *him* to not be stressed. It seemed like the long-term goals of harmony in our relationship and the band's success should outweigh my concerns over one incident.

We were both hungry and still wanted sushi, but we might run into the others if we went to Avenue A, so we found another restaurant nearby on Irving Place. It wasn't exactly the kind of romantic dinner I had hoped for—we were both emotionally drained from the argument, and our conversation was forced, with Steve not wanting to say much. But we felt solid enough to call Emily Goldberg to tell her we'd meet her at Meow Mix in about an hour and a half. Barb would be bartending. Barb had assured Steve and me that it would be quiet on a Sunday night, and the drinks were on them.

We strolled back to the hotel and climbed the stairs to our room. Steve said he was tired and wanted to lie down. I decided to lie down, too. After a few minutes, I checked my watch.

"Look, we'd better get ready to go if we're going to be on time to meet Emily."

Steve let out a long sigh. "What?" I asked. Steve turned to me.

"I'm too tired," he said. "This all has just worn me out. I need to go to sleep."

It wasn't even 9:00 P.M. yet, but I knew that sleeping was often his way of dealing with stress. I felt stuck in the same dismal pattern again.

"Are you sure?" I pleaded. He was drifting away, right in front of me, and I felt gutted all over again. It was going to be too painful to me to just sit there. He would probably sleep until morning.

"Are you sure?" I repeated, not wanting it to happen. He nodded. I took in a deep breath. "I've got to go out," I explained. "I can't stay here like this. I can go to Meow Mix, meet Emily, and say hi to Barb. Are you going to be okay if I leave?"

"Yes. I'll be fine."

I touched his hand, remembering the time in Prague when I was afraid he would kill himself while I was gone. He seemed peaceful.

"Let's get you tucked in," I said. A sad calm washed over me. I helped him pull the covers up. I leaned down for one more kiss. He looked so sad and fragile, the wisps of hair falling away from his forehead. Letting him sleep seemed like the only way I could help. "I don't think I'll be gone long," I said quietly. Then I pocketed my keys and left.

The Meow Mix was empty, as Barb promised, except for three people at the bar: Mike, Jendeen, and Pandora. I froze. They had been furious the bar had canceled the show and said they never wanted to set foot there again, yet there they were. I trembled as I took a seat at the other end, leaving about eight stools between us. Barb came over wearing an Itchy Trigger Finger T-shirt with the sleeves rolled up, looking like an impish boy, as usual. I spoke to Barb in a low voice, not wanting to be overheard.

"I don't want to be with them now," I whispered, giving a little nod to my left. "They haven't been treating me . . . I don't know . . . I'm feeling a lot of hostility from Pandora."

"You want a drink?"

"That would be great, thanks." They set a gin and tonic in front of me.

"So what happened?" Barb was speaking quietly, too.

"I don't want to go into it all now, but Steve is obsessed with making sure they're all happy, and not able to focus at all on our relationship. We just had dinner, and he couldn't stop worrying about the rest of the band." Barb made a few sympathetic sounds. They'd been in several bands and knew how those dynamics could interfere with relationships.

"You should go up to Liquid and talk to Hillary. She's managing tonight." Hillary was Barb's partner. Barb continued, "Hillary's had to deal with this a lot from me. It's a band-wife problem, completely normal." I nodded, blinking hard to keep the tears from dripping. "Go up there and tell her all about it. She'll understand and help you get through it."

"If Emily Goldberg shows up, can you let her know that Steve isn't coming down here?" Barb nodded. I finished my drink and chopped at the ice with my plastic straw. I looked down the bar toward Mike, Pandora, and Jendeen. "I've got to let them know Steve isn't coming so they won't be looking for him," I whispered. "And they can tell Emily, too." Barb nodded again.

Mike was the closest to me. I felt safe talking to him because of our work together on the radio show. I slipped down the bar to the stool next to him.

"Mike," I said, but I couldn't finish my sentence. Pandora had stood up and walked around Mike to confront me.

"Where's Venus?" she said. She looked stricken, and there was a catch in her throat. The gurgle made it sound like she thought I had murdered him and stuffed his lifeless corpse into a closet. I stood up.

"Venus isn't coming down here," I said sharply, willing myself not to shout it at her.

"But where *is* Venus?"

"Venus isn't coming. Venus is fine." I didn't want to tell her my spouse was at the hotel, sleeping. It was too easy to imagine a scenario where Pandora would head back there to comfort him. That was all I needed. I grabbed my bag and left, not putting on my coat until I was on the other side of the door. Then I strode north, toward Liquid, in search of someone who would see me as a human being.

Meow Mix was a punkish lesbian bar with live music; Liquid was almost its opposite, with warm, copper-colored walls that echoed the tonier vibe of Union Square and Gramercy Park. Liquid also opened early in the day for coffee, and Hillary and Barb usually sent us home with a free bag of Starbucks beans. Hillary was happy to see me and completely sympathetic. After a few hours of her reassurance that this sounded like band crap, and fuck 'em anyway, it wasn't about me, I felt buoyant again. I had the strength to go back to the hotel.

I unlocked the door. I had let myself half wonder if Pandora would be there, and what I would do if I walked in on them embracing, but it was just Steve, still asleep. I kissed him awake.

"I'm back," I said quietly, letting a little melody into my voice. He blinked, smiled, and sat up. He really was okay. "I'm ready to go to sleep now," I said. He smiled again and lay down. I got in and spooned against his body. It felt like it was all going to work out.

■ ■ ■

Our normal pattern in the morning was to have coffee in the small shop below the hotel, the Loon Loon. We all spent so much time there that we got to know the owner, Setsuko, and she didn't seem to mind the whole band using her shop as a living room. I sat in one large, stuffed chair, sipping coffee and reading the newspaper, while Steve worked on a pen-and-ink sketch and drank coffee. We were quiet; Pandora had come in and was sitting nearby. I finished the newspaper and wanted to figure out what was up for the day and plan accordingly. The band was playing at CBGB's, so that probably meant a late-afternoon/early-evening load in, but there were six or seven more hours to imagine and plan for.

"So . . . what's the schedule for today?" I asked. Steve's face flooded with worry.

"I've got to change my strings, I have to make sure I have new batteries, I need to make sure the set lists are in order . . ." He trailed off, overwhelmed. This was a familiar sight.

Shannon, Emily H., Jendeen, and Lynette in front of Loon Loon, New York, 2002

"Okay," I said. "I can get out of your hair. Do you want to plan for lunch together?" He looked at me, bewildered.

"I don't have time to eat today," he responded, his voice getting raspy. This was unexpected. Surely he didn't mean it literally.

"So . . ." I fumbled for what to say. "Does that mean I'm on my own for lunch and dinner?" He nodded. I felt my jaw tense as my body hesitated between fight, flight, and freeze. My brain stopped, and my vision blurred through tears I blinked back furiously. Steve was now a distorted, watery figure on the couch across from me. I could not be seen crying in public, especially not in front of Pandora. I was shocked he didn't have even half an hour in the day to eat something with me. I stood up. My flight response had won. "Okay," I said. "I'll be off. I've always wanted to see the New York Public Library." It was true. It was on my list of possible places to see on this trip. I had read that the library had the original Winnie the Pooh stuffed animals there and other interesting artifacts, as well as a bazillion books. "I'll check back with you later," I added, quickly kissing him on the cheek. Then I fled.

It was so early that the library wasn't open yet, but I had nowhere else to go. I didn't feel emotionally safe going back to either the hotel or the Loon Loon. I ordered coffee at a counter across from the library and waited for it to open. I was beginning to think that coffee was the cause of my upset stomach.

After several hours at the library, I felt bored. I hadn't been able to find the Winnie the Pooh stuffed animals. It was about one o'clock, and I was hungry. My disappointment of the morning had cooled, and it seemed entirely possible that Steve might have overestimated how much prep he had to do. He never liked to eat dinner before a show, but maybe he would want lunch.

I was walking up Twenty-Fifth Street, nearly at the hotel door, when I saw Pandora and Steve turn the corner together from Third Avenue onto Twenty-Fifth. She carried a bouquet of flowers, and they were both smiling and laughing about something. Steve looked at me, still smiling.

"Hey, we just came back from lunch. Too bad you didn't come back earlier. You could have gone with us."

My brain went white-hot. Had he forgotten what we'd said to each other three or four hours earlier? And here they were, a pair, essentially a couple, who might have invited me to join them for lunch. Actually, only Steve wished he could have invited me. Pandora had stopped smiling and didn't say anything. I finally lost it.

"You told me this morning you didn't have time to do *anything* with me today, not even a lunch break, but you decided you had time to go to lunch with *her*?" I shrieked, jabbing a finger in Pandora's direction. She stopped, embarrassed, then ducked her head and walked around me to go into the hotel. I had no desire to follow. Steve was the real object of my rage. "How could you do that?" I yelled. Heads turned, and I didn't care. I knew I had put up with a lot, a lot more than most other people would have done. I was done locking my feelings in some godforsaken oubliette.

"I never . . . I never said that," Steve stammered.

"Oh yes you did," I retorted. I pointed to the window of the Loon Loon next to us. "You sat right there this morning, and I tried to figure out what our schedule would be for the day. When I asked you if that meant you didn't even have time for lunch or dinner, you said *yes*."

"I don't remember doing that," he repeated.

"You said you didn't have any time at all for me the entire day, yet you were fine making plans for lunch with *her*," I snapped.

"But she was just being nice," he replied. "She could see how upset I was after you left so quickly."

"Fuck you!" I roared. "I had to leave because you, my own husband, rejected me once again! I had to get out of there because I was starting to cry!"

At that moment, Emily Goldberg and Adrian Dançiu

rounded the corner, pausing a moment to look at us. *Fine*, I thought, just like all those tawdry reality TV shows: exactly the reason I hadn't wanted anyone to make a documentary about the band in the first place. Now I didn't care. I was ready to give them a show. But they kept going, opening the door to the hotel and disappearing inside.

"Let's go upstairs," Steve said grimly.

"Fine." My anger had not diminished, but I didn't feel like fighting in public.

We continued arguing in our room. Steve was totally clueless about our conversation in the morning. It felt like a double whammy. If he really wasn't aware of what he said, how could I trust *any* kind of communication or plan with him? More than that, he'd tuned me out again, this time in an epic way. If he was able to do that, how could I trust his words when he said he loved me?

"I need to make sure everything is okay with Pandora and the rest of the band," he said sternly. They had to get ready for the show. At least this part was predictable. I nodded my head in exhaustion. He disappeared out the door, and I sat on the edge of the bed, looking at my shaking hands. He was back a few minutes later and said that he'd apologized to Pandora and that she was okay.

"But I need you to be away from the hotel while we're getting ready. I don't want any of the band members to have to see you or interact with you until after the show," he said emphatically.

"You mean, leave this room?"

"Yes, at least until after we've left. We need both rooms for everyone to get ready."

"Can I go to the show?" He took a deep breath and looked at me.

"I don't know," he said. I couldn't say anything else. If I tried to speak, my voice would garble from the heaving gasps that thrashed inside me.

Once on the sidewalk, I tried to figure out where to go. I

felt alone, exposed. I couldn't just stand there. I couldn't go to Fitzgerald's because we knew all the bartenders and they'd ask how everything was going. Maybe they'd seen me screaming at Steve. I walked down Third, looking for a place where I could sit in peace and not engage with anyone. Barfly was nearly empty and quiet, so I stopped there until I realized that I was gulping drinks too fast, and I would get drunk if I stayed longer. I decided to walk, to explore, to pass the time. It would help me stay warm. It worked for a while. I found another thrift store, then the East River. Then it started to get dark, with that rising chill that sets in an hour before sunset. I thought maybe I could work my way back to the hotel and watch from somewhere to see them leave for the gig. Then I would go back in and warm up.

In the dusk, I found a shadowy area near a grate next to the D'Agostino grocery store, kitty-corner from the hotel. I crouched down. Anyone walking on the sidewalk would see me, but from the opposite side, maybe I wouldn't be noticed. I wondered if this was what homeless people felt like. I felt the cold from the concrete seep through the soles of my shoes into my body. I watched feet pass by. A beige plastic bag bounced down the street, buffeted by the conflicting currents of cars and wind.

Then I saw them emerge from the hotel, lugging guitar and drum cases down the sidewalk to the corner of Twenty-Fifth and Third. Third was the busier of the two streets, so that's where they would hail the cabs. I saw Mike and Jendeen climb into one cab with half the equipment. Pandora and Steve got into the other with the rest of it. Then they were gone. I stood up, my legs numb. It didn't feel real. It felt like watching the end of a movie.

I crashed onto my bed, trying to sleep, but my thoughts wouldn't stop scuttling on their hamster wheel. I really wanted to go to the show—I loved Steve and his music—but I couldn't bear another rebuke. Then there was Pandora. He was taking her side. It wasn't something I could pretend I imagined anymore.

■■■

Years later, my therapist used the phrase "emotional affair," and everything crystalized: the appearance of friendship, the long hours together, and most significant, the prioritizing of Pandora's interests over mine. Emotional affairs are just as corrosive as sexual affairs—perhaps even more so, because they break the trust of emotional intimacy. I think Steve just wasn't motivated anymore to put the effort into paying attention to my feelings. Yet even after that revelation in the therapist's office, I didn't have the courage to talk to Venus about that period of our lives. More than a decade later, after we'd turned another corner, I began trying to write about it. It took me that long to start telling my truth.

At that point I still occasionally called my spouse Steve, mostly in private. She hadn't yet asked me to call her Venus. More often, I called her Sweetie. I could call her Venus when talking with other people, referring to her in the third person. That didn't challenge my sense of intimacy with her. I was reluctant to call her Venus directly because of how it conjured the image of Venus and Pandora striding away from me.

"So, I'm at the part now where I want to write about what happened to us then, and I need to clear something with you. I've never told you this before, but my therapist gave me a term for it. I want to know if you think this is accurate." Sweetie nodded. "She said you and Pandora were having an emotional affair. You were closer to her than me, confiding in her, that sort of thing."

I heard a deep breath, then a pause.

"Yes, that sounds like what it was." There was another pause. "Yes, that's probably what it was."

I was shocked. I'm not sure what I expected, but I hadn't

been prepared for this decisive agreement. Something like rage burbled inside me, but it wasn't rage. I'd already experienced that. This tasted more like sadness and regret, with some kind of metal-cogged bitterness that coated my tongue. Yet I felt an odd tremor of relief. I hadn't been crazy.

"But how . . . how did it happen?" The confirmation was so candid. Was it a conclusion already reached without telling me? "I don't understand," I prompted.

Sweetie explained that back then, she had been so focused on being successful with the band that whenever I complained about something not going right with our relationship, she felt like it got in the way of things, and that maybe we were destined to "slip away" from each other. Sweetie told Pandora about our arguments and how I didn't understand what she was trying to do with the band. Pandora listened.

In "The Goose Girl," the princess makes a terrible mistake in expecting that the social order she's known and trusted will continue. Perhaps the waiting-woman seemed like a faithful family friend, someone she would never expect to threaten her.

"Do you think she might have seen me as a rival the whole time?" I asked, cautious. I had to wonder if that was her impression of me when I kept on hearing what a great person she was, that maybe she'd disliked me longer than I'd thought.

Sweetie considered this a moment before responding.

"Yes, it's possible," adding that perhaps that was why Pandora had later quit the band so suddenly and refused to talk about it.

■■■

As I lay on the bed at the Carlton Arms, wondering what to do, someone tapped on the door. I got up.

"Hello?" I said, without opening it.

"It's Emily." It was Emily Hooper. I remembered I hadn't seen her get in a cab with the others. I unlatched the door.

"Aren't you supposed to be at CBGB's?" I asked. She laughed.

"Oh, they don't need me for all that setup. I wanted to take more time getting ready. You wouldn't happen to have any scissors, would you?" I did, and found them for her. "Thanks," she said, "I'll get them right back to you. Want to cab it over there together?"

I sighed.

"There's a problem." I looked at Emily, still her usual, chipper self. "Pandora has been acting angry toward me. I don't know why. Steve and I argued about it, and now he wants me to stay away."

"Oh," she said, only slightly surprised. "Don't worry about Pandora, she's just like that."

"Uh, are you upset with me at all?" Steve had made it sound like everyone in the band was upset with my outburst.

"No, of course not," she chided me. "You'll see, come along and everything will be fine." So I agreed to go with her.

When we arrived, Steve was standing near the front of the bar, talking with Matthew, who was acting as manager at that point. I could see that Pandora and Jendeen were farther down the room, toward the stage. I walked over to Steve and gave him a questioning look. He put his arms around me and kissed me. I couldn't understand how he alternated between being so angry and then so loving, but for now it seemed I had been forgiven, so I decided to accept it. Still, I kept my distance from the rest of the band that night.

I talked to Matthew, briefly explaining what had happened. He was surprised I had been made to feel unwelcome.

"If anyone ever behaved that way toward me, I'd call them on it, right then and there," he exhorted. "I would *not* take it." Yes, I thought. Matthew is my astrological sign-mate, and I had wanted to do exactly what he said I should do. But it seemed that Steve was angry with what I felt in my heart. I swallowed the words I wanted to say, and they traveled deep inside to unmapped recesses and began to root.

22

■×▲♣✱■∧●■

2001, New York City

About a year later, two jetliners flew into the World Trade Towers. A third demolished one side of the Pentagon and exploded in flames, and a fourth crashed into a farm field in Pennsylvania, short of its intended target. The whole country careened from shock to sorrow to anger and back to sorrow. For a while, most of the world sympathized. An acquaintance from London called us in Minnesota—more than a thousand miles from either coast—to make sure we were okay. I thought about this as I walked around the Ground Zero perimeter two months later. I seemed safe from the jet-fuel bombs, but other assaults threatened.

Before the September 11th tragedy, the band had scheduled a tour of England that would start from New York in November of 2001. Emily Goldberg would join them to film it. We made many frantic phone calls to confirm that clubs were still open and wanted the band to perform. I was back to my regular teaching schedule in Rochester, but I could take a long weekend to go to New York before they flew to London. I'd join them there over my Thanksgiving break.

In the story of the Goose Girl, the princess seems stuck between a misguided promise and the truth of what actually happened. It's a fairy tale, so we don't hear about her emotional journey—we don't get any of her internal dialogue. Every day she walks by the severed head of her horse, who reminds her that something is terribly wrong, but she is stuck, powerless to change the situation. She must have felt tormented by her inability to prevent the disaster that led to the death of her horse, her own diminished state, and her bewildering promised silence, making her complicit in the warped state of things. I know I did.

■■■

After my outburst at Steve and Pandora in 2000, things seemed okay when we got home. Then, about a week later, he came back from rehearsal.

"I'm sorry to tell you this, but the band has decided you can't come on any more trips with them. They're finding it too distracting."

I had intuitively known I needed to stay by Steve and grow with the gender exploration and music career or be left in the dust. I was doing that as much as possible. I was on sabbatical and finally had the time to travel and help out, and now he was telling me the band had given me the boot. I was furious. I had been there from the beginning, spent hours fending off creeps from behind the sales table, running errands for whoever needed something, and this is how they thanked me. All the funding for Steve's costumes, instruments, travel, studio space, and more—which the other band members benefited from and used—came from my financial support. I had come up with the names for all their special theme nights (Fin de Siecle, Fleurs du Mal) and even named the fucking band. I didn't have words to express what part of my marriage I handed over to this band—and now they wanted to vote me away.

But a year later, here I was in New York, again with the band.

I told Steve I wanted to see the Ground Zero area, but as usual he had other things on his mind and didn't have time for it. I decided to go by myself, perhaps as a pilgrimage to a disaster, a good way to ruminate on various explosions and their aftermath in my life.

At first I was dismayed by the gray stretches of chain-link fence that blocked the streets—a grim, galvanized web that left me on the outside, peering in. A few blocks later, I began to smell it: burned metal and oil. It reminded me of the time a car in a neighbor's garage caught fire. When it reached the gas tank, it ignited a gasoline fireball that shot high in the air and burned the whole building down. A tarry, choking smell. I grieved for this city that I loved, the city that always set my heart racing and tracing possibilities.

I had a map of what the area used to look like, a neat little guide that disclosed the streets in three pop-out folds of Upper, Midtown, and Lower Manhattan. I had caught a subway as far as it would go and started from the north end, near Church Street, below Canal, where small throngs of people stood, looking in the distance. It was frustrating to not be able to see anything. Most of the walls were solid wood, with chain link on the pedestrian side to keep people out. I was disadvantaged because I was short; the taller people could see more. Every so often, there would be a place where other people climbed on railings and parked vehicles to get a better view, but I didn't want to do that. It would be another violation. I kept walking, hoping for some better gap to open up so I could see, feel, and understand.

When Steve told me I couldn't travel with the band anymore, I knew I couldn't express my outrage without starting a bigger argument, so I formed an eggshell of protection around my rioting emotions. I played it calm. There were only four voting band members: Steve, Pandora, Emily, and Jendeen. I asked Steve if I should try to talk to each person individually, to hear them out and reassure them that I wouldn't let whatever was going on with me interfere with their shows, and that I was around to help. To my relief, Steve thought this was a good idea, and I started making appointments.

Emily Hooper said she had no problem with my joining them in the future. She had not voted to keep me away. That made me feel a lot better. Maybe my quest wasn't hopeless. Next I talked with Jendeen, who said something that surprised me. She had been following Venus's lead, she said. When the subject came up, Venus hadn't made any argument in favor of allowing me to come on future trips. Jendeen interpreted that to mean that Venus didn't *want* me to come along anymore, and so she voted against my joining them. She said if Venus wanted me to come along, she would be fine with that as well.

I also talked with Jendeen about my perception that Steve was more concerned about Pandora's feelings than mine.

"Yeah, well, Venus and Pandora do kind of have a thing," she said, agreeing.

"*What?* What do you mean?" I hadn't expected a confirmation. Jendeen quickly corrected herself.

"Oh, I don't mean they're having any kind of affair or thing like that," she said hastily. "It's just that . . . well, they sort of have a groove together. They're in tune with each other. It's different than with the rest of us band members."

A chill passed through me like a ghost. I hadn't imagined it. There was an odd link between them, I had sensed it already, and it was pushing me out. It was strong enough for other people to notice.

■ ■ ■

As I started walking around the Ground Zero site, I came upon the first of what would be many makeshift memorials fixed to the chain-link fence—bouquets of flowers in cellophane bags stuffed through the gaps, notices with photographs asking if anyone had seen this missing person, like one might post for a lost dog or cat. But these notices were for someone's husband or wife. Brother, father, sister, mother. Child. Where they had last been seen or heard from. Some of the posters were in protective sleeves, others bare to the elements, the paper wrinkled and stained with rain. Some were several pages long. The individual and collective pain was heartbreaking. I wished Steve could see these things with me.

A few people on the street didn't linger to look at the site. Despite the devastation, they were still going to and from work. The New York Stock Exchange was open, and police let the people with authorization pass through a few checkpoints. There was a street vendor underneath some scaffolding with a stand not much bigger than a card table, selling souvenir pins. It felt strange to buy something, but I remembered he needed to make a living. I bought a small rhinestone American flag pin, the only flag pin I have ever purchased, and a brass pin of the two World Trade Towers, with windows and banded levels pressed into its surface and a tiny antenna jutting out of the North Tower. The base of the pin read, "New York." It would have been a normal, kitschy souvenir before September 11th. Now it was a sad memento.

I considered what I knew about the World Trade Center prior to the disaster. I had stood in front of the buildings and walked between them when I was a college student visiting Linc and Marsha. They and their friends scoffed at the towers, complaining about how ugly they were, austere and monolithic. The plaza had been incredibly windy, and I had to grasp the sides of my billowing peasant skirt to hold it down. I didn't go inside either building. Only people dressed in business suits seemed to enter and exit. It didn't look like the kind of place I'd be welcome. Walking around the site now, I wondered how different my life might have been if I had stayed that summer in New York like I'd planned.

■■■

After talking with Jendeen, I was still afraid to talk to Steve about my concerns. It wasn't just me; Jendeen had recognized a special relationship between Steve and Pandora. But I didn't know how to voice my distress anymore. He might not understand what I was saying and somehow make it my fault. Even before the disastrous communication the morning of the CBGB show, I'd already noticed that sometimes when I talked to him, he would hear only 25 percent of what I said and make up the other unheard 75 percent with whatever his brain was working on at the moment. When I brought up a tricky subject, like a financial problem, in hopes of coming jointly to a solution, he would get defensive and switch into making it all about his inadequacies. He acted like I'd accused him of something terrible when I was just trying to come up with a way to address the problem together. If I brought up Jendeen's description of Steve and Pandora's relationship, it would likely backfire. Steve would end up siding with Pandora even more.

I thought maybe he tried to keep her happy because he depended on her for the band's success. Moreover, the stage validated who he was at that time: someone searching—definitely not conventionally male, not typically female, either. It gave him a confidence he didn't have offstage. So it made sense he wanted her in the band to maintain that validation.

Another puzzle was how she had become so hostile toward me. It's true that Emily Hooper said Pandora could be grumpy, but Steve never reported anything negative about her when we'd have supper at the end of the day and recount what we'd done and who we talked to. He told me about her hopes and dreams, her worries about her cat, her plan to buy a house someday. Sometimes I thought the problem must be me because there were occasions when *Steve* didn't seem to like me, either. I was too conventional, not cool enough.

I did tell Steve part of what Jendeen had said, how Jendeen had voted to ban me because Steve didn't speak in favor of my coming along, and that she took that as a signal that he didn't want me there. He was the leader of the band, after all, and his opinion counted the most. I wanted to know why he didn't stand up for me. Steve said something vague about not wanting to argue against what the other band members were saying. He hadn't voted. This struck me as strange, but sometimes he could be oddly passive in the face of conflict. He said he still wanted me on band trips. I had him repeat that several times before I decided to trust it. As far as I was concerned, I had only one person left to persuade, and if push came to shove, she was already out-voted three to one.

Years later I would discover that Pandora was the *only* one who said I shouldn't be allowed on band trips. Steve hadn't disagreed with her, and then, after dropping her off at her apartment, drove home to tell me that the whole band had decided I couldn't join them anymore.

■■■

South of the Stock Exchange, I was still in a canyon of tall buildings, but cranes and sunlit edifices began to appear in the distance. Fewer people walked around this end of the site. I kept trying to find the loop of the circle, looking at my pop-out map of how the streets had once appeared and comparing their names with the street signs. Sometimes I was surprised to see dust and debris still clogging the crossing signals.

From the south end of the perimeter I could see some kind of large temporary building with small windows, the type one sees at construction sites, only bigger, blocking what would have been a north-south avenue. This is where I began to see the wisps of black smoke rising from some spot in the blocked-off area. The odor I smelled earlier was stronger.

Something in there was still burning, some acrid combination of metal, concrete, and plastic. An oily smell. A melted-wires smell. A burned-out vehicle. I did not want this to be me.

As I moved west toward the Hudson River, it seemed as if I was in a neighborhood. Small trees graced the boulevards, and they appeared undamaged by the devastation nearby. Along another chain-link fence, this one dividing the sidewalk from what might have been a tiny park, scores of teddy bears, most of them pink or blue, were set in a row along the fence, some with dust masks. As I looked at the flowers and read the notes, I realized this was another memorial.

My heart broke with tenderness for people I would never know. I had begun the journey around the site feeling sorry for myself, sad that my spouse often chose other people's company and interests over mine, sad that when everything between us seemed to be going fine, another crazy hitch would burst in out of nowhere. But my sorrow was nothing like the sorrow these people must have experienced.

■■■

Without knowing it had been Pandora's idea to ban me from tours, I continued to move forward. Before meeting at her local coffee shop, I asked Steve to give her a seven-and-a-half-page letter I'd written, attempting a sympathetic *maybe you didn't realize* tone. It was agonizingly apologetic. I was trying hard to appease someone who I knew, deep down, didn't want to be appeased. I reminded her that I'd always considered her a friend, mentioning umpteen special dinners and other social occasions at our house we'd invited her to. I explained what was going on between Steve and me prior to and during the trip. I also described how Steve and I had agreed to take care of each other emotionally, what Steve had forgotten about the agreement, and described in detail how I felt slighted with some of her specific behaviors. I wanted to be accurate. Accuracy, I thought, was the one thing I could depend on being true. I also acknowledged how the extra stress of having the film crew around perhaps had made things difficult for all of us.

What exactly did the Goose Girl say into the old stovepipe about her story? Did she feel the need to get every single detail right because she feared someone would question its accuracy?

In some translations of the fairy tale, she doesn't tell her story into a pipe, she climbs right into the charred, black oven to whisper her story—a kind of metaphorical death, if she's on a hero's journey. Maybe she's afraid the king will turn on the oven while she's in there, because she says something he doesn't want to hear.

■■■

Despite my wretched misgivings, I plowed ahead, doing everything I could think of to make it better. Yet it was so clear, as she sat quietly across the table from me, shoulders high, eyes only meeting mine in short, angry bursts, that not only would she never see me as a friend, but perhaps she never had. It bewildered me. All I had to go on was that Steve seemed to think she was a nice person, yet I could tell she hated me.

■■■

I began to look up at the skyscrapers around the Ground Zero site and noticed many of the ones that once faced the World Trade Towers had large, crumbling gouges. I felt sorry for the buildings, too. Their lines and arching symmetry had been beautiful. What kind of repairs would be necessary to fix that, I wondered. Would it even be possible, or was their structural integrity at risk? Was Steve's and my structural integrity at risk?

Matthew Hopping had gotten the band an appointment with a music lawyer in New York, and that's where everyone else was while I walked around Ground Zero. As we understood it, connecting with a music lawyer was now the route to being signed by a record label. A lawyer with connections takes on a band, discovers what's possible out there for them to enter the perplexing and tricky music industry, and, due to expertise with similar contracts, is able to negotiate something reasonable. I asked if I could come along. It seemed important to be there.

"No."

"Why not? This is important to me, too."

"I'm worried you'll upset . . . people." This I knew was code for pointing out that I was on a non-speaking, eyes-averted basis with Pandora. Steve worried I would cause a scene. *I* knew I wouldn't, but it was futile re-explaining to him what had happened a year earlier. Still, it seemed a miracle that we remained together and that I continued to feel welcomed by everyone else on these trips. "Besides," he continued, "I think I'll just feel distracted if you're there." I had the uneasy sense that he might be thinking he'd be more marketable as a rock star if he didn't have an obvious wife. Whatever "distracted" meant, it was his band. I couldn't attend the meeting with the lawyer. So I chose to walk around Ground Zero instead.

Many of the surrounding skyscrapers seemed undamaged. Later that afternoon I would find out that the meeting with the lawyer had been in one of these buildings. The office where they'd met had windows that overlooked the former World Trade Center site, the center of all that devastation. They'd all stood there and looked at the rubble and the workers still searching through it before the meeting started, before everyone sat down around an expansive, granite conference table to talk.

Maybe Steve had been looking out the windows as I found my way around below, like an ant in a terrarium. When he told me he'd been up there, I felt puny and insignificant. Strangely, that's not how Steve saw it when we compared our experiences. He marveled that we'd been experiencing the same thing at the same time from different places, as if some kind of invisible thread had stretched out and connected us. He might have been right, but at the time I found that interpretation hard to agree with. I couldn't shake the sense of abandonment. The band would travel from New York to England, and I would go back home alone. I wished we had *shared* either of the two vantage points, but he'd taken in a rapid bird's-eye view of the site, while I moved at a literal pedestrian pace around things. They were two sides of the same circle, but I felt exiled as the sole traveler on my arc.

I used my journey around Ground Zero to brood and grieve. In Minneapolis, there were all the times that Steve was late getting home because he had to give Pandora and Tiffany a ride home, or he'd have to rush out the door to give Pandora and her cat a ride to the vet. At least the open tension put an end to the post-rehearsal drinks at the Monte Carlo. Even though she hadn't revoted in my favor, I was still able to accompany the band whenever I wanted. To keep Steve happy, I had to stay out of her way, which was perfectly fine with me.

■ ■ ■

I'd been walking around Ground Zero for an hour now and still hadn't closed the loop. I was getting tired. Toward the northern edge, I found a viewing platform. Here again were the small crowds, this time patiently waiting their turn to step onto the raised wooden deck. When it was my turn, I found the area I wanted to see mostly in shadows. It was anticlimactic: there wasn't much more than what I had already taken in. For me, the raw grief of the countless bouquets of flowers, notes, and stuffed animals along the chain-link fence had said it all.

Still in a walking mood, I headed north on Broadway. I stopped at a convenience store for a bottle of water and was surprised to find a little booklet, *Wall Street Rising*, listing the important sites of Lower Manhattan, organizations and businesses that were still open in the area, with pleas to utilize them so they could stay open. I grieved for the people and what they would have to do to recover, day after grinding day. I wanted to do something to help, but all I could do was walk. I continued north, and the familiar activity of the city came back to me. The smoke smell faded.

I returned to the hotel to find that Steve had gotten there before me.

2001, New York City

"What happened? How did it go?" Exercise had put me in an optimistic mood.

"Oh. We won't be working with him," Steve replied.

"What? I thought this was going to be—I thought this was what you needed to make it—to get signed—or something!" I was stunned. I had been pinning my hopes to the lawyer more than I realized. Now we were at a dead end. "What did he say?"

Steve explained that the lawyer liked their music and thought he might be able to do something for them, but there was a hitch.

"The lawyer asked me if this was the way I really was, or whether it was a stage act." Steve gestured indignantly at his face, his hair, his clothes. "Of course I told him it was the real me."

The lawyer had responded regretfully that he thought that's what Steve would say. He appreciated what they were doing, what Steve in particular was doing, but the music industry wasn't ready for it. The lawyer wouldn't be able to find anyone to sign them. And Steve wasn't going to disavow his identity.

"I'm not going back in the closet again," Steve said emphatically. "I told him that expressing who I am is the very thing that got us noticed this far. I'm *not* giving that up."

"I know, I get it, but what did the rest of the band say?" There must have been some wiggle room, maybe a temporary compromise with a way to renegotiate once the band reached a wider audience. There'd been five other people in the room. Didn't they have an opinion?

"Oh, they all agree with me," Steve said. I was surprised. Steve had told me several times now that Pandora was concerned about not making enough money for all the time she was putting into rehearsals and gigging. I thought the others might feel the same. "They thought it was the right thing for me to do," Steve reiterated.

A few years later, I talked with Steve about this a little more. In fact, the other band members hadn't said much of anything at the meeting. They'd all followed his lead. I shook my head when I heard this. Maybe I should have tried harder to go with them. It might not have made a difference, but I was probably the only person willing to disagree with Steve and work to find some kind of middle ground both parties could agree to.

The loss left a bitter taste. They never did get a recording contract or any other kind of industry support. They never even got another appointment with a music lawyer. Steve (eventually Venus) continued being the songwriter, publisher, booking agent, publicity person, and record label. It was a lot to juggle, and there was never enough money. Band members would drop out, and they would need to find and train in someone new. There was a hard future ahead, and it saddened me to watch him struggle.

I also knew the response to the lawyer was motivated by a need for self-preservation, an urgent drive for survival. I couldn't say that was wrong.

23

■ ★ ▲ ✿ ■ ♠ ● ■

2000–2001, Minneapolis

It seemed that maybe people—Pandora, Jendeen, some band fans, and maybe even Steve—had less regard for me because they didn't see me as a creative person. I was already on a trajectory to write and perform more poetry, and I had connected with other people in the writing world. Now I pushed myself harder. I wasn't going to sit at home pining for Steve to get back from rehearsal. I went out and participated in as many readings as I could and invited Steve to be part of the line-up or audience, whatever applied. Often he came with me. I played keyboard for a performance art show he did at Intermedia Arts. I was determined to prove everyone had underestimated me.

I started reading with poets who had a sort of beat/music vibe, the Bosso Poetry Company. As part of that collective, I began to read to beer-happy audiences at Art-A-Whirl—a huge tour of open art studios and parties in Northeast Minneapolis. I drew on my earlier love of jazz improvisation and experimented with reading mash-ups with other poet friends. I began reading to improvised music and sometimes jammed on violin while other poets read.

In the story of the Goose Girl, there's an odd interlude where the princess has begun tending the geese, and she unpins her hair to comb it out. Conrad, the young man who tends the geese with her, is fascinated by her golden hair and wants to pluck some out. To prevent that, she charms the wind into blowing his hat far across the fields, and by the time he has caught his hat and marched back, her hair is all done up again. She still has some power. If I'd stupidly given away a lot of my power, I was determined to get it back without losing Steve and the music and art I loved being a part of.

Through *Write On! Radio*, I met Emily Carter, author of the acclaimed story collection *Glory Goes and Gets Some*. I loved the gritty, rock-and-roll vibe of her writing and told her so, explaining this was probably because my husband was in a band.

"Oh, yes," she said, giving me a broad smile. "I know who your husband's band is. I know who Venus is."

We became good friends, and soon I was inviting her to read as an opening act with All the Pretty Horses. It was refreshing to have someone in my camp to talk to at shows, someone who liked and appreciated me, who didn't dismiss me because I wasn't in a band. But I still felt precarious. Pandora was still there at every rehearsal and every gig. Steve didn't come home talking about her as much as he used to, aware of the cold war between us, but it still seemed any disturbance might tip us back into open conflict.

In Emily's documentary *Venus of Mars*, there's a scene where we're all in Duluth, the day after some gig, and most of the band and entourage has stayed overnight at Steve's mother's house. A few others who stayed at a nearby motel pile into the living room in the morning for bagels and cream cheese. Steve's mom, Lillian, is interviewed, then his Aunt Irene comes in, and she's interviewed, too. Everyone is sitting on chairs or the floor of my in-laws' small living room, where I've been hanging out for almost twenty years, often opening Christmas presents in the corner where I'm sitting in the documentary, sewing up some clothing item that started coming apart at the seams.

If you look carefully, you'll see I'm not interacting much with the other band members, not even making eye contact

Pandora and Venus at Slimelight, London, 2001

with them. It was filmed just three months after Steve told me the band had decided I couldn't travel with them anymore, and my feelings about it were still raw. Obviously, I continued to travel with them. I was trying to be my regular, affectionate self with Lillian and Irene, whom I loved. It was a difficult balancing act. I was trying hard to be true to my perceptions of what had happened and at the same time not upset the people I loved.

On that same trip, Emily Goldberg and her cameraman Matt Ehling wanted to film Steve and me walking together in the snow—the two of us venturing into the bleak North Shore tundra. We walked along snowy railroad tracks in Lester Park and across the mounds of snow down by Lake Superior, both familiar places. It was odd to have a film crew trail us, but most of the time they were out of earshot, especially as we traipsed along the icy railroad bed. With the house full of band people, Steve and I didn't have much time for just the two of us, so we used the opportunity to check in with each other.

"How're you doing?" he asked.

"I'm okay. Thanks for asking. I think it's working just to stay away from her. She doesn't seem to want to engage with me at all."

"Okay. That's good."

"Hey, your mom and Irene really seem to like having everybody over."

"Yeah." He laughed.

"I wasn't expecting Irene to stop by."

"I wasn't, either."

"You know, she's really a creative person. I'm sure that's why she came to see everybody. I remember her doing all those art projects."

"Yeah. You know, I didn't think of that."

"I'm just reminded of it now. Hey, I really like—what's his name—Rockula? He's good energy. And funny."

"Yeah, he's a drummer, he's been helping Jen with the tech stuff. Jen seems to really appreciate it."

"I like the line where he said she was making him sleep under the truck."

"Ha! Yeah!"

"I think we've gotten to the point where we're supposed to turn back now."

"Okay. Here we go." He smiled at me as we turned back.

I hadn't been keeping score, but somewhere along the line Emily Goldberg had started to film more scenes of our relationship. She went down to Rochester, filmed me teaching, and interviewed some of my colleagues and students. She filmed me running the board at KFAI and reading poetry. She came out to the barn with us for a boarders' potluck, inter-

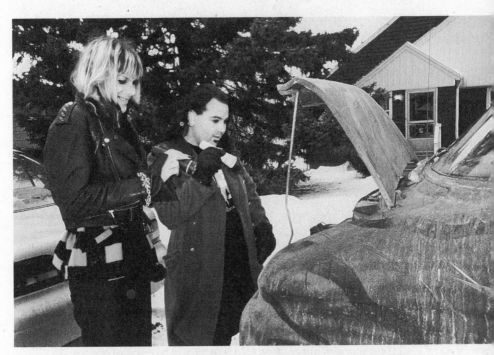

Venus and Rockula (Robert Knott) outside the Grandells' house, Duluth, 2001

viewed people there, and filmed us horseback riding. Steve had always pitched the documentary as a band vehicle that would give them enough fame to jump to the next level, a financially successful level, so that's how I saw it, too. Without either of us realizing it, though, the focus had changed. And when Emily resisted filming my outburst at Steve and Pandora on the corner of Twenty-Fifth and Third, choosing not to venture into the marrow of bad reality TV, she earned my trust.

24

2001, London

At Thanksgiving break I met the band in London. As I rounded the corner by the hotel, I saw Steve striding toward me, and my heart swelled with joy. Then I noticed that Emily had set up a tripod on the sidewalk outside the hotel to film our reunion, a classic scene where we would walk toward each other and kiss. I wondered if Steve was being nice only because Emily was filming. To my relief, he seemed equally happy to see me off camera. My luggage was delayed, and the next day it was delivered to the hotel next door, where Pandora and some of the other band members were staying. Pandora apparently recognized it was mine and let Steve know. I was surprised she did that—I had so soured on her that it was hard to imagine she would ever help me.

Everything about the trip unfolded the way I'd hoped. The musicians and people hanging around the band were friendly and seemed to respect me, and Pandora and I stayed so far apart that I don't think we ever spoke to each other. True, Steve was mostly in band mode, completely focused on whatever gig was happening at least twenty-four hours in advance of the show and usually in the twelve to twenty-four hours after the show. I felt a particularly bad decision had been made just before I arrived: Gossips, a London venue, had told soundman Matthew Hopping there was no backline (drums and P.A.) at the club, so Steve and Matthew borrowed the equipment from the support band they'd been working with up north. However, they had no vehicle to get the equipment to London. They decided to have Matthew take it in a cab, which Steve paid for on a credit card. It was a great distance, from somewhere near York to London. They didn't reveal to me how much it cost. I thought it was something like $200–$400—for a show they made $75 on. Many years later, Steve told me the true bill was more like $1,000–$2,000. And when they arrived at the club, all the backline they had needed was sitting in a room backstage.

Steve laughed about this at the time and turned it into a joke. I refused to do that, even when I thought it was only a few hundred dollars, because all the band's bills would eventually come back to me. Steve had multiple credit cards and accounts, and he never seemed able to make more than the minimum payment on each one. We owned the house together, and eventually I learned that we could avoid the outrageous credit card interest rates by refinancing the house. We did this at least four times. I was the person who paid for the house, utilities, all its upkeep, groceries, cars, and insurance. If I ruminated on it too long, the financial responsibility made me feel like a mule. So I didn't. But I didn't know how much longer it could continue if the band didn't somehow command a bigger audience.

The band's London gigs were at places Steve and I had discovered during our private trips there together—Gossips and a huge warehouse called the Slimelight, a play on New York's glitzier Limelight—so it felt like a kind of homecoming for me. The managers of the bed-and-breakfast where we stayed remembered us from previous visits and were very friendly. I don't remember who had suggested that we check out the Slimelight on one of our earlier trips. It must not have had normal licensing or something, because it wasn't advertised.

"So how do we find it?" I asked.

"Get out at the Angel tube station in Islington, and follow the goths."

We did, and it worked. There was a doorman who scrutinized the people lined up. Then we noticed a sign at the door that said "Members Only." Uh-oh. But we were still more dramatically dressed than many of the others, Steve in new boots and his usual torn fishnets, and me not quite so impressive but still wearing very black and shiny patent leather. Steve took my hand and led me around the line to the bouncer at the door to get in, looking impatient. The bouncer motioned us in, deeming us sufficiently gothed-up/alternative and obviously confident that we belonged inside.

The interior was a raw, artfully crumbling space, with music booming on at least three floors.

"I have to get the band a gig here," Steve had said, looking around. I nodded in agreement.

In contrast, Gossips was a much smaller place in Soho, a basement dance and music club that catered to the punk and goth crowd. The first time we went there, for Goth Night, we joked that the London goths didn't dance, they just leaned against the walls. That wasn't true of the Slimelight, but Gossips was easier to get to with its central London location—we'd usually walk to it from one of the Gower Street hotels. With both locations, I felt like a seasoned veteran of the London scene compared with Steve's bandmates.

Maybe my increased confidence made the trip go well— plus we weren't sharing a room with Pandora. Despite the ongoing money problem, Steve and I were able to joke about things, share observations, and snuggle with each other. On a day off from performances, Matthew Hopping joined Steve and me for a boat ride from Westminster to Greenwich. We saw the *Cutty Sark* clipper ship, laughing that prior to this we'd all assumed it was just a brand of Scotch. We traipsed through the museum of timekeeping devices and stood on the prime me-

Ariel Cafarelli, Ted Ammerman, Lynette, and Venus, New York City, 2001

ridian together. We looked out over the green hillside below the museum and longed to have a picnic hamper with us. Then we found a pub near the bottom of the hill and had a few beers. When the boat dropped us back in Westminster, Big Ben began to toll. This was *the* London experience, Matthew enthused. Steve and I agreed. Then we were back in Minneapolis, where our happiness carried into the holidays.

25

■ ★ ▲ ✦ ✦ ■ ♠ ● ■

2001–2002, Minneapolis

By now, Steve's standard way of dressing for stage included shedding his patent leather bra early in the performance, displaying nipples covered with black electrical tape to stay legal. I didn't like him showing his breasts, and told him so. There was plenty of nudity in performance art, but the bar scene was different. He said that he had to present his authentic self to the audience. I argued back that he was appealing to a sexist fixation with women's breasts, and he countered with an argument about being true to himself. I knew I couldn't stop him when it came to self-expression. I also wasn't confident that his argument was completely wrong. I wasn't transgender. The closest I could come to understanding what my spouse was going through was imagining what it would feel like if someone forced me to wear clothes I felt horrible in, day in and day out, clothes that led anyone seeing me to make negative assumptions about who I was. I knew it wasn't a sufficient understanding. I had to trust Steve when he told me what he needed.

But Steve's openly erotic stage presence made people curious about sex between us. I don't like to broadcast my sex life, so it was an unwelcome intrusion. I felt like a lab specimen, invisibly poked and prodded by prying eyes. For Steve, it was different. He wanted to stand in front of an audience every night, tear his clothes off, and shout, "This is who I am!" He wanted to hear the crowd roar back with approval.

I also resented the spoken and unspoken questions about our sex life because of the gender double standard: it was always men, heterosexual men, eyes glittering, asking me how we made love. They were especially interested in how our sex life worked with Steve's newly budding breasts: "two partridges" is how my friend Emily Carter described them. Some were friends, some were strangers, and their treatment of us felt objectifying and sexist. I channeled some of my frustration into writing, finding that if I was playful and slightly outrageous, the poem would go over well in a bar. Then we could all laugh about it, with no more questions asked. In truth, I wasn't someone who got excited over breasts, and I missed resting my head on his previously smooth chest, but I loved everything else about how our bodies joined together.

Steve presented as a strong, fierce person who had both male and female characteristics, which drew interest and respect from the local fetish community. Inspired by what we'd seen in New York, he put together theme nights that often showcased not just bands, but also a fashion show, flogging demonstrations, vendors of fetish gear, and so on. Fetish was a big fashion movement in the 1990s and 2000s, an offshoot of punk. Even Chanel marketed a black lipstick, and the *New Yorker* ran a profile of a major Manhattan dominatrix. Ground Zero nightclub in Minneapolis—so named before September 11th—had opened its doors, and Matthew Hopping and a friend from college started the city's first Bondage-A-Go-Go night there. We added the club to our circuit because Steve could wear more fetish-oriented clothes there than at the 90's. It didn't hurt that Michael McManus was a regular and could get us in for free. I could deal with Michael as long as he didn't get drunk and start taunting me with "Oh, LEE-net . . ." in some kind of fake French accent.

I found the fetish community interesting. For one thing,

there were specific rules. It was like grammar. The canons of it hit me when I stepped into a warehouse trailing Steve and Pandora for a Pretty Horses show. The doorperson asked me to pin a small, color-coded button to my chest that signaled dominant, submissive, or neutral. She also handed me a sheet of paper with at least twenty rules. I came to a full stop.

"What do I do?" I whispered to Steve, pulling at the elbow of his floor-length black coat before he walked forward. "I don't want to do anything wrong."

"Just take a button," he prompted.

"Yeah, but I don't want to . . . um . . . get involved in anything."

"Then do what I did," he said, smiling and pointing to his button indicating he was a dominant. "I don't want to get involved in anything, either."

Basically, you couldn't do anything to anyone without their permission, not even touch them, and the button indicated whether you welcomed being approached or not. It was Vaga-bondage, invitation-only, not fashion, but a night of the real thing. We were there because the event promoters invited the band to play a set.

As we walked by the examining tables and chairs where practitioners administered delicate electric shocks for willing clients, or strapped clients onto tables for various versions of medical procedures, I was reminded how bondage and discipline didn't feel very erotic to me. I'm more of a person who likes back-and-forth interaction, like a good conversation between equals. But I appreciated that there were rules to this scene, and that adhering to them was what made people feel safe as they tested their limits, whatever their personal reasons. I also appreciated that this was a scene where women were respected.

Putting together big fetish shows at places like First Avenue and the Gay 90's introduced us to many people in that community. Shannon Blowtorch had joined the band as a dancer and brought the Horses' performances to a new high point of the show: the band would riff, and she would ceremoniously buckle

The Grinder with Emily Hooper, Venus, and Shannon Blowtorch, at Don Hill's in New York, about 2001

on metal, studded underwear. It looked like a chastity belt. Then Steve would plug in an angle grinder and nearby band members would don protective eyewear. Steve pressed the grinder to the raised knobs on the metal underwear, sending a cascade of fiery, metal sparks into the air. It looked like the fireworks of pleasure.

I loved Shannon's being in the band—she was direct and had a ton of new ideas. And she respected my relationship with Steve. This may have been because she was a lesbian. Lesbians and most gay men seemed to accept my relationship with Steve more readily than straight people did.

I may have inadvertently sent dom signals to a lot of people in the community, after all those years of classroom teaching, as well as working with horses. It's not natural for me to accept abuse from or pander to other people.

The shows introduced us to Rebecca Holmberg (also known

as Amanda Wildefyre), a dominatrix and Brown University graduate who possessed a marvelous sense of creativity and ability to construct elaborate props. When we met her, she was moving beyond private sessions. She taught classes and did performance art and theatrical spectacles, some in her backyard, some at Intermedia Arts. When she took us on a tour of her dungeon, I liked the fact that it was *not* in a basement and was sparkling clean, with white carpet and plenty of chrome.

When she discovered I went horseback riding, she wanted to know more. She'd ridden horses when she was younger and wanted to get back into it. Would I help her do that?

"Sure," I said, then backpedaled a little. "Well, at least I can try. I can introduce you to Maureen, the woman who owns the place, and we can go from there. Sometimes there's a horse or two for lease."

Within days, she picked me up in her enormous purple pickup and drove me out to the barn. I introduced her to Maureen, who found a horse for her. I gave her a refresher on how to tack up, and we headed out on the trail together. She made plans with Maureen to lease the horse.

A strange thing happened as we drove home. She said she was thirsty, so I pointed her to a convenience store. She pulled the truck up in front and put it into park. Then she looked at me and asked me to go in to get her a soda. I peered at her, confused.

"But I don't want anything from there. I wasn't planning on going in."

"Oh." She turned the ignition off, got out of the cab, and walked into the store. She was back within minutes, soda in hand, and started up the truck. As she pulled back onto the highway, I began a conversation about something completely unrelated.

When she dropped me back at the house, Steve asked how it had gone.

"Oh, it was great. I think she wants to do it again. But you know, something kind of weird happened." I told him about the soda incident. Steve started laughing.

"You know what . . ."

"What?"

"I think she was testing you." I gave him a puzzled look. "You know, she has all those slaves doing her housework and gardening for her."

"Testing me?" And then I got it. "Oh gawd," I laughed. "I think I failed the submissive test."

I don't know if that was really true—I was too embarrassed to ask her about it—but Rebecca was certainly smart enough about human nature to be able to set up that kind of test. We went out to the barn together a few more times, then she was on her own.

This new circle of friends gave me an idea. In my drive to be a poet, I had developed the convoluted notion that if I wrote a novel, and people read it, they would also want to read my poetry. Inspired by the band's emphasis on fetish shows, I thought I had a good idea for the book: something about a dominatrix who goes through a great loss and comes out of it healed and wiser in the end. I had a friend who led fiction workshops out of his home, so I signed up and spent the next few years working on the book. When people in the fetish community heard I was writing it, they were interested. Some wanted to help with research, inviting me to sessions that would normally be private. I hesitated to accept their offers because I had begun to sense a certain sadness in the fetish community. That was really what I wanted to write about.

I began to feel like more of an imposter than a supporter, and that worried me. Though both clients and practitioners said they felt their work was healing, a kind of therapy, it still seemed that something was missing in the "cure." It seemed wrong to make intimacy a paid commodity. I never thought what dominatrices did was similar at all to prostitution. Every single step required negotiation and consent between both parties. Still, to me it emphasized the separation between humans and the inability of some people to find loving intimacy. I wasn't sure what the "cure" for that separation was, but I was afraid that the fetish scene might be reinforcing that gap. And perhaps subconsciously, it paralleled worries about my own relationship with Steve.

Still, I went to a private session to better understand everything. I could see that for my friend being bound, gagged, and strung up between two metal posts, it was a return to feeling small, meek, and powerless, yet still finding the courage within to bear it. It was an affirmation that one *is* strong enough. Maybe that's where I sensed the kinship. I, too, was learning how much I could endure.

When I thought I was far enough along to have a sense of the whole possible novel, I gave Rebecca the first few chapters to read, hoping she would find them authentic-sounding enough. I had spent a lot of time researching. I had learned what the tools were called, how the different sizes of cattle prods worked, and how flogging can injure the kidneys if not done right. When we met a week later, she handed the pages back to me.

"Well, what did you think?" I asked nervously.

"Well, I never like a book that starts with a dead dom," she remarked dryly.

She was right, of course. And it wasn't just the dead woman in the first chapter (and why had I fallen into the stereotype of the dead-woman-in-the-first-chapter?). I'd set out to write something new, something with a fresh, insightful perspective, and in over two hundred pages had re-created just about every bad stereotype about the fetish community. I may have had a good idea to start with, but somehow I'd turned it into something else. I went back and wrestled with the thing a few more months, but there was no fixing it.

The truth is that I don't like hierarchies, period. I like working *with* people and animals, not ruling or being ruled by them. I wasn't the person to tell that story. Even more, I wasn't able to see myself and my own fears clearly enough to write an authentic story about human nature.

■■■

Pandora was still very much in the band, as they maintained a heavy schedule of rehearsing and performing. She was present in Steve's life through rehearsals and shows, and he probably still gave her a ride to and from rehearsal. But we weren't having dinner with her, not at home and not on the road, at least not if I was along. Steve didn't come home from rehearsals telling me everything she was up to. Many of the new people we met, people in the performance art community, the fetish community, and the literary community, were the people we socialized with. She wasn't included.

For the Valentine's Day Fetish Ball at First Avenue, Steve decided to make a big splash by coming to the stage on stilts. Shannon said they could borrow some from Bedlam Theatre, a cutting-edge theater company then located in Minneapolis's West Bank neighborhood. Shannon would also enter on stilts, adding a nice symmetry to the spectacle. Both of them would appear to be ten feet tall. To do this, they had to practice a lot down at the studio, and every time they did, I sat at home worrying that Steve would fall and crack his head open on the concrete floor.

It wasn't an idle fear. He now often ran his guitar through a remote pickup, which gave him the freedom to walk around in the crowd, playing his guitar, while the band stayed onstage, hammering the beat forward. Sometimes he'd get up on the bar, still playing guitar, and walk down its length showing off his legs, his wasp waist, everything. Surprised patrons would quickly slide their drinks out of the way and look up with wonder as he walked by.

But once, at a show at the Saloon in downtown Minneapolis, I'd seen him fall. The performance stage at that time flanked the dance floor next to a long bar, with a divider that masked most of the view from one side to the other. The band was playing a loud instrumental break, and Steve left the stage to hop up on the bar's shiny surface. He began to walk. I stood at the far end, enjoying a vantage point where I could see everyone pull their drinks out of the way as he walked toward me. Then, about a third of the way down, he wobbled a bit, gave a strange, small smile, and crashed into the bar pit, completely disappearing from view. I raced over to where he fell, frightened and trying to push through the onlookers, then saw him pop up again out of the bar area, now with a broad, silly smile on his face. He scrambled back to the stage, guitar still in hand, and finished the song. Without pause, they started up the next song on the set list.

I made my way to the stage area, concerned. Was he in shock? What if he'd hit his head, and no symptoms of an injury showed up for a while? The song ended, and I gestured to Tiffany that I had something urgent to ask.

"Is he okay?" I said anxiously. She gave me a look of confusion.

"Venus. Is Venus okay?" I asked, gesturing toward him.

"Oh, Venus is fine," Tiffany assured me, then stepped back to her mic and prop area for the next song.

None of the band saw what happened, and they didn't find out until the show was over. Steve had hopped back and switched to his backup instrument. He told me later that all his guitar strings flew off in the fall. Miraculously, he hadn't even cut himself on broken glass, though he'd managed to smash through several dozen clean glasses. He was a little sore for the next few days, but that was about it. He decided to retire the bar-walking stunt.

I imagined a replay of that when he told me about the stilts. He scheduled an evening rehearsal for stilt walking with Shannon a week before the show, assuring me it wouldn't take as long as a regular band rehearsal because it was just the two of them. When the time came and went for him to be home, I got concerned. I called the studio line. No answer. Maybe he was driving home now. I waited another half hour and called again. Still no answer. Maybe it was taking longer than usual to get home because he was giving Shannon a ride. I waited another half hour. No Steve, no answer on the phone. Dammit. He might have fallen and hurt himself. Maybe Shannon didn't know how to get ahold of me. Or maybe she'd left and he decided to practice by himself and fell. I should have gone to bed to get up for classes the next morning, but I was too worried to sleep. I got in the car and drove down to the studio. When I unlocked the door, the two of them were standing by the desk area, laughing about something, surprised yet happy to see me.

"Why didn't you come home?" I'd driven downtown for no reason at all. "I was so worried about you! When you didn't come home or answer the phone, I was worried you fell and got hurt." Steve and Shannon looked at each other, perplexed.

"Oh!" Steve said, looking at a clock. "I'm sorry, we completely lost track of time."

"Two hours? And you didn't answer the phone."

"Yeah, I don't know about that. Maybe it got turned down. I'm sorry. Really, I'm sorry. I can see how stressful this was for you. But guess what? The stilts work great."

I nodded. I couldn't switch out of my emotional mood as fast as Steve could. Shannon recognized that.

"Hey, it's later than I thought," she said. "I gotta go. See you tomorrow?" she nodded at Steve.

"Yeah, that's good. I'll see you tomorrow," he responded.

At the Fetish Ball, I watched from the floor as the screen in front of the stage rose revealing Steve and Shannon standing on stilts in front of the band. They began the first song. I was reassured that they'd be okay when I saw that they actually didn't move around a lot on the stilts. They looked like two fascinating monsters, swaying and stepping slightly as they towered

Venus on stilts at First Avenue, 2002

above the audience and the band below. The crowd loved it. It had been the right decision, and I was relieved when they hopped off the stilts and started the next song. I began to walk around the audience, saying hello to people and admiring the costumes everyone wore. By now I had enough of a wardrobe to fit in, especially since I'd found a real patent leather corset in a cardboard box marked "Clearance" at a shop in London's Camden Town. It had pointed cups with spiral stitching, like something Madonna would wear.

I saw Rebecca and said hello. She gestured to one of her clients who'd come with her. He was wearing an elaborate costume, mostly padded leather, that included aluminum extensions ending in hooves for his arms. It enabled him to walk around on all fours like a horse without awkwardly crouching forward. She'd put a saddle and something like a bridle on him.

"Want to get on?" she asked.

"Oh, no. I couldn't," I said, laughing.

"Are you sure?" she asked again, grinning. "He wants some-one to ride him. You know how to do it." She gestured for me to come closer and introduced us. I shook my head at him.

"I'll be too heavy. I'll hurt you."

"No, I can handle it," he said. I remained skeptical. "Look," he said, "I'll let you know if it's too much." I studied him closely. He was big and built like a leather man.

"Okay." I'd never have a chance to do something like that again. I put a leg over, got on, and watched the dance floor clear for the two of us as he spun around underneath me.

"You okay down there?" I shouted to him over the loud dee-jay beat.

"Yeah, all good!" he shouted back.

The whole thing lasted only a few minutes—I continued to worry I'd give him a back injury—but both he and the crowd were stoked by our show. I slid off, happy I'd done it.

26

■ˣ▲♣✦■♠°■

2002, New York City and Minneapolis

The band made a quick trip to New York without me for a show at CBGB's Gallery in February. When Steve got back I found out everything had gone wrong. Something malfunctioned with the bass amp. It blew a circuit, and important journalists in the audience had to wait for the music. They eventually patched the bass through the board, but Steve couldn't use his guitar effects, and the sound wasn't the same. And then the manager for a photographer who took Civil War–style promo shots of them on a previous trip got mad because he thought the band broke its end of the bargain. It was unclear what was wrong because they'd had a verbal agreement, and as I understood the situation, each party was going to use the other's work/image to develop their careers. The pictures were wonderful, long exposures shot on glass plates. Everyone looked appropriately grim and gothic. But the argument made Steve resolve to never use the pictures again. It was a plagued show.

That trip may have created stress in the band that Steve didn't communicate to me. Perhaps he himself wasn't fully aware of it. He kept plugging away, hoping the next gig would lead to some bigger break. In contrast, it seemed like the stress in our own relationship had lessened. Steve and I were closer when I was with him. I felt that glow reflected by the new people we met in the arts, LGBTQ+, and fetish communities.

■■■

In May the band hosted another fetish event at the 90's, coordinating bands and deejays on two second-floor stages as well as headlining. But something was wrong. There weren't enough people in attendance, which meant not enough money was being collected through entry fees at the top of the stairs. Well into the evening, Steve tried to piece it together. There were rumors that someone from the 90's had taken the entry fee at the front door, leaving people upset that we asked them to pay a second time at the top of the stairs. I never figured out what really happened, but the night ended with the bar patrons being told to clear out as usual. My wristband identified me as crew, allowing me to stay to break down the stage and carry equipment out the back door. The staff wanted us out of there as quickly as possible, but the band was still in the dressing room, going over the pay. I lingered. No one had pointed me toward anything to carry out.

Suddenly the dressing room door slammed open. Pandora stomped through the doorway, red dreadlocks flying. She grabbed her bass, set it on top of her rig, and propelled it all down the hall toward the elevator. Pushing that much equipment so quickly, on small coaster wheels, seemed a recipe for a disastrous tumble. But the angry determination on her face made me keep my distance. I heard the elevator ring, then a few moments later I heard the doors close.

A minute or so after that, Shannon came out of the dressing room, aghast.

"Pandora just quit the band!" she exclaimed.

I was stunned—and nearly giddy with delight, but I couldn't show it. "Oh. What happened?"

"She got mad about the money and then just got up and said she was quitting!"

"How is Venus taking it?"

"I don't know," Shannon responded. "We've got to get her back. Where did she go?"

"She took her stuff to the elevator."

"Come with me. We've got to get her to come back." There was no way I wanted to be part of that project, but I didn't want to let Shannon down, either. I reluctantly followed her down the stairs to the alley-side back door. Shannon opened the door. It was pouring rain outside.

"I don't want to go out in that," I said unhelpfully.

"I will." Shannon dashed down the alley while I held the door ajar to prevent it from locking. I peered out but couldn't see anything, just wet pavement and brick. Shannon was back a few minutes later, her mohawk slumped to one side with rainwater. "I found her, pushing her rig down the sidewalk in the rain. She was crying, but I couldn't get her to come back."

I was sorry that Pandora was crying, and I was sorry to hear she was pushing her equipment along a sidewalk in the pouring rain. She didn't have a car and probably didn't want to wait for a cab. Or maybe she didn't have the money for one. Steve had given her a ride this night, as he did to all the gigs. But overall, I was thrilled she'd quit. I felt she'd spent the last few years trying to destroy my marriage; I hadn't ever given Steve an ultimatum, always fearing he would choose her over me. And now she was out of the band. I wanted to do the happy villagers' dance at the end of Sylvia Plath's "Daddy," saying emphatically, "they are dancing and stamping on you." I wanted to sing the refrain from the song in The Wizard of Oz: "Ding dong, the wicked witch is dead." Then I felt ashamed of myself. But only a little.

Later that evening, as we sat up in bed, I asked what had happened.

"I don't know, she was just really upset about the money," Steve explained. Years later, he would start to think that maybe she had warned him she was going to need to quit soon, but it hadn't felt definite. Then a few years after that, he said that yes, she had definitely said she wanted to leave the band and was just trying to pay off what she owed for plane tickets (about $200 at the time, I think). They had already been looking for another bass player.

"The numbers just didn't add up," he continued. "When I started paying out what everyone was promised, we were still over $400 in the hole, so I decided to cover it out of my own money." I cringed. The overage was coming out of *our* money, which meant it was coming out of my paycheck. But the result had been Pandora's leaving the band, so I wasn't going to make an issue of it. "When I had to tell her that no one in the band could get paid, that's when she got upset," he concluded. Many years later, he thought she might have gotten upset at the suggestion that she was doing it *only* for the money.

All I knew then was that she got angry about money and quit. I wasn't going to tell Steve that deep down I was very happy this had occurred. I knew there were going to be some difficulties because of it. Someone had to be found quickly and trained in to cover the upcoming gigs. That someone had to be a permanent bass player Steve felt comfortable working with to develop song ideas. I didn't realize how difficult that would be. I just became more optimistic about our future together.

27

■ ⋆ ▲ ✦ ✷ ■ ♠ • ▶

2002, New York City

We stayed at the Carlton Arms so often that Steve longed to paint a room there. He showed slides of his paintings to two of the managers, John Ogren and Hugo Ariz. Would it be possible to do an installation in one of the rooms? They said yes. Steve scheduled a performance to coordinate with painting the room. The band would do a show July 5, playing for Zenwarp, a theme night that moved from one club to another, at someone's party space in Chelsea. After the show, the band would fly home, and he would stay to start working on the room. Did I want to stay and help him? Yes, of course. The hotel would give us the room free for about three weeks in exchange for our painting it. I couldn't pass that up.

We landed the morning of July 4, just in time to drop everything at the hotel and head to a rooftop cookout in Brooklyn that Matthew Hopping invited us to. By then, he had moved to New York and was living there with Eddy Kennedy. Steve and I felt a proprietary delight in their relationship, because we'd seen them meet at Meow Mix on a night the band wasn't playing, when Matthew left to get us drinks, started chatting at the bar with a guy with neon-green hair, and didn't make it back to the hotel with us. When he explained it all later, we knew he was in love. After a year or so enduring a long-distance

Matthew Hopping and Eddy Kennedy, about 2002

relationship, they both moved to New York, and from there, Matthew began to manage the New York shows.

The weather for the Fourth was typical for a New York summer: stinking hot. Around six in the afternoon, I stood on a roof next to a waist-high parapet wall to look over the nearby buildings toward the New York skyline in the distance. The parapet was too rough to rest my elbows on, but I could balance a drink there if I was careful. The sun was getting low, but it was nowhere near sundown. I wanted it to get dark so we could see the fireworks. The sky started to cloud over, the way New York weather shifts when the ocean moisture rolls in. Matthew

Lynette, Fourth of July in Brooklyn, 2002

stood next to me, on his phone. He was wishing his mother in Virginia a happy Fourth of July.

Since it was the first Fourth since September 11, high levels of security surrounded anything going on in the city. On every trip from the airport, all vehicles were stopped at a security checkpoint before being waved toward a tunnel or bridge into Manhattan.

As Matthew talked on his phone and I stared at the skyline, a dark, wedge-shaped airship dropped out of the clouds and hovered, silent and surreal. It was so close, it seemed we could reach out and touch it. Realistically, that couldn't have been possible, but that's how near it seemed. It sat there motionless for about two seconds. Then it silently darted back into the clouds as if sucked into them, as spookily as it had appeared. *What the hell?* I thought I must be hallucinating.

I turned to Matthew, who had stopped talking to his mom and was gaping at me.

"Did you see that?" we said simultaneously, instantly relieved we weren't losing our minds. Yes, we'd both seen it.

We figured it had to be some kind of stealth craft. The Air Force was patrolling the skies for potential terrorist attacks, and of course they had to check us out because we were on top of a roof. What they found was a bunch of punk rockers, scantily clad for the weather (Steve in a ripped-up bare midriff T-shirt and short-short cut-offs by this time), drinking pitchers of gin and tonic and other assorted alcoholic refreshments.

When someone said Zenwarp would take place in a condo, I imagined something small, but when I stepped into the space, it was like no condo I had ever seen. At least three floors of a warehouse had been mostly gutted and redesigned in an open plan, with exposed wood beams and glass and metal railings. On the level where the dungeon was said to be, I could see a man stretched out supine, maybe on a board, suspended and slowly revolving in the air. The band would provide the live entertainment, a break from the normal deejay tracks. The audience loved the performance, so much so that the band loaded out a lot later than expected.

There'd also been a lot of drinking, which probably explains why it was hard to get people going the next day. Five of us were crammed into room 5D on that trip. Eden Taylor, a short, spunky woman with blond hair dyed red at the ends, had replaced Pandora on bass, and she and Emily Hooper shared one of the double beds. Steve and I shared another. Shannon, who was becoming more of a booking manager, crashed on the narrow floor between the beds. Jendeen was staying with friends, which is why Steve decided to economize and put us all in one room. Since I was still asking Steve to bring home some kind of band income, I didn't criticize the plan.

The room was on the fifth floor, the one we called the Egyptian floor due to the art in the hallway. This would seem a drawback when carrying band equipment up all those flights of stairs, but when you got to the top, you were rewarded with the most beautiful hallway in the whole place. The walls and woodwork were painted gold. In relief on one side, two life-size figures stood out, also painted gold and sculpted from plaster, or maybe something more durable. One was a head and torso of a man wearing an elaborate Egyptian headdress, his eyes kohled black, his expression regal and resolute. The other was a woman, naked, her arms stretched to reveal large, stylized wings spread behind her. Her eyes were also rimmed black, and she wore a regal expression. A smaller gold band encircled her head—a hooded cobra rising sternly at the front. She reminded me of the goddess Isis.

On the other walls of the hallway, busts of people wearing similar headdresses in rich blues and reds jutted from the wall and bore names underneath them: John, Hugo, Ty, Matsuko, and so on. We recognized them as the people who worked at the hotel. Rows of stylized Egyptian figures and raised hieroglyphics covered the rest of the corridor, as if telling some kind of a story. John Ogren told us the figures we'd first seen were of the husband and wife who had created the hallway.

The morning after the show, I was the first to wake. We needed to start painting the room, but everyone else remained asleep. We'd given ourselves nearly three weeks for the project, but when we arrived John said there would be an art opening and he wanted the room ready three days earlier than expected. Then we'd used up more days with the Fourth of July and the show, so now we really only had two weeks, and Steve still had to paint everything white to create a fresh canvas.

I stepped around and over the sleepers to go into the bathroom and change into painting clothes, hoping the noise would wake my roommates. It didn't. I groped my way back to the bed and whispered to Steve about the problem. He wasn't sleeping, either.

"No, we've got to wait until everyone is up," he whispered back. "It won't be long."

I shifted a corner of the curtain to let a small triangle of light enter the room and sat in bed, reading, waiting for them to start waking up. Nothing. It looked like they were going to sleep in until noon, at least, which would cut it close for their afternoon flight back to Minneapolis.

Steve already had an idea of what he wanted to paint in the main room. First we'd have to paint over the previous art—a cold gray and dark red depiction of morose-looking people painted by an artist who had done at least three rooms in the hotel. Then Steve would pencil in the floor-to-ceiling trans-figures—what he called them at the time—that would dominate the room. The figures were like the ones he painted and drew in the pen-and-ink sketchbook, and perhaps how he saw himself: a blue, otherworldly figure, sometimes with hair on their head but often not, a figure with breasts and a penis. When Venus had heart surgery many years later, one of the blue figures in her drawing had the skin in the middle of their

Venus painting, Carlton Arms, 2002

chest peeled back to reveal the valves of their heart. Still later, when Venus formally changed her name and had bottom surgery, the blue figure had sutures where their penis had once been.

I was happy to be the assistant, doing the background painting, some blue wash and yellow, swirly stars that Steve had used in other installations. I would also paint a few poems where they fit. But that morning, surrounded by sleepers, I couldn't do anything in the big room. The bathroom, however, was a blank canvas. I decided to start there.

I painted the feet of the claw-foot tub gold, inspired by the Egyptian hallway. We'd found a gallon of gold paint in the hotel's art-supply closet, and from that I'd learned more of the place's history. The building dated from the 1880s and had housed one of the city's earliest elevators. But that ceased working long ago, and now a linen or supply closet occupied the space on every floor where the elevator would have stopped. The art-supply closet was a dragon's hoard of materials left over from previous projects, everything from paint to fabric to hardware to brightly dyed feathers. Steve and I glommed on to the gold because we'd already used the color for most of the ceilings of our house back in Minneapolis. For the large swaths of wall space we would use paint that came by the bucket from a nearby hardware store, and Steve had gotten tubes of acrylics from Pearl Art for the details.

The bathtub feet done, I began to paint a gold stripe along the outer shell when Emily Hooper began to stir. I moved out of the bathroom to give her privacy, then she grabbed a towel and walked down the hall to shower. Others also began to move, quietly looking for space to put their luggage to finish packing. Shannon, the soundest sleeper, still lay inconveniently on the floor between the beds and was the last to get up.

After the group left for the airport, Steve and I began to work in earnest, putting down tarps and painting the walls white. Someone from the hotel staff came to take one of the beds out to give us more space. We discovered that one coat of white didn't adequately cover the previous art—the ghosts of it remained. A second coat would eat up precious time before we could paint the images on the walls. But we had art to make and a free place in New York for the next two weeks.

We quickly settled into a routine. We woke in the morning, Steve started working on the main figures and some bending, stylized skyscrapers that spread onto the ceiling, and I went someplace to get us coffee and sometimes a little breakfast, like croissants or berries from the grocery store across the street. We worked a few hours like that, then when we were really hungry, I got us lunch, usually at Lamazou, a deli up Third Avenue that I adored. They had Yorkie chocolate bars and all kinds

Lynette and Venus, New York City, 2002

of wonderful cheeses. I typically got us sandwiches and chocolate, and then perhaps another treat, like Orangina, to take
back to the room. We would have a little picnic on the floor,
then go back to work, pulling in tandem like a team of horses
that read each other's signals.

I became familiar with the hotel and neighborhood. I knew
what items were located on the various floors. I knew where to
go if we needed more towels, cups, or soap; I knew where to get
more brushes, who was working in the office and when. I got to
know everyone a little better. Often I ran up and down the stairs
and through the hallways barefoot. Once an older woman staying at the hotel scolded me for running around barefoot.

"You might pick up diseases or step on something," she cau-
tioned sternly.

I didn't contradict her—she meant well. I was wearing shoes
in the room where we painted, and I would slip them off to run

a quick errand in the hotel to avoid tracking paint in the hall-ways. But I didn't tell her that. I was comfortable in my element. I just smiled and thanked her for her concern.

One day, John took us down to the basement, where they kept the unused furniture, in case there was a castoff we could re-style for the room. The basement was dark, with all the am-bience of a crypt. Off to the side lurked an ancient-looking cylindrical hunk of metal that rose above my shoulders. John saw me studying it.

"Ah, you've discovered our furnace," he chuckled.

"Furnace?"

"It's what heats the hot water for the radiators," he ex-plained. "It's an old steamship engine."

Steve and I stared in wonder at this new, fantastical creature hidden in subterranean New York.

We planned to make the room comfortable for us to stay in. On previous trips with the band, there had never been enough mirror space or lighting—in a glam band, people are con-stantly working on makeup and costumes. I scoured the thrift stores and found a handsome pair of matching mirrors that we hung in the bathroom. The hotel used bedsheets as curtains, and I hand-sewed some scarves onto them to make them more opaque. I also found some glitzy-gold tassel material in an-other thrift store to tie the curtains back. It was fun running errands to the hardware store and going with John Ogren to a store a few blocks away to choose new carpet. It seemed as if everything we needed was right there.

This was the summer before the hotel installed air condi-tioners in the rooms, so we kept the windows open and a fan going constantly. One night, as we slept next to the half-open window, I heard some voices that seemed unusually close.

"Look at this!" the voice said. I thought I was dreaming, but it seemed to come from right next to me. Then I heard the zip of the window going up and forced my eyes open. A man on the fire escape was trying to come in, two feet away.

I summoned all my vocal power (not an easy thing to do when one is shocked) and yelled at him in an unearthly, guttural voice to get out. At this point Steve was awake enough to see a pair of hands clad in black, fingerless gloves reaching through the window. Then the hands pulled away, followed by some kind of exclamation. I grabbed my robe, and we heard running footsteps pound through the adjacent room. By the time I poked my head out into the hallway, all I glimpsed of the intruder was half a silhouette and the bottom of his shoe as he slammed through the wooden fire door at the end of the hall.

We went down to the front desk to wake Jeff, the night manager, to explain what had happened. But there was no sign of anyone lurking around. No one was staying next door, in the room the intruder had run through; in fact, hotel bookings were far below usual after September 11th, and there was hardly anyone on our entire floor. After making sure the intruder wasn't still on the premises, we went back upstairs and pondered how to get back to sleep.

Perhaps an hour had passed, and the grinding sounds of a garbage truck below weren't helping us sleep. Steve looked out the window in the murky dawn and saw the workers tossing bags of garbage toward the vehicle. He noticed that one wore fingerless gloves, and a light bulb went off. There was a dumpster on the sidewalk below the fire escape. Perhaps a sanitation worker had figured out that the room we were in was always vacant—there was a reason why the hotel staff were letting us paint it over. Maybe he had heard about the hotel and discovered he could shinny up the fire escape, climb through the window, and then walk down the hallway, admiring the art on all the hotel floors before quietly exiting. Maybe he was even going to show it all to a buddy, which would explain why I heard voices.

It made more sense than any other scenario. If he was trying to rob a hotel room, he would have chosen a time when he thought the guests were away. If he had meant us physical harm, he wouldn't have spoken first or been deterred by my yelling. We were never able to figure out how to check with the sanitation department to see who had been assigned to that area, but we slept with the windows closed after that.

■■■

The first poem I painted in the room was "As We Drove." With Steve's coaching and occasional assistance, I had finished painting the inside of the closet with a black-and-blue "rain" pattern that Steve had used in other installations, including the big blue doors of Rifle Sport Art Gallery in Minneapolis. Steve didn't want to put any of his own images in there, so I started painting the lines of the poem, thinking it would be a fun treasure for a future visitor to find. It wasn't until I was crouched on the floor painting the last lines that I realized the supreme irony of the placement.

Around this time, Steve dreamed that two octopuses saved him from drowning and then, to his horror, that the people on the beach were getting ready to kill and eat them. He decided to paint a large octopus on the bathroom ceiling and wall. It cradled one of the blue figures in its arms. I wrote up his dream as a poem and painted it next to the image. As I painted, it occurred to me that I needed to see the words as objects, not as an entire poem that someone in the room would read from start to finish. The way the viewer's eye fell on the expanse of wall would make it difficult to take in a whole poem. I started to put up shorter poems or just phrases from poems—words that could be taken in at a glance. It became an interesting exercise in form.

Sometimes we got stressed out by the time constraints, but I loved working together. I began to see my poetry in a different way, and I began to think of art more consciously as an expression of love. Inspired by that vision, I painted the phrase

Lynette's poetry, Carlton Arms, 2002

"I have always loved you" on the wall opposite the octopus. I had initially been thinking of the love the octopuses had, then I began to think about the many struggles Steve and I had been through. It seemed we had finally recovered our rapport. Steve told me later that when he read that phrase, he cried.

We got the room done in time for the opening and then had a few extra days to enjoy it before returning to Minneapolis. I basked in the temporary calm of having no performances, no last-minute crises. But of course it couldn't last.

In Minneapolis the band was back to its usual schedule of rehearsals and shows, some of which I attended. In the fall, Steve flew Barb Morrison out to Minnesota for a long weekend to record the album that would turn into *Creature* at Pachyderm in Cannon Falls, a town I drove past each day on my commute to Rochester. They had recorded the previous album, *Ruin*, there when I was at an out-of-town conference. When Steve came home that time, he had played a video of them goofing off in the studio and bragged about how Pandora got to sleep in the same bed as Kurt Cobain and Courtney Love. It had made me feel shut out. This time, I would be able to stop by for a night to see how it all worked.

But being at Pachyderm was anticlimactic. Things were falling apart. There weren't any working lights between the house and the studio, which made the terraced steps treacherous in the dark. The house technician met us when we arrived and sourly showed Steve, Barb, and Jendeen around. Then he left. The pool had been drained. Barb complained that the studio didn't have adequate drive storage, so I was sent back to the Twin Cities to get something from the Apple Store that would work. Someone told us later there had been a divorce, and the owner couldn't afford to keep up with repairs anymore. It showed.

I should have paid more attention to the uncanny parallels: there were many deferred repairs Steve and I still needed to make to our relationship.

28

■★▲✦✸■♠●■

2003, Venice

Steve's focus had switched to finishing and promoting the new CD. He talked about another tour of England.

Mine had switched to finding a tenure-track job closer to home. I loved my Rochester colleagues, but the ninety-mile drive was grueling, especially in winter. I hit a deer on the highway as I drove home from a night class, totaling my car, and once a year there was some other major breakdown. More insidious, something was wrong with the right side of my back from having my foot on the accelerator too long—my car didn't have cruise control. When I leaned forward over the kitchen sink, the muscles on my right side ached, and when I sat in the saddle and looked down at my knees, my right leg inched farther forward than my left. I had a couple of interviews before the sabbatical, but nothing had materialized. When I began the year of teaching required after the sabbatical, I started to look again. By spring, I was rewarded with good news. I had a job offer from Normandale Community College, only eleven miles away from where we lived. Everything was finally coming together.

We were now at the twenty-year-anniversary mark of our marriage and decided on a return trip to Venice. Maybe we could do it properly this time. I loved the city, with its luminous atmosphere, arched bridges, and curious architecture, its sound of water lapping stone. I loved the quiet canals and lack of cars, and the overall sense that it crumbled but still miraculously continued to rise like a goddess out of the water. I especially loved experiencing it with Steve.

But the truth is that almost no one there, from servers and *pensione* keepers to the vast numbers of people milling in the streets, recognized us as a couple—two people romantically together. One sunny afternoon, as we came down the steps of a small bridge, we stopped, entranced by the wistful sound of a cello through an open window above. We turned to each other and kissed, then opened our eyes to the hiss of nearby commotion. Some men were shouting and booing at us. Steve and I had experienced all kinds of slights before, and I usually tried to shrug them off. This one I couldn't shrug off. After twenty years of marriage, I wanted us to express our love openly. Their yells bruised that experience.

Venice was a lovely yet often hostile place. When we took a gondola ride, the other gondoliers yelled something in anger to the boatman who guided our boat, pointing at us. Relief flooded his face when he realized we couldn't understand what they said, and he steered us off the route toward a quieter canal.

Yet another time we stood in a bar in the early evening. To our surprise, a tall, lovely trans woman came up to us and began to talk, mostly in English. We were on the verge of thinking perhaps we were making a new friend when I realized she had started excluding me, angling her body toward Steve and conducting the conversation about eight inches above my head. She seemed to be trying to impress him and flirt with him, telling him where she lived and all the important people she knew. As I tried to assert myself more in the conversation, both verbally and with my stance, she glanced down at me and said, "Merde." I didn't know much Italian, but I knew enough French to recognize when I was being called a little shit. I put my hand on Steve's arm to signal that we had to go, but he didn't get it and ignored me. Was this his hatred of conflict? But a confrontation was already happening. I decided to call her on it.

"Look, Angelica," I said, "I know what you're saying, and I don't appreciate it." She gave me a smug little smile and shimmied her head. That was it. I splashed my drink at her, set the empty glass on the bar, and walked out, hoping Steve would follow. He did. He apologized to me, saying he hadn't been able to read the situation, and that once he started to figure it out, he didn't know what to do. To me, it was just another galling episode of how he rolled out a welcome mat to flirtatious strangers. I wrote a funny essay about the incident and read it for a slam back in Minneapolis, but the experience still stung. Somewhere in my gut, the words I really wanted to say, the ones I'd swallowed during the Pandora years, continued to fester.

It made me wonder if I would ever be enough. It seemed that no one understood our relationship, not even us. We kept making it up as we went.

A few days later we were in the Correr Museum, a building off St. Mark's Square with spacious galleries, when my phone rang, the waltz melody jarring the hushed calm of the museum. No one but Steve ever called me, so I hadn't thought to turn it off before walking into the museum. I fished it out of my purse, trying hastily to answer and silence it as I walked toward the door. An angry guard stopped me, saying something I couldn't translate but understood to mean this wasn't the place for phone use. I nodded and kept walking. I looked at the screen and recognized a Duluth area code. The person on the other end of the line was a nurse at Chris Jensen nursing home in Duluth. My mother had been there since January.

"You said you wanted to know how your mother was doing," the nurse explained.

"Yes," I laughed, nervously. "I'm sorry I didn't start talking to you right away. I'm out of the country, and I was in a museum. The guard didn't want me talking in there."

"Well, your mother has gotten worse," she said. "It looks like pneumonia."

"I see," I said. "How long . . ." I couldn't finish the sentence.

"If it were my mother, I'd try to get here right away," she responded. I explained that I was out of the country but had a flight back in a few days. Would that be soon enough? She was noncommittal. Maybe she thought only the most heartless of daughters would vacation at a time like this.

"Does Dr. Smith know?" I asked. "Dr. Smith" was my older brother Harvey, who checked up on his own patients a few times a week at the nursing home and stopped in to see Mom while he was there. He had always been closer to Mom than I was. They'd even taken a couple of trips to England together. He was there in Duluth, not an ocean away. And he was a doctor.

"I'll let him know," she assured me. I thanked her for calling and hung up. I didn't know what to do next. I walked with Steve along the hot pavement, explaining what the nurse had said.

It wasn't a surprise to hear my mother was dying. She'd struggled with increasingly frightening dementia the last several years. I suspected she'd wanted to leave the world for a long time, and now she had what some called "the old person's friend"—pneumonia. But I couldn't help feeling that I had failed her.

■ ■ ■

We had never been close, too similar in our mutual stubbornness to get along. Still, we had developed a kind of understanding about ten years earlier when she decided to sell the house in Duluth. I had been free for the summer and helped her decide what to keep, give away, or sell. From there, she moved into a senior-living apartment, then a few years later decided to move into assisted living in Duluth. Someone from her church told me that she couldn't keep track of paperwork anymore, so I took over managing her finances.

It seemed like something I could handle: my sister lived far away and had her own family issues to attend to, and my brothers were of a generation that left most family matters to women.

Soon she began to show signs of dementia. It was not Alzheimer's, where she might slowly regress back to childhood. We didn't have a name for it at the time, but later I learned it was called Lewy body dementia, characterized by frightening hallucinations and paranoia. She also began to lose her ability with words. When she said something, I could tell from the context that she'd used the wrong term and meant to say something different. Then she got kicked out of the assisted-living home in Duluth's downtown area. She had become combative and was hitting people. The staff called me then to explain she was in the Duluth hospital's psych ward. I was stunned: my independent, churchgoing, classical-music-loving mother was in a psych ward. When she was released, I would need to find a memory-care facility for her, and she didn't want her friends to see her anymore.

This was all going on while Steve focused on the band and I battled the Pandora effect. A year or so later she was kicked out of the memory-care facility, again for being combative. That landed her in a full-fledged nursing home with bedridden, trapped residents. When I went to visit, I would find Mom in a residents' lounge, strapped into a putty-colored vinyl La-Z-Boy chair. The staff explained that the lap belt was for her own safety, so she wouldn't fall, and that there was a warning bell that activated if she tried to take it off. By now, she had lost most of her ability to use words, though I was told she still had lucid moments. But usually when I visited, I would find her sitting in the chair, frustrated, and swiping in anger at the air below the chair arms. She kept trying to shoo away imagined children, or little gremlins. Another time, she tried to wordlessly get me to take her diamond-engagement/wedding-ring set from her finger. I felt I couldn't do that while she was still alive. It was hers, after all. I thanked her for thinking of me and told her, not now.

■■■

Mom was still alive when we returned from Venice a few days later on our originally planned schedule. She had pneumonia but was stable. Steve threw himself into band gigs—one took place just two days after we got home. I drove the three hours up to Duluth by myself to check on Mom, staying overnight at my mother-in-law's house. I felt very alone.

Once Mom moved to the nursing home, Steve had not come with me once to visit her in the six months she'd been there. We might be in Duluth together, but when it came time to make a visit, it would be me alone driving up Arrowhead Road and pulling into the parking lot lined with dirty, icy snowbanks. It would be me alone looking for her as I walked through the hallways, not sure if I would recognize her shrunken body slumped in a bed or chair. Steve explained that he worried his appearance would scare my mother—he had dyed his long hair black, wore black clothing, and applied heavy goth/femme makeup. I knew this was possible, but on some subconscious level, I must have known that *I* was the one who needed him there. Yet my sense of how to advocate for myself had been worn down, and after arguing back and forth about it a few times, I gave up.

A few weeks after we got back from Venice, I got a call again that Mom was not doing well, this time from my brother Harvey. Steve and I drove to Duluth, and I went to the nursing home. Her eyes were closed, and she looked small and fragile in the white linens of her bed. I clasped her hand and told her I was there. She gave a light squeeze back. I murmured to her a while longer, then gave another squeeze. This time there was no squeeze back. She was sleeping, and I left.

Harvey phoned early the next morning. Mom had passed away around 5:00 A.M., and he had been there. I stood, looking out the window of my mother-in-law's house as the sun brightened the grass of the backyard. Birds were singing their dawn songs. The oddest sensation came over me. I was now an orphan.

I didn't expect that feeling. My father had passed away shortly after my twenty-second birthday, and I had felt independent of my mother for decades. Yet now I felt completely marooned.

My extended family came to the rescue. I don't remember much of the funeral, but I have pictures of me and Steve there with my brothers, sister, and so many cousins, aunts, uncles, nieces, and nephews, standing in front of the church doors, like a family reunion. And I also have a photo of me standing next to the tallest urinal any of us had ever seen in our lives, discovered by my cousin Bruce in the men's choir robing room.

It still felt like a time of failure to me. I told myself I should have moved her to Minneapolis to be closer to me. When I went to the nursing home to pick up her personal effects, I asked about the ring. The mortician hadn't seen it. The nursing home staff didn't know anything about it, either. That's when I realized my mother had not been trying to let me know I could have her ring. She had been trying to give it to me because she knew there was theft at the nursing home. It's possible someone had tried to steal it earlier, and that spurred her to offer it to me. She was smart enough to understand that, even with her dementia. I had been so stupid.

29

■⋆▲⋆✦■⋀●■

2003, Minneapolis

Within a month, Steve and I were at another funeral. I don't
think I was conscious that so little time had passed since my
mother died. The band played two out-of-town gigs that I
hadn't gone on, and I felt the grind of Steve's emotional ab-
sence even when he was home, because he was in band mode.

It was August, and we shuffled through dry grass along the
iron fence at the edge of Lakewood Cemetery in south Minneapolis. Wiry, dead lawn scratched at my sandaled feet. Lakewood was huge, 250 acres of green space studded with shining
mausoleums, memorials, and obelisks that abutted several of
the city's wealthier neighborhoods. But a late summer drought
had stolen some of the setting's beauty—the automatic water-
ing system didn't make it all the way to the edge of the lawn.

The conversation Steve and I had been having wasn't going
the way I planned. We were supposed to be there to support
Tanya Warwas. She had fallen in love with and married Steve
Moldenhauer, and now she had lost him to melanoma.

We had first argued because we were running late. When we
arrived at the large cemetery chapel, an astonishingly beautiful building in a Byzantine style, with a soaring mosaic gold
and green dome that rose over the sanctuary, we paused at the
back, both of us overwhelmed by the large turnout. The service

hadn't started yet. Steve Moldenhauer had been active in the Twin Cities punk rock scene, and the people in the pews represented a who's who of local music luminaries. The place was so full I worried we'd have to stand at the back for the service, but someone in the last row motioned us over and encouraged everyone else to squeeze together to make room.

First there were the friends with fond reminiscences, telling their stories of funny things Steve had done. Then there were stories from friends describing how he and Tanya had met at a party at someone's apartment, laughing and play-wrestling each other. Others spoke of their loving bond with Steve throughout the melanoma ordeal. The whole congregation was in tears, moved by the stories.

I couldn't stop wondering what it would be like when either Steve or I passed away. Would anybody be able to say things like this about us? Since my mother's death it seemed we'd gone back to an earlier pattern of arguing—we even argued about what to wear to the funeral and the fastest way to drive to the chapel. I had thought the tension would leave our marriage once Pandora quit the band, and it had felt like we were kindred spirits again for a while, but as summer ended, the negativity returned. We were like mismatched gears. Something kept halting our forward movement, always finding a new problem to get stuck on, and Steve's anger would rise, usually about something that made no sense to me.

I still didn't know how to mourn, and all I could think was that something was wrong in how we related to each other. Yet I didn't want to give up on us. I had faith in our common bond. I thought, if we could just stop the escalating arguments, we would be in tune with each other again.

We walked down the stairs of the chapel together, wondering what to do with ourselves for the hour before a reception began nearby. I decided to explain what I was thinking, carefully.

"That was a beautiful service, wasn't it." This was more a comment than a question. Steve nodded. I couldn't read his face, but it seemed clouded over with sadness. He didn't want to talk to any of the acquaintances we walked by. I steered him across the drive, toward some trees that promised shade from the relentless sun.

"You know," I began, "while I was listening to everyone speak, I couldn't help but think about us." I stopped, still trying to read his facial expression. I plowed forward. "I couldn't help but wonder, if there were a funeral for one of us, what people would say about our relationship." Now I seemed to have his attention. "It was so clear how much Tanya and Steve loved each other, from what everyone said during the service." I took a breath. "I'm worried that if there were a funeral for you or me today, that people wouldn't be able to say the same things about us." Steve grimaced and looked away. Then he looked back at me.

"What do you want me to do?" he asked, his voice low yet emphatic.

"I just want us to act more like a loving couple." I didn't have a list of items that could be checked off for us to become that couple. I couldn't conceive of love that way. I just knew there was something wrong in how we were interacting.

"You don't understand how much I'm trying to do, and I'm trying to do all this for you, too." His hands agitated the air as he spoke. I didn't understand what he meant by "all this." His anger was definitely not what I wanted.

We were now in the spiky grass near the cemetery's fence, some of the turf completely bare where even the roots had died and been blown away. I could see the dusty soil darken my toes and the tops of my feet. It felt gritty, like fine sand. He turned and looked back at the throng of people standing outside the chapel, then turned to me. "I don't want to argue here in front of all these people," he said. I nodded, saddened that we couldn't even attend a funeral right.

We made our way back to the car and got in without speaking. After a few blocks, Steve said, "I don't think we can go to the reception."

"I know," was all I could think to say. I was so tired of this roller coaster of emotions, where everything between us seemed wonderful one moment and in the toilet the next.

As we drove, I retraced the past months. Pandora's quitting the band and my relief. Steve's training Eden in as a new bass player, then the relentless schedule of gigs that seemed as if they would translate into some kind of progress but never did. My new job at Normandale. Our Venice trip. I somehow forgot that my mother had died a month earlier.

We parked in back of the house and walked in, both of us silent and sulking. I wasn't ready to give up. I went to the living room and sat on the couch.

"Look," I said, "how do you think a loving couple acts toward each other?"

"It's not like this," Steve hissed, "It's not arguing."

"Oh, come on," I said. I was pretty sure he was the one who had gotten heated first and started arguing. We went back and forth like this a few more rounds.

"I can't take this anymore!" he finally shouted, and stomped upstairs. I leaned back on the couch, trying to slow my breathing and calm down. I just had to deescalate things. Soon he was walking downstairs again, carrying a soft-sided overnight bag.

"I'm done," he said, measuring his words. "I've packed a bag, and I'm leaving. This is it." I wasn't expecting this at all. I sprang to my feet and ran across the room to embrace him.

"No, no, this isn't what I meant! Don't go!" I pleaded.

"I'm going," he said grimly, shrugging my arms away. He walked out the door to where his car was parked in front of the house. I heard the car start, and he drove away.

I sat in the living room a long time, watching the light grow more slanted, then dim, then darken. He'd driven away in anger before, and he'd always come back.

This time he hadn't said where he was going.

Sometime before the sun went completely down, I got a call from Emily Carter. Steve had phoned her, explaining he'd left me. He wanted her to check up on me to make sure I was okay. Now it felt terrifyingly real. I didn't want her to come over to comfort me. I didn't want anyone to witness my total collapse. But she came anyway.

I don't know where he slept that night, and I don't remember when we talked on the phone again. The gaping wound of our relationship seemed to shock Steve as well, and he expressed sadness about it, but he didn't return. When I realized he wasn't coming back, I set Elton John's version of "Sorry Seems to Be the Hardest Word" on infinite repeat and sank to the floor next to the stereo. The wood surface felt cool against my skin, almost calming. I lay faceup under the dining room table and stared blindly at the raw oak of its backside, surrounded by a barren forest of chair legs, sobbing and half groaning the words along with the recording, internalizing them. Where had I gone wrong? Above me, I noticed the capital letters Steve had scribbled with a Sharpie to show where the extra leaves went. But they weren't there. A didn't meet A. It met C.

The song rang through my head over and over. What did I have to do to make him love me? And why did this happen every time I tried to talk with him about my feelings? The song told me to say I was sorry, but hadn't I done that already? Or had I asked for too much? It cycled back to the first verse, and I felt struck down all over again. I rolled to one side and convulsed with a new torrent of tears.

We didn't know where to go from there, but we agreed to not tell anyone else we had separated. Part of this was to protect Steve's mom, who had her own health issues, and part of it was that I didn't want to start teaching at a new college with a visible storm cloud labeled "marriage problems" hanging over my head.

The storm cloud was there, of course. Maybe the idea that we could keep this fracture hidden from other people was delusional, but holding that idea was how I got through it. We bought a horse for Steve after I got tenure in Rochester because

Venus and Misia, mid-1990s

he said he wanted to go riding with me, and I'd jumped at the chance to do something with him that didn't involve me watching him from the audience. My cousins who owned the farm where we currently boarded the horses probably wondered why Steve wasn't coming out to ride with me, but they said nothing. My colleagues may have wondered why Steve looked so nervous and shaky at a department dinner we'd been invited to as the semester began, something I'd confidently RSVP'd for before he suddenly left, but they also said nothing.

I contacted a therapist we'd done marriage counseling with. Very slowly, she helped me see that I had let myself get talked into ignoring my intuition. I don't think it was just Steve who talked me into it, though he was a big part of it. He radiated a kind of charismatic confidence, especially when onstage. His fans and band members trusted his leadership in everything. It didn't help that most social messages told me to be less assertive. Once, when we were having happy hour drinks with a male friend, Steve wanted to order a pizza. I said no, we couldn't afford it. But he kept at it, arguing how easy it would be, until I snapped and said firmly, "No, we're not getting a pizza. We can't afford it." When I saw the same friend the next day at work, he berated me for having made him feel uncomfortable by arguing with Steve in front of him. I explained the situation to him, but he was having none of it. I opened my mouth to say more, realized the futility of my words, and closed it.

I had subconsciously resisted many social messages by becoming secretive. But they still seeped in—they watered my roots—and I grew to believe I didn't *have* any intuition. Like the Goose Girl, I had given away my power. I needed to figure out how to get it back.

30

2003, Minneapolis

Two weeks after Steve left, I was scheduled to guest-host Gender Blur at Patrick's Cabaret. I'd been invited to put together a show of six gender-queer artists, each doing a performance piece that lasted up to fifteen minutes. The event had been set for months, and I had been proud when asked to do it—concrete evidence that an artistic community I admired accepted me. Now I felt like a fraud. I wasn't blurring my gender, my spouse was. And we'd just split up.

We still talked. We still liked each other. We still *loved* each other. I couldn't turn off the urge to see the band perform, so I went to their in-town gigs. At some point, we began to hook up with each other, on the large blue velveteen couch in his basement studio at the warehouse. I always made sure I had some kind of blanket near to throw over myself in case someone else with a key (band member, roadie, whoever) came in—there were five or six studio keys floating around.

I started to like living alone. I'd never been completely by myself before—I'd always lived with my parents, in a dorm, or with Steve. Maintaining the house and yard was time-consuming, but I felt a strange delight when I hauled out the ladder and decided what to scrape and paint. Steve asked if I would deejay for an in-studio party at the Colonial Warehouse.

Yes, I replied, and told him to list me in the promotions as DJ Blonde. We couldn't stop twining our lives together.

Pressure to make a decision about getting back together mounted when the documentary, *Venus of Mars*, was accepted for a world premiere at the Amsterdam Film Festival. The band would be on tour in England, then go to the festival from there as special guests, performing after the premiere. The big question was whether I'd be there, too.

Emily Goldberg knew we were separated. Ironically, from the clips we'd seen, our love for each other had turned into one of the film's major themes. It was one of life's cosmic jokes that we were separated now, before it even premiered. But I was adamant: I did not want to go to Amsterdam and pretend everything was fine if it wasn't.

I felt Steve had to be the one to initiate any kind of return— he was the one who had left. I wanted to reconcile, but if he wasn't motivated, didn't feel the desire strongly enough, our reconciliation would be doomed. The pain of all those rejections through the years bubbled just below the surface. We'd sit on the couch in what had once been *our* living room. Maybe we'd watch a movie and have a couple of drinks, or maybe we'd make love on the couch and talk about Amsterdam afterward. I never let him go to our bedroom on the third floor, our crow's nest at the top of the house. As far as I was concerned, if we were separated, he wasn't sleeping over. That was one boundary I could control.

Yet his talk about coming back dismayed me with its emphasis on the practical. I didn't sense the deep emotion I needed to hear. I hungered for the sound of something strong and true, something that could help him leap past the hurdle that often made him angry or inattentive. Even as we talked, I could hear his frustration. His just saying he loved me wasn't enough. I knew now that I deserved a loving relationship, and that I'd made too many compromises.

Therapy had taught me how to honor my own emotions

again. Part of that process was reflecting on what I saw and recognizing that my observations were valid and real. I don't know when I stopped believing in my own judgment, but it had happened somewhere along this branching path. The therapist gave me exercises, essentially baby steps, that guided me back to my sense of self, my intuition, my own true nature.

One morning, I sat in my tiny backyard, trying to catch some of the early sun. A cardinal chirruped away in the high tree nearly above me, and various sparrows and chickadees provided a steady chatter of birdsong. I was practicing observing, as my therapist suggested. The smaller birds were swooping between some of the lower tree branches and the bird feeders in those strange, random patterns that also suggest an intentional choreography. *Now these, now these.* I could hear the air rustle through their wings when they fanned past me. *Now us.* Suddenly, I realized I understood what they were saying.

I was astounded by the expansiveness of what I was feeling. This was what it meant to listen. I had always loved listening. It was what brought me to music and what brought me to poetry. I loved the simple cadences of instruments and voices, and now I could hear them in the animal world. In the flock's flight patterns, it was as if I could see the notes of their unheard harmony drawn across the sky.

After, I listened to Steve's voice as we sat in the living room, as he said he wanted to move back in. It didn't have the solid sound I sensed needed to be there. I listened for some kind of tone that resonated with his words but heard just glimmers, like fireflies that winked and faded into darkness. We had resumed going to concerts and dinners, and we shared the mundane details of our lives. I still felt that rapturous afterglow that bonded us when we made love. Yet on a day-to-day basis, what seemed like band-related issues often absorbed more of Steve's attention. He didn't act like a full partner. I longed for him to be someone I could talk to about *my* day when I came home from work, hearing what *I* said, instead of changing the subject to something about the band or another thing that concerned him. He had been that person once.

■■■

Years later, when we learned that ADHD affects a person's ability to direct their attention, some of these behaviors began to make sense. For someone with ADHD, the world is a jumble of information coming at them, and various things pop out—often the new things—while others fade from view. People with undiagnosed or untreated ADHD can come across as irresponsible and selfish but are often bewildered when others are upset by their behavior. This was exactly what had happened to us. Of course the gender issue created tremendous stress, because society wasn't ready to accept my spouse for who she truly was, but ADHD interfered with our ability to handle it together, as a loving couple.

In the early years of our relationship, I envied how Steve was able to turn off the world to focus on a project. He was great at concentrating on one thing at a time, able to spend an entire day fixing some kind of electronic gadget, or brushing in the details of a painting. But now I think that type of focus was less a choice and just the first thing that rose up out of the jumble to command attention. In the years that followed, he wasn't *choosing* to be inattentive to me, he just had his attention pulled in other directions, usually to some new band problem. But there was no way for me to know that. Instead, I found myself on a baffling merry-go-round, responding to his changing emotions.

Then there was Steve's tendency to assume the worst about my wishes and motivations. This may have resulted from a lack of self-esteem, rather than the ADHD, and it had an even more corrosive effect. Is it an overreach to call it PTSD, due to the strong pressures of society that caused him to hide his gender reality throughout childhood and most of his adult life?

I don't think so, and that would certainly explain the sudden mood swings that led to suicidal thoughts. Moreover, he often exuded confidence and certainty, and said he felt comfortable being between genders. I didn't understand how insecure he really felt.

■■■

As the weeks stretched into October, we had to decide. The documentary would premiere in Amsterdam in late November, when I would be on Thanksgiving break. I ached to go, but knew I shouldn't if we weren't actually reconciled. I waited for some other signal. I couldn't articulate what it was, but I knew I couldn't move forward without it.

Steve and I were standing in our living room, having just gotten up from the couch, a long, sturdy piece of furniture he'd made for me as a surprise Christmas present in the early years of our marriage. We were putting our clothes back on. It was dark out, but darkness came increasingly earlier as the months moved toward winter. Steve asked me again what I wanted to do.

"I don't know, I just need to feel that you really want to be with me, that you really want to be in this relationship." I threw out my arms, palms up, a gesture that admitted I didn't know any better way of putting it.

Steve sat back down on the couch, eyes cast down. "I don't know what else I can tell you," he said, frustrated. "I love you. I've told you I love you."

I nodded. Yes, he'd said these things. He'd said them often. He even said that he loved me to other people—they told me so. But then he would act differently. He had gotten enraged, packed a suitcase, and left when I'd worried out loud that we weren't expressing our affection for each other as much as a couple should. Maybe I needed actions, not words, because I'd been let down by words. Right now, he was forming the right words, but the music in his voice sounded like an angry anthem, as if this was some kind of test I was forcing him to take.

He stood up again and came toward me, close, putting his hands on either side of my waist. He leaned down slightly to look into my eyes. His face was serious, his gaze riveting.

"Look," he said, his eyes never wavering from mine, "I'm sorry for all I've put you through, but I really do love you and only you. I really do want to stay with you." His voice was a little louder this time, more emphatic, and the tone different. I didn't say anything for a while. We just looked into each other's eyes. His gaze did not waver. There was a stronger sense of energy between us, almost like an electrical charge.

I felt a flicker of hope. "Can you just hold me a moment?"

"Of course." His long arms connected and strengthened around me. I could feel the tears welling in my eyes and closed them tight, trying to hold it all in. I didn't want to disturb the stillness. Something in his actions felt like the message I'd been seeking to reassure me that maybe we had a chance together. And his voice. It had sounded like a love song.

"Okay," I finally said, pulling him more closely in our embrace. "Please come back home."

31

■×▲✦✚■♠●■

2003, Amsterdam

A month later I was on a plane to England. The band was already there, traveling from somewhere in Yorkshire, so I'd have a day to myself before joining them in Brighton, where the person organizing their tour was based. A friend teaching in an exchange program in Oxford invited me to meet her there, where in approximately twenty-four hours she treated me to a concert, a visit to the chained books at the Bodleian Library, then drinks at the pub where J. R. R. Tolkien and C. S. Lewis had regularly met, an evensong, holiday shopping, and a morning choral service. Every hour or two, distant bells echoed, reverberating with the stone buildings. I was in an enchanted city. I loved it.

Brighton, unfortunately, was the opposite. Steve met me at the train station. Initially the visit felt good, but that high began to dissipate as we walked. Steve pulled my suitcase helpfully along the two-mile walk in the dark but didn't give promising answers as to where we were going. He said I shouldn't expect it to be a happy gathering at Jim and Jill's, where we were staying. They were having relationship problems, and everyone had hunkered down in their rooms.

Supposedly we were lucky because we didn't have to bunk with the other bandmates, but it didn't feel that way. Steve and I camped in a room someone told me belonged to a teenage daughter, though I never saw her. It was painted theater red with various drapes piled around the edges. Someone had tacked heavy blankets over the windows, leaving the atmosphere perpetually dark. There was no furniture. Instead, stuffed animals, loose glitter, and scattered, half-used makeup containers littered the floor, where we slept. It reminded me of an extremely messy version of Sarah's bedroom in the Jim Henson movie *Labyrinth*. When I woke up the next morning, I checked to see if any detritus had stuck to my skin.

In Amsterdam, someone held up a sign for the band at the airport, and we piled into a few cars the film-festival organizers had arranged to drive us to our hotel. The weather was breezy yet sunny—much warmer than Minnesota or even Brighton had been. The hotel was a couple of miles from the central film-festival venues, which made us dependent on volunteer drivers or cabs. The film would screen at Paradiso, a famed music venue, and be followed by a question-and-answer session that included me. Then the band would play. The main meeting place for the festival was a café next to the venue.

I kept searching for opportunities to see other parts of the city. I'd been in Amsterdam a few days as a college student with not much more than a Eurail pass—no credit card, in the days before ATMs. I'd loved gazing at the paintings in the Rijksmuseum and the Van Gogh Museum. I hoped to carve out a few hours in the afternoon to show them to Steve.

But as far as Steve was concerned, we were there for a film festival and performance: all work. Emily Goldberg had already been there a few days and was sightseeing with her boyfriend. Not being a band member or filmmaker, I spent a lot of time sitting in the central café, reading festival materials and looking out the large glass windows onto a square where hundreds of bicycles were parked. Bicycles seemed to be the main mode of transportation for getting around town, even in the rain.

In the late afternoon, the performance venue opened so the

band could set up and do a sound check. I stood in the entrance, awestruck. Paradiso was a soaring space, an old church, darker and more gothic than the Limelight, with stained-glass windows on the upper level behind the stage and two balconies along the sides and back. The capacity was immense, with several hundred chairs on the floor. I knew the size of the room—and the thought of how to fill it—would trouble Steve, so I sat up in the gallery to one side and studied the stained-glass windows, trying to puzzle out the stories they told. After sound check, we had only a few minutes to get back to the hotel to change. Then we were back for the film's premiere.

It felt odd to find a chair with my name attached to it near the front. I had hoped to hide in back somewhere, but obviously they wanted us to have a clear path to the stage for the Q&A period. The film began with a montage of band performances and clips of fans talking about the band, then scenes of the two of us doing normal things at home. Soon I was watching myself lead our horses in from the pasture, the two of us at a barn picnic, and footage of us galloping up a hill. I teared up at the sight of us being so normal, so happy together. It was the first time either of us had seen the entire film, and somewhere along the way I found myself gripping Steve's hand. Scenes unfolded with family-member interviews and one of my classes in Rochester. I watched myself on the gigantic screen, running the sound board at KFAI and carrying equipment at shows, glammed up with extra red, blue, and black extensions clipped into my pigtails. There were scenes of us walking through the snow hand in hand and scenes of us kissing.

At the end, a frame announced that we'd celebrated our twentieth wedding anniversary in June, and a cheer went up. The audience continued to cheer during the final frame, which showed a note dedicating the film to Emily's parents, who also enjoyed a long, happy marriage. I felt honored and humbled that Emily had seen things *I* couldn't see in our relationship, and that the audience wasn't cheering just for the band, but for *us*. People were affirming our love for each other.

I continued to feel that support from the audience as we moved onto the stage to answer questions, but I also felt exposed. I thought my experience as a classroom teacher and radio host would prepare me for this part, but I didn't anticipate the questions about our sex life, how I felt about Steve's breasts (again, questions that only men seemed to ask), and queries about why we didn't have children. Not being able to have children was still painful to me. I wasn't ready to tell anyone I'd tried and failed. I declined to answer those questions.

■■■

Perhaps I was also unsettled because everyone was calling Steve Venus now and referring to him with she/her pronouns. It had started as a stage name, just a little over four years earlier, not long before Emily began filming. Emily readily began using the name Venus, as did many of the people involved with the band and new people in our lives. But a lot of people still used the name Steve, including longtime friends, family members, and me. (De Mars as Venus's last name was still years away, a name inspired by the documentary that Venus would begin to use when she began a solo career without the Pretty Horses.)

Steve had repeatedly assured me it was okay for me to use whatever name I wanted. I found "Venus" disconcerting because the name made the person I knew as my spouse remote, a person up on a stage and encased in some invisible, hard shell. With the film, I could see that the name Venus and the pronoun she had now entered the public consciousness as his *only* name and pronoun. To avoid confusion, I already used "Venus" and "she" when referring to my spouse in third person in a public setting. But if I had to call across the room to him in public, I called him Sweetie, and in private, I still called him Steve. I

couldn't figure out another way to feel a close, intimate relationship with my spouse and avoid getting confused or angry
looks from the people around me. The double-thinking was
beginning to get exhausting. But as the band absorbed more
and more of his attention and new acquaintances began to call
him Venus, I didn't want to follow suit—there was distance every time I felt the name on my lips, as if I was one in a massive
audience on the floor looking up at an untouchable person on
the stage.

I kept asking for reassurance. The typical query went like
this:

"A lot of people are calling you Venus, but I'm still calling
you Steve. Is that okay with you? I mean, you haven't changed
it formally or anything."

"No, that's okay, you can call me whatever feels comfortable
to you."

"What about pronouns? Some people are referring to you
as 'she.'"

"Oh . . . I don't know. I don't feel comfortable with *any* pronouns. You can call me what you want."

■■■

I stayed near Emily Goldberg as we watched the band run
through its set after the premiere, the audience wild with applause. Emily had noticed how some of the questions during
the Q&A had made me feel uncomfortable and assured me that
my responses were fine. Her boyfriend, Chris, had also joined
us, and Emily was glowing. The film was a triumph.

The performance ended, and everyone was sweaty and energized. The party moved to the café next door, where Steve
and I hoped to get some food, since we hadn't eaten anything
since early afternoon, but by then the kitchen was closed. Steve
had been so concerned about setting up the equipment that
we'd skipped dinner, and we'd also been the last ones out of

Paradiso after the show, so we'd missed a second opportunity to eat. There was a dance party in the back room, but no food. I suggested finding something at a nearby restaurant—Paradiso was in a busy square, and there had to be something nearby. It would be nice for the two of us to get away from the crowds and talk about our reactions to the film and everything else. I hoped to find a cozy, romantic little spot out of the developing drizzle.

Steve agreed, and we walked out into the mist, gazing down one dark, meandering street, then another, looking for lights or something else that would indicate a restaurant. Since the café had stopped serving food, we thought we'd better hurry to find something. But about five minutes into our exploration, Steve became increasingly frustrated, saying something about needing to get back to Emily. I thought he meant Emily Hooper, and it sounded to me as if he wanted to swoop in like a mother hen and rescue another band member from some crisis I didn't understand. We had just seen ourselves on-screen as two people with a deep and committed love for each other, and now he wanted to search for another band member instead of spending a few minutes having dinner with me. Exasperated, I said, okay, we can go back after we've found something to eat—I was feeling a little lightheaded. We had just passed a kabob place that was open. It looked tough and grubby from the outside, but it had food.

The inside confirmed our initial impressions. The walls were a kind of yellowish gray, lit by a dim overhead light bulb. We sat at a counter, and the other customers eyed us suspiciously. We were both dressed in glam-goth clothes, and that wasn't how people were dressed for this place—they wore T-shirts and workman's clothes. And we likely carried our argumentative vibe as we walked in. Steve went mostly silent and wouldn't speak to me, wouldn't even look at me. We ordered some food, ate a few bites, then got up to go, leaving most of the lumpish meal on our plates at the counter.

While watching the film, I'd ridden a high, feeling like one-half of the world's greatest love story. Now I felt reduced to a zero—not worthy of attention or respect, not worthy even of some kind of response. Certainly not loved. It was as if the entire movie had been a lie.

I couldn't recognize that Steve's lack of eye contact had more to do with the other people in the restaurant than with me. Back home, he rarely dressed to "pass" or blend in by wearing conventional women's clothing. His makeup by this time was dramatic, with Cleopatra-style eyeliner and maybe a bindi in the middle of his forehead. During the day he usually wore a black vinyl vest with zippers that he'd gotten at a fetish shop and skinny leather pants modified either with leather lacing up the sides or knee-to-floor fake-fur bell-bottoms. It seemed to me that he *wanted* people to see him in all his complexity—but then sometimes he panicked at the possibility of a negative reaction. This was not an idle fear: a lot of violence is still aimed at trans people, especially trans women. We'd heard about Brandon Teena and seen the film *Boys Don't Cry*, and neither of us was dressed to blend in that night. If I'd had more insight that night, Steve's lack of eye contact might have reminded me of what I'd seen back in eighth grade, when it seemed he was trying to disappear into his hair.

We had a therapist in the early 1990s who tried to help us sort out how Steve's developing gender awareness affected our marriage. A gay man himself, he was sympathetic to Steve's situation and took him to the University of Minnesota Health Sciences Library where together they could look up the latest psychological research about being transgender. When Kevin met us at our next counseling session, he told us the experience had been a revelation to him.

"We walked into the library together," Kevin explained, "and all the heads turned to look at Steve." He was shocked, explaining, "That never happens to me. I can't imagine the pressure of being under that kind of scrutiny, what that must feel like every day." Steve and I nodded soberly. It was all true. And there didn't seem to be anything we could do about it. This kind of scrutiny made him afraid for many years to hold my hand or kiss me in public.

But in that kabob place, I just wanted some expression of love from Steve, the kind I had heard in his voice in our living room just a month earlier. And I couldn't understand how we could experience such a high at one moment only to crash into a pit of despair the next. We got back to the party, and it was still going, though with fewer people than when we'd left. Steve led me to Emily Goldberg, and I realized it was *this* Emily he had wanted to get back to. I was still confused as to why. She seemed to be doing fine and was getting ready to leave. She and Chris were at a different hotel and would stay in Amsterdam a few more days, so we said good-bye. For some reason, he couldn't find the words to tell me that he wanted to get back to the party because he thought he might meet someone there who could help the band's career.

We were in Amsterdam just that one night. Someone would drive us back to the airport in the morning. I would have another day or two with the band, then fly back alone. They still had another week of gigs in southern England before they headed home.

We cabbed it back to the hotel in a dejected funk. While Steve seemed worried about the band and other members of the entourage, I stared out the window into the dark, wondering what invisible sights we were driving past. I was completely frustrated. What had felt like a pinnacle of romantic partnership was morphing into a shitty veneer. The whole experience felt like a fraud that I'd bought into. We said very little to each other during the short ride, clamming up and trying to avoid looking like we were having an argument, though I'm sure the driver could smell the tension fuming off of us.

Our room at the hotel was on a lower level. The place itself had seemed nice enough when we'd arrived earlier, but now the hallway looked gray and dim. Our room had windows, but the curtains had stayed shut because we'd been in such a tear to change clothes for the premiere. I never did get a chance to see what the windows looked out on. Two double beds loomed in front of us, one for the suitcases and one for us. Everything now seemed murky and monochromatic. Emily Hooper and Shannon were across the hall from us, and the rest of the contingent was spread to the upper floors of the hotel.

I couldn't stand the troubled silence between us any longer.

"What just happened?" I asked. Steve sat on the edge of one bed, his eyes trained toward the floor. I sat cross-legged on the other bed.

It took him a while to answer. "I had to see Emily," he finally said. "I needed to be there."

"I don't know what you're talking about." Now I was really getting angry. "We wasted money at a shitty restaurant and then went back to the dance, and she was fine. She was great! What the hell is going on with you?"

Steve shook his head. "I just . . ." his voice dropped away, and then he started again. "It was just an emotional time for me."

"An emotional time for *you*? How do you think *I* felt, watching myself on film as one-half of this great romantic partnership, only to have you not want to spend even a couple of minutes having dinner with me?" I paused. I was just getting started. "All of these issues, all of the things you led me to believe were solved so we could get back together again, was that all just a big, fucking lie? Because that's what it feels like to me right now!"

By now Steve had started crying, and between choked sobs he muttered that I could just leave him if I wanted to. But I didn't want to, so now I was crying, too. I got up off the bed and sat down at his feet, hoping he would look at me. He wouldn't.

That made me cry even harder. I slid away from him and lay on my side on the blue carpet at the foot of the other bed, hugging my knees to my chest.

For at least two hours, we kept spitting our hurt toward each other in short, frustrated bursts, then we'd both be quiet, traveling frightening paths alone in our own minds, waiting for the other person to say something to make it better. That never happened. Whatever the other person said only made it worse.

Then Steve stood up and said he needed to go for a walk, and maybe find a canal to jump into.

"No!" I cried. Steve was already pulling on his tattered leather jacket. "No!" I cried again. I tried to put my arms around him. Touching and hugging had often calmed him before.

"I have to go! Let me go!" he shouted. He pushed me away, hard, and I toppled to the floor. I scrambled to my feet to try to put my arms around him again, but he was already at the door, turning the knob to open it.

I leapt at him, entirely on instinct, hanging onto his shoulders to try to stop him from leaving, but he shook me off and opened the door. I leapt again, but this time he was moving so fast all I could catch was a foot, a steel-toed combat boot, clanking down the hallway, dragging me. I screamed for Emily or Shannon to come out of their room to help, that Steve was going to drown himself in a canal. There was no response. No one came out of any of the rooms along that hallway. I must have been dragged thirty feet, with the side of my face scraping along the carpet. With a jerk of his foot, Steve shook free and turned a corner, exiting a side door. I had lost him. I slowly got up on my knees and breathed. My face and hands burned. Then I got to my feet, went back to the hotel room, and closed the door.

What could I do? My hands were shaking. I had to stay calm, to think. I remembered that a friend-of-a-friend's husband had committed suicide while they were in some European country.

Was it my turn to experience that nightmare? The band and I had an early morning flight back to England the next day. When should I tell them we needed to call the police, to start looking for a body floating in the canals? Should I call the police now? Then again, what if it was the same as when Steve would bail out of an argument and get in the car and drive for hours? I remembered his crisis in Prague. If I involved the police, maybe we'd be delayed, and that would make things worse. And if I called the police, what would I tell them? Where had he gone? Didn't someone have to be missing twenty-four hours before the authorities would begin to search?

The right side of my face still hurt, and I had prickly sensations around my right eye. I went to the bathroom mirror, trying to figure it out. Some of my eyelashes were missing. I looked for glass shards to pull out but couldn't find any. Maybe it was just grit.

I walked back to the bed, trying to make myself ready for whatever might happen next. My last thought was that I shouldn't fall asleep, but I did anyway.

A few hours later, maybe two, I woke up when the door opened. A trace of dawn light glowed at the edge of the curtains. Steve was back, standing inside the door.

I raised my head, blinking, focusing my attention to make sure it wasn't a dream. "Are you okay? I was worried and didn't know what to do."

Steve shook his head. "I walked and walked all night, looking for a place to jump in. But I never found a good place. And then, when the sun started coming up, I felt stupid. So I came back." He paused a moment. "I'm sorry," he said.

I got up and hugged him. I was really, really, really happy he hadn't committed suicide. But this time I knew all this wasn't something that I would be able to put aside. It wasn't something I *should* be able to put aside. Many things were wonderful between us, but something was also profoundly wrong. I wanted to fix it, but I now saw that I wasn't the person to do that.

I considered that although I wanted to be in a relationship with Steve, and I loved him, I might not be able to live with him. It might not be good for either of us to live together. I started imagining alternative scenarios where the two of us could love and respect each other, but not be emotionally dependent on each other. All those scenarios involved separation.

32

■ˣ▲✦✱■⋔●ᴈ

2004, Minneapolis

We flew back to England, and the band played a dispirited gig that night to a half-empty house. The next morning, back in Brighton, Steve tried to make up for the utter failure of our time in Amsterdam by walking around downtown with me for a few hours before I got on the train to head to Gatwick. It was cold, and most of the shops were closed. We walked out on a windswept pier over the ocean, and I tried to imagine what it might be like in the warm summer months with scores of tourists. Then I was on a plane and back at work. I didn't tell any of my colleagues what the trip had been like—I had just started teaching there and didn't really know anyone. And how could I tell anyone anything when it seemed like the whole documentary was a fiction?

The band kept Steve busy with local gigs in December and January. We got through the holidays and our January birthdays, but I was emotionally detached from the relationship, a sort of watchful balloon tethered above. I tried to enjoy our time together when it was good but hovered for the next crisis. Things seemed to go horribly wrong when I cared too much.

In late January, Steve wanted me to hear a recording of a song he'd been working on that he thought I'd like, one that he'd written for me. I was touched, and looked forward to hearing it. He cued it up and I sat on the couch to listen. The song was called "Stars for Eyes," but all I could make out of the lyrics was a chorus that repeated "I hate you" over and over. I couldn't stand it.

"Turn it off," I said emphatically. The balloon had landed, and I had no more tolerance.

"But you haven't listened to the whole thing."

"I've heard enough. I don't want to listen to a song about how much you hate me." I was appalled that he expected me to listen to something like that.

"But that's just the chorus. It gets better."

"I said turn it off!" I stood up and stomped upstairs. I wasn't just angry; I was humiliated. What did he think I was, some kind of idiot robot? Would he have done this to anyone else?

Steve followed me upstairs, explaining that maybe the song needed some more work. Right. I couldn't see any way of fixing it. I'd already heard the chorus.

Years later, he showed me the lyrics and played the recording again. It starts deceptively beautiful, quietly, with the lyric, "One day / I will be ..." and then it's hard to make out the words. The intended words were that he would be my knight in shining armor. But his voice is muted in that part of the recording, losing the beginning and end consonants. It's still difficult to make out the lyrics to that section, even when reading them on the page. After about three minutes his voice gets louder for the bridge, "Of course I know / you hate me ..." and then to the chorus of "I hate you," eventually followed by a quieter "I love you" and "Could I ever / forget you." He later explained he'd written it when we were separated, when he didn't know if we could get back together. I honestly still don't know why he thought I would want to hear a song that said he hated me.

We'd planned to go to an art opening that night at SooVac, a gallery on Lyndale. Moreover, we were expected—Steve might get a show there. I wasn't looking forward to doing *anything* with him after "Stars for Eyes" but somehow pulled myself together and went. I was numb and enraged over the song, then looked at the art on the walls and felt disgusted. The exhibit was called "Hysteria," a group show that included paintings smeared pink and black. I don't remember the genders of the artists, but I felt appropriated—ripped and stuffed into some dank drawer by someone else's version of being a woman. It didn't help that Steve spent his time talking to people who stepped in front of me to gush over the band's performances. He didn't make space for me by his side, didn't even seem to notice the trespass. That made me even angrier.

I strategized. I willed myself to remain calm. In a day or two, I would tell him we had to separate. I mentally walked through all the techniques I could think of to address it in a loving way, a way that told him I cared for him, but I couldn't live with him. I had been studying peace and reconciliation the last few years with a group at my church. I admired Desmond Tutu and his Peace and Reconciliation Commission in South Africa as apartheid ended. Tutu had even spoken at the church, and as an usher I greeted him, amazed that such a strong and visionary man was physically so tiny. Such a person would know that the only way to overcome the massive force of self-righteous anger would be through offering love and forgiveness when it was least expected.

I felt sad this had happened so quickly after the release of *Venus of Mars*. It seemed the entire movie had gotten it wrong. But I couldn't live my life feeling so unloved. Steve and I were enduring opposite sides of a civil war. We needed to end that war and move forward.

I didn't trust him to take care of the house and all the bills associated with it, so I would ask him to move out. If that felt right, probably in a few months' time we could start looking at divorce. It would be complicated, but I thought that if I could remain calm and logical and follow all the techniques I knew of, it would work out for both of us. We would be able to go our separate ways, still maintaining some kind of love and admiration, but without the kind of interdependency that had often left one of us feeling deserted.

I planned what I would say to Steve the next morning. It had to be in the morning, when we were both at our calmest and most rational. So the next day, after we'd had a few cups of coffee, I said I'd like to have a conversation. We sat side by side on the couch, Steve wondering what it was all about. I told him that I loved him very much, and that I felt bad things had gone the way they had. I said again how much I loved him, but that our clashes were not good for either of us. I wanted him to have a good future, but I didn't think I was able to go forward together in it anymore. I didn't think the relationship was healthy for either of us. Steve was stunned, but in the face of what I said, he couldn't disagree. We both knew I was taking care of all the bills for the house, so it was obvious I would stay there and continue taking care of it. I gave Steve some space to pack things to take with him, and once again he moved out.

When we separated the first time, I was in shock. I felt ashamed. We both kept it a secret from most people because we had some underlying sense we would get back together, and neither of us wanted the baggage that came with people separating and friends choosing sides. But this time felt different. I wasn't proud of what had happened, and I wasn't making any big announcements, but it would be pointless to cover it up. If the mood seemed right, I told whatever friends I ran into that we were no longer together. I expected that Steve and I would have a few strained but calm meetings where we decided how to divide things up. I imagined I'd have to take in boarders to keep the house, and I hoped I could keep the cats. I was pretty sure I'd be able to keep the horses. Of course it was only right that Steve would keep all the art. Most of it was in his studio in downtown Minneapolis anyway, a place I didn't even have keys to.

Once again I was alone in the house. It felt odd. I fed the cats and walked through the rooms and thought about being responsible for it all. Of course it wasn't the first time I'd felt this way, but this breakup had been *my* decision, and I continually pondered whether I'd made the right choice. I didn't want to give up. I still wanted to figure out how to do it all. I mourned the death of sharing an inspired and creative life with Steve, but with each day that passed I felt stabilized by not having to negotiate his mood swings. I no longer experienced sudden rejection by the person who knew me most intimately. Maybe I could figure out a way to have the life I wanted without him.

I bent myself toward resuming a normal life, whatever that was. Part of a normal life for me was getting out of the house, but it seemed insurmountable to go to events by myself if I didn't have a plan to meet friends. I'd been the same way when I was single, and now I was single again but not interested in starting a new relationship. I still had a pair of season tickets to the St. Paul Chamber Orchestra. I asked Neal Karlen, a longtime friend, if he'd like to go. His girlfriend had just broken up with him, and both of us felt lost with Valentine's Day approaching. We talked ahead of time, agreeing to go just as friends, and it felt good to get out. Neal is an incredibly funny person, a writer, another lover of words, so all felt fine as we settled into our seats at the Ordway's main stage.

That feeling lasted until intermission, when we went out to the lobby to pick up a few drinks. We ran into Donn and David, men Steve and I often talked to at orchestra intermissions. We'd developed the habit of joining them post-concert at the St. Paul Hotel bar for a few drinks. They were happy to see me, and looked at Neal quizzically as I introduced him.

"Where's Venus?" asked Donn, the more talkative and uninhibited of the two.

"Oh, Venus can't be here tonight," I said evasively. "Venus is busy. With band stuff." Neal shot me a look.

I switched the subject. I couldn't get into explaining things, not with the intermission bell ready to sound in ten minutes. Donn and David would want to know more. Donn was a gay man in a committed relationship, and David was his straight friend who enjoyed sharing a concert series and rounds of golf with him. David had experienced his own marital ups and downs, and I knew both of them would want to get to the heart of things. I couldn't bear to do that now.

"So what's new with you guys?" I was relieved that the response to that query lasted until the intermission bell sounded. I don't remember if they invited us to meet them at the hotel bar afterward, but I was ready to make an excuse if they did.

Neal wondered when we got back to our seats why I hadn't told them Steve and I had separated.

"I know, I should have told them, but I just couldn't right now," I said lamely. We knew Neal through Emily Goldberg, and perhaps all those scenes from *Venus of Mars* had shown him only an idealized version of our marriage. He must have been surprised that the woman appearing in that film could be so bitter about events in the relationship that she wanted to end it. I myself knew I was still in love with Steve; I just couldn't see a way to be in the same room with him, much less a marriage with him.

A month later I wanted to go to a show at the Guthrie because it was getting rave reviews. I didn't want to miss it just because I wouldn't know what to do with myself during intermission. Again Neal came to the rescue, and we snagged two last-minute tickets.

As I watched the scenes unfold, I realized I'd been an idiot to go to this particular play. It was *Romeo and Juliet*, and though I've never thought of the play as particularly romantic, there were a few scenes that drew me back to earlier days, days when I'd been blissfully happy with Steve. Now I felt like a loser. When I read the program, I felt even worse. There was a familiar name in it: the cute guy who'd sat behind me in a junior high art class tossing spitballs at the back of my head was listed as the fight and swordplay director. He had been one of the kids who hung out smoking under the spruce trees across the street from school. In contrast, I'd been a rule follower and tried to excel at everything in school. Now he was some kind of New York–based theater expert brought in by the Guthrie. What had I done with *my* life?

It didn't help that my face had broken out—I was forty-four years old, and I'd had some version of breakouts since the end of graduate school, much worse than anything I ever experienced in high school. The dermatologist called it "adult acne," which I'd never heard of before. None of my friends had it.

Was it stress? At the time I blamed it on a garbage burner that had gone up on the north side of downtown about a year before the pimples and redness began to break out. But those were also the years of job searching and mounting relationship issues, the years of going to the Gay 90's and wondering if my spouse loved the fawning men there more than he loved me. The night Neal and I went to the Guthrie I had a large blemish southeast of my mouth, and the more I tried to camouflage it, the worse it got. I took to turning my head, trying to keep my face shadowed. I willed myself to forget about it.

Afterward, Neal and I went to the Chatterbox Bar to talk about the play and catch up in general. It was a place I liked to go—a friendly neighborhood spot, with a well-worn wooden bar, unpretentious high, dark, scuffed-up wood booths, an assortment of vinyl albums hanging from the walls, and vintage video and board games to borrow in the side room. A friend of a friend and his wife had started it, and I'd been going there with Steve since its early days.

As I strode confidently through the door, I realized I'd made an error, but it was too late to turn back. Jay, a tall, good-looking man with a blond ponytail, who could easily have been a bouncer, was bartending and nodded at me. He'd been onstage as a go-go dancer with the Horses a few times, most memorably in leather butt-less chaps, and I always talked to him if he was working. Usually I was there with Steve. I motioned for Neal to move past the long bar, nervously searching for a booth to hide in. I found one three-quarters of the way down and slid in. But instead of a server coming to take our order, Jay stepped out from behind the bar.

"Hey there, how's it going?"

"It's good," I said, nodding noncommittally. Should I introduce Neal? I decided to. Jay shook his hand warmly.

"Where's Venus?" he asked. I inhaled deeply, getting ready.

"We're separated," I said, trying for a tone between matter-of-fact and soft. "I don't know what Venus is doing now."

Jay's whole body stiffened. He hadn't been expecting that. For the life of me, I couldn't figure out why this was a surprise to anyone. Yes, I was still in love, but I'd been through hell and wasn't interested in going back there ever again. Hadn't anyone else been able to see this?

"Oh," he said. He might have said something about being sorry, but he might not have. He politely took our drink order and backed away from the table.

I explained my history with Jay to Neal, why he might have reacted that way. Neal nodded sympathetically, but there was nothing he could do. When I excused myself to go to the bathroom, I checked myself in the mirror and was horrified to see that my blemish was bleeding.

Normandale's spring break had started, and I was grateful for the time to get my face back in order, away from other people. I had an aloe vera plant that usually healed various cuts and scrapes, so when I got home I broke off a leaf and applied it to the blemish. The next morning I woke up, felt some pain in my jaw, and looked in the mirror. The lower left quadrant of my face was completely swollen. I didn't think I could even go out for groceries. I foraged the fridge, hoping the swelling and redness would diminish by the time I really needed food, or classes started up.

The next day I had to show up to record a phone interview for *Write On! Radio.* My co-host at the time, Ian Leask, met me at the front door to the KFAI building.

"What happened to you?" he exclaimed.

"Oh, I think it's a bad reaction to medication." I wanted to simplify the discussion and end it.

"Geez, it looks like someone punched you in the jaw," he said, as if he was sure that's what had happened. Embarrassed, I assured him that wasn't the case. Now I knew that I really, truly wasn't fit to be seen by anyone.

I drove home from KFAI, constantly checking myself in the rearview mirror. Ian was right: I looked terrible. As I pushed open the back gate to drive the car in, I stooped to let my hair hang over my face, ashamed a neighbor might see.

I stared out the windows at the sunshine outside, the melting snow and ice. I had an entire week free for spring break, and I didn't even want to take the garbage out until it was totally dark. I felt like I was in jail.

I went through a day or two of this, lonely, not satisfied by the opportunity to catch up on reading. I couldn't even see my horse because I was sure to run into other people.

I finally decided to get something done. I'd put off contacting Steve to negotiate an upcoming show we both promised to participate in before we imagined being separated. A friend of ours who went by the name Future Lisa did a cabaret with guest performers at various venues around town, most often at the Turf Club on University Avenue in St. Paul's Midway area. It was a midsize bar with a decent stage and a long, admired history of supporting local bands. The Horses had played there many times, and now Steve was on the bill to do a short solo electric set. I had planned to read poems. We confirmed that before the separation. I'd been thrilled at the time that I was being invited to read more, and I didn't want to cancel now just because Steve would be present. But I also wanted to make sure we didn't create some kind of ugly scene, so I punched in his number.

"Hi, it's me."

"Oh. Hi."

"I'm calling because I was looking at my schedule, and I see we're both doing the Future Lisa thing on the twentieth. Is that okay with you? I'm reading poetry." There was a long pause.

"Yes," he said flatly. "That's okay with me."

"Have you told her we're separated?"

"No, I haven't told her."

"Okay, well, let's just both reconfirm. I don't want her to worry there will be any drama or anything."

"Yeah." He paused. "Yeah," he said again, "let's leave the relationship stuff out of it."

"How's everything else going? I saw from your band emailer that Eden is quitting the band. 'Taking a sabbatical' is how you put it."

"Oh that." Again there was a pause. "The New York trip did not go well."

"Oh no! What happened? I thought she fit in so well with you guys!" I was genuinely concerned.

"Oh, Eden got really drunk at the CBGB's gig." He then proceeded to tell me, blow by blow, what had happened. Eden had been fine at the late-afternoon sound check, then left for a while and returned drunk and angry. Backstage, she continued drinking and shouted at anyone who tried to take the bottle she had away. When they got onstage for their set, they weren't even sure she'd be able to stand, let alone play the right notes. It was obvious to the entire audience that something was wrong, but the band kept going as if the bass wall of noise were planned. During the last song, she pulled the strap over her head and started swinging the instrument by its neck. Shannon, dancing fiercely onstage next to her, tried to pull it away, but Eden turned and started swinging the bass into the stage floor, smashing it like an ax splitting logs again and again. When the body was smithereens and completely detached from the neck, people rushed the stage to grab souvenir pieces of what was left.

"Oh, that sounds terrible!" I exclaimed. "Did she have an explanation?"

"No. She seemed to be okay the next day, and Shannon and I had a talk with her when we got back. We can't do that again. She doesn't even have a bass to play anymore."

"Oh, poor Eden. I know she loved playing bass." I silently pondered what had happened. I knew something must have gone deeply wrong for her, and I wished I'd been there to somehow avert the crisis or at least talk to her about it. But I was in no position to tell Steve how to run the band.

"Yeah. Well."

"And obviously poor you." I knew how hard it was to get decent musicians to play with the band. They had already been through ten or thirteen drummers by that point.

"So you have your poems worked out to read at the Turf Club?" he asked.

"I'm trying to revise some old stuff. I might write something new. I have a lot of time on my hands stuck at home this week."

"What do you mean?"

"Oh . . ." now it was my turn to pause. "You know how my face breaks out sometimes."

"Yeah."

"Well . . ." I looked out the window at an ice dam dripping off the roof. It glinted in the sun. "I thought it might heal up faster if I used an aloe vera leaf on it, but I think I had an allergic reaction instead."

"What do you mean?" He sounded concerned.

"Oh, just that the whole lower left part of my face swelled up. Ian said it looked like someone punched me."

"Are you going to be okay?"

"Yeah, I think the swelling is starting to go down, but it still looks terrible. I think it's going to take the rest of the week for this to even start healing."

"Well, sorry. I know that's hard."

"Yeah. And the worst part of it is that—" I was looking out the window now at the swelling lilac buds on the bushes in the side yard. I wanted to slip outside and touch their plump greenness. "I just feel trapped here. I want to get out and enjoy the sun. I feel like a loser."

"Don't feel that way."

"Well, I *do* feel that way."

"Look, I was going to go for a walk around the lake. You could come with me."

"I don't want anyone seeing me like this."

"It's not that warm out. There aren't a lot of walkers out there yet. Besides, you could wear a scarf or something." The invitation was tempting.

"Okay," I finally said. "I'll go."

When Steve pulled the van up in front of the house, I held my head to the side again, trying to shield my face with my hair. Steve studied my face as I got into the van. I felt nervous and vulnerable.

"You don't look that bad," he said after a moment. "Don't worry about it. You look fine." I found that reassuring.

We parked along the road that circled Lake of the Isles and got out, looking across the frozen surface to the stately mansions that ringed it. The lake was about three miles around, with frequently used bicycle and walking paths. I don't remember what we talked about as we walked, but it felt freeing. My spirits were lifted so much that I suggested having a bite to eat at a restaurant we liked that was usually quiet that time of day. Steve paused before responding, weighing something.

"Sure," he finally said.

We got there in time for happy hour and a few snacks. I made sure to sit by a window, with the left side of my face away from the server. I felt protected.

We didn't see or talk to each other until the Turf Club show a week and a half later. My face had healed by then, and I was feeling much more confident. I read some poems inspired by the frustrations of the last few years, including "Poem to Be Burned":

> To all attachments, destructive, self-destructive, fattening, addictive,
> I renounce you.
> To the money that makes me happy and sad, commanding mood swings, snake-charming, writhing in awful directions,
> I renounce you.
> To hatred and a sectarian spirit that says if you are not with us, you must be against us, and waving our flags we will cast you away,
> I renounce you.
> To the weird bodies that huddle in my mother's brain cells driving her mad, squinting monsters that are fighting and fighting,
> I renounce you.
> To the news that my mother does not want to eat or drink, and I am glad because it tells me she knows, still, what she is doing, and then I feel shame for thinking it is good that she is capable of taking her life,
> I renounce you.
> To all fears that when I am on the top of the world, screaming with joy and naked, blissful, and you can see everything, how ugly I look, and how average, that you could fake your love for me,
> I renounce you.
> To the gorgeous, haughty, and untouchable that have gotten too close to my skin and broken my heart,
> I renounce you.
> To my skin that bristles and smarts at painful memories that have nothing to do with living and therefore must be let go,

I renounce you.

Tonight I put on a fabric of new skin, resilient, sensitive,
    guard hairs standing straight out to a point, ready.

A friend since the Rifle Sport days, Ted Lofstrom, was in the audience. He congratulated me on the reading and said that particular poem reminded him of Buddhism.

"Yes, you're right," I told him. "I've been reading a lot of books by the Dalai Lama. Trying to learn how to detach." I thought another moment, and then decided that Ted, married with two kids, would probably understand my relationship problems with Steve. "The truth is," I continued, "we've been separated the last couple of months. We're trying to remain friends, but it's hard."

"Oh." Ted didn't register a lot of surprise, but he nodded. "I'm so sorry to hear that." I gave him a sad smile.

"Yeah, it's . . ." I trailed off. "A complicated time. We're slowly telling people."

"I know how that goes," he replied. "Let me know if you need anything."

"Thanks."

Steve was up onstage now, summoning a deep resonance in his voice as he went through his set. I was struck by how soulful he sounded when not surrounded by the spectacle of the band, the dancers, the flashing lights, and the sparks of an angle grinder on metal. Now he was able to speed up and slow down for emphasis. Even more interesting was that even though it was just him and his electric guitar, the sound was about three-quarters of what the whole band sounded like. Using various noise pedals, he'd come up with a way of putting together enough bass line, rhythm guitar, and lead to fill in the sound pretty well. The only things missing were the drums and occasional backup vocals, which I sang softly to myself from the audience. I still loved watching and hearing him play.

I wanted to talk to him after the show, remembering the

closeness I'd felt walking around the lake. I knew it would be a bad idea to approach him as he got off stage and talked to fans—too awkward. So I waited until people started filtering out and he began to pack things up for load out.

I don't remember what I said to him, but it was something he responded to negatively, so I snapped back, and there we were again, having an argument. It was the last thing I'd wanted. On some subconscious level, maybe I had begun to think that our relationship had a future, if we could just clear up a few things. And now we stood between the central pillars that divided the bar side from the stage side in the middle of the Turf Club, arguing. Neither of us wanted to be that kind of person.

"I don't need to listen to this anymore," Steve said hotly and walked back to the stage to load out his guitar, amp, and speakers. I felt the moisture fill my eyes and didn't want anyone to witness me weeping. I fled back to Minneapolis, tears streaming down my face and nose, wailing and screaming at the headlights of the oncoming freeway traffic. What had happened? Maybe he was upset at what I'd read, though he hadn't said anything about my reading. Probably I'd expected too much, hoping for the usual friendly smile at the end of a gig. I shouldn't have expected a hug or a kiss, but I'd wanted some kind of friendly acknowledgment, a reassuring signal, something like what I'd experienced when we walked around the lake. I'd gotten the opposite, and it seared me.

Once home, I sat up a while, thinking and crying, trying to see things from Steve's point of view. Of course he'd been angry. I'd asked him to leave. I wasn't supporting him anymore. I had gone back to that daydream where I thought that if the friends he was staying with would charge him rent, he'd learn how to set money aside and be more financially responsible. But that wasn't happening, and I should have known I didn't have the right to ask him for special attention or anything else. We were probably getting a divorce. I'd wanted him to treat me as someone he cared about. Maybe that's what was really behind my wish to somehow remain friends with him. I still wanted to be significant to him. I could see how that would be impossible now.

I was ashamed that I had asked for too much. I had broken whatever fragile tie had existed between us. I decided to call and apologize. I knew he'd be up a few more hours because that's how it went after a show. My call went to voicemail. Of course he wouldn't pick it up, even if he had the phone in his hand.

"I'm so sorry we argued," I sniffled into the phone. "I know I can't be asking you for anything anymore." I still wanted to talk to him. "Look, if you're still up and want to talk, please call me. I'll be up a little while longer." I paused again. What more could I say? What did I even deserve to ask for? I rambled forward: "I feel terrible that I caused us to argue again, that was the last thing that I wanted to do." Another sniff. "I know you probably don't want to talk to me, but it would be really good to hear your voice again." Sniff. "Okay, that's all. Bye now."

Half an hour later, he called back, and we began to talk.

33

2004, Silver Spring, Maryland

Within weeks, we were dating again, mostly low-pressure activities like walking around Lake of the Isles or the path along Minnehaha Creek. I saw Steve do a solo cameo at First Avenue for a fundraiser dreamed up by Mary Lucia, a local deejay with a whiskey rock-and-roll voice. The event was a benefit for cat shelters. It featured well-known local musicians, each covering a song by David Bowie. The official title of the night was "Rebel Rebel," but most of us referred to it as "Rock for Pussy." Steve played "Space Oddity." I watched him, sitting alone on a stool in the middle of the stage, singing and strumming his guitar. I listened to the appreciative sounds from the audience and quietly sang along with my beloved glam-punk warrior who seemed like Major Tom sometimes, lost in the ether.

When he got to the lines about delivering a message of love to Major Tom's wife, I stopped singing and furiously tried to blink away an unexpected torrent of tears. Steve's behavior made it so hard for me to rely on him loving me. Maybe being onstage was a little like traveling in outer space. Sometimes he'd stepped away from the capsule and lost his tether. Maybe he'd continue to lose his tether—and someday, maybe it would be permanent.

When he got off the stage, he was happy to see me there. He'd been the second performer of the night, and the crowd hadn't been as large as he hoped. Most of his fans showed up later and were disappointed they'd missed him.

We'd gotten to the point where we were romantically involved again, making love, and thinking maybe we wouldn't get divorced. There were late-night make-out sessions in the Colonial Warehouse studio again. But I didn't want to repeat the tsunami of feeling unloved and unsupported all over. I was more adamant about what I needed from our relationship. Steve crashed at either Emily Goldberg's or Ted Ammerman's apartment, depending on what week it was, and I wished they would make him pay rent. I was weary of being the lone voice nagging him to figure out how to support himself. Maybe he only wanted to be with me to have someone who could pay the bills. When we went on dates, I now insisted that he pay his own way, which led him to devise a lot of picnic dates.

By late May, Steve couldn't stay with Emily Goldberg anymore because her boyfriend was moving in. He didn't want to stay with Ted Ammerman because Ted was having problems of his own. Living out of the Colonial Warehouse was also a no-go, because the building wasn't zoned for that. Steve would lose his lease if management discovered he was living there. It was earlier than I wanted him to come back home, and he still spent any money he had on the band, but I didn't know how else to make things work. I caved.

Complicating the decision was that in a few days the band would tour New Zealand in conjunction with a film festival featuring *Venus of Mars*. After that, they would all fly to Silverdocs, a documentary festival put on by the American Film Institute in Silver Spring, Maryland. It wasn't Sundance, but Emily seemed to think it was the next best thing. The institute was happy to fly me out to Silver Spring and pay for the hotel for me and Steve, with band members in separate rooms.

But I worried the tiny spark that held us together would flicker out with Steve in New Zealand for weeks—and he'd be there on our anniversary. More important, I didn't want to walk into another fight like the one we had in Amsterdam.

My therapist suggested making little gifts for each other that we could open each day to remind us we were thinking of each other. These were small, inexpensive sentimental things, like little cards, pictures, or booklets that wouldn't add much bulk or weight to a suitcase. I wrapped up a crystal and a few small, beautiful stones from Brighton Beach in Duluth, where we'd been very happy, and a small shell from a beach on the Lido in Venice, where we'd waded in the ocean and watched the sunset over the lapping waves. I also gave him a tiny jack-in-the-box. When you cranked it up, a purple bird with an enormous beak popped out. Steve gave me a miniature porcelain mouse with large ears, expressive dark eyes, and a tiny tail, and also a drawing of a figure he'd created that we usually referred to as "Bug." It was a bird's-eye view line drawing of a big-eyed child staring pleadingly up, holding a balloon in their hand that read, "I love you."

I was anxious when I got on the plane. The gifts helped me feel as if Steve still loved me, but there remained the shadow of the last time I'd flown to a premiere.

The Silverdocs driver told me the band had already arrived and dropped me at the hotel, about a block from the American Film Institute. I found Steve in the lobby waiting for me, no band members in sight, with a big smile on his face. We kissed and gave each other long, avid hugs. So far, so good.

Most of what I remember from that trip was the bright sunlight that reflected off the pale stone and concrete walls, and how new everything looked. Festival Central was a glass-box lobby of the AFI with nearly constant free food and drinks for festival VIPs, which included us. We ran into Shannon and Tempest, the new bass player, on the sidewalk between the hotel and the AFI. Emily Goldberg was at Festival Central. But I was eager to have time for just the two of us to catch up, and

when I quietly said this to Steve, I could tell he was torn between keeping track of band members and demonstrating that
our relationship was a priority. Finally, he figured out whatever compromise he needed to make with himself and we
walked out together.

We found a public square behind the AFI building, with a stage
and outdoor film screen, and little tables and boutique shops.
The screen was where they would project a new Joe Strummer
documentary, *Let's Rock Again!*, and All the Pretty Horses would
perform after that. The square initially seemed attractive, but
something about it felt as stiff and uncomfortable as a wrought
iron garden bench. I could imagine Stepford Wives congregat-
ing there to drink zero-calorie sparkling water out of wine gob-
lets. The cafés catered to more of a business community, and
now they were between hours, not serving lunch or dinner. We
searched briefly for a cozy restaurant, then went back to the Festival Central lobby so I could eat something. Steve miraculously
managed to not get sucked into band business.

An hour or two later, we sat together watching the movie in
the square, and then went back to the lobby so Steve could set
up for the band performance. Usually in this sort of scenario,
Steve would have fidgeted in a distracted state the entire afternoon, but he managed to quell himself this time. I was impressed. A reception followed the performance with the usual
festival talk and schmooze.

The next evening they screened *Venus of Mars*. We settled
into velvety rust-colored chairs and watched the images of
our lives roll by. I was getting used to this. It was like watching a well-produced home movie. I found myself wanting to
see more of what had been left on the cutting-room floor, like
many of the scenes of us riding. The fleeting barn scenes remained my favorites, maybe because it was just the two of us
enjoying something unencumbered by audience and stage.
The frames that flickered on the screen already made me feel
nostalgic for those times.

After the roar of applause, we took our seats for the Q&A. We agreed that Steve would step in quickly to field the awkward questions about why we didn't have children, so it felt good to talk about our story. That trip was the beginning of several film-festival trips we participated in together, if the festival wasn't held when I was teaching and was willing to pay my airfare. We flew home together, determined that we would do better at letting each other feel loved and appreciated.

The film no doubt reinforced our equilibrium. It provided validation we were indeed a couple to the world. I had been so maddened by our individual incidents and emergencies, things like an unexpected credit card bill in the mailbox or Steve's scheduling a show when we had our own tickets for a concert, that I hadn't recognized the role the atmosphere around us played as it reinforced or undermined our relationship.

The perceptions of the people around us affected me differently than Steve. I saw it as a frustrating stumbling block we could work past. When Steve didn't want to do something I thought would be a given in any other committed relationship, like holding my hand or linking arms, I felt it. He wouldn't tell me why— too caught up in his own feelings of paranoia to explain. He must have worried he'd be read as something, but what? If it was as a woman, that would make us two lesbians; if it was as a man, perhaps that would hurt too much. Perhaps he was too afraid that someone would yell at us. Whatever the reason, the result was that I'd feel hurt, as if the terms between us had suddenly changed and I was no longer allowed to feel or act affectionately. It always sparked a fight. We'd even had marriage counselors who didn't understand why we wanted to be together.

There were people who accepted and supported my spouse as trans, but that didn't necessarily mean they saw us as a couple. Sometimes they thought that since Steve was trans, he was promiscuous—a stereotype neither of us was aware of until we started to run into people who came onto him, expecting that he was. One fan in New York, after he realized we were seriously together, mailed us a book called *Open Marriage: A New Life Style for Couples*. We laughed—it was so completely opposite of what either of us wanted. Steve called him to relay how much we'd enjoyed the gag gift, then discovered it wasn't a gag. It was a serious proposal, which Steve emphatically declined.

It's possible that some of the people supportive of Steve saw me as a relic of his previous life, and now that he'd come out as trans, it was just a matter of time before he cast me aside like a piece of outgrown clothing. Maybe that's what Pandora thought would happen. That perception may have grown as more people began to call him Venus and referred to him with she/her pronouns. They didn't understand why I still called him Steve. At the time, I knew only that "Steve" named someone I felt close to, whereas "Venus" was attached to an unhealed wound. So I would ask again if it was okay to call him Steve.

The truth was that not only did the person I love not completely identify as female at that time, but also I didn't know where I stood in the relationship if that person *did* become fully identified as female. The word "husband" to define Steve was already problematic, but the word "wife" didn't fit his role in our relationship, either. "Spouse" felt like a cold, clinical term. It's the word I use now, but it would take me many years—not until the Supreme Court made same-sex marriage legal in 2015—before I felt truly comfortable using that term.

When the documentary about Venus was made, the trans community was just beginning to be more visible. The word "deadname"—the name given to someone at birth instead of the name they'd chosen in their new, genuine identity—was not in use, but the concept definitely existed. If someone asked me about it, I explained that the Venus name had a different history, and that Venus said it was okay for me to use the male name. Yet there was also ambivalence. When people asked which pronoun was preferred, Steve/Venus wouldn't tell them one or the other, preferring *no* pronoun.

Somewhere along the line, he began to wish I would call

him Venus and use she/her pronouns. But he was afraid to tell me, fearing that I would leave.

I wish he had asked. I never threatened to leave over any of these changes. But whenever we'd gone through major milestones in Steve's/Venus's journey of self-discovery, like cross-dressing, going out publicly, wearing full makeup every day, and hormones, I would usually answer my beloved's queries honestly. If asked how I was going to feel about some kind of change, I'd say I didn't know how I'd feel until after it happened. I had no prior experience. I was making it up, playing jazz. With no role models for either of us, our behavior was analogous to free jazz, a style that broke down conventional forms.

In the meantime, I had tried running a couple of other names past him—names I could use that, to me, conveyed more intimacy than "Venus." One was "Stevie," which he didn't like at all. He liked the other possibility, "V," but we had a friend who went by V, and it would have been too confusing.

I don't know why I didn't consider using she/her pronouns without calling her Venus. It's possible it was one last vestige of something old that I was trying to hang on to, but it seems odd to cling to a pronoun. For most of this time, I saw Venus as fairly gender-fluid, and while *I* never presented that way (remember: I was very disappointed with my appearance as "Lars"), I was often angered when stereotyped as female. This is why I liked camp and anything else that functioned as a poke in the eye against gender stereotypes.

It would be another fourteen years before Venus asked me to call her Venus—in the context of saying she wanted to have a legal gender and name change. That's when I began using Venus as a *real* name. By then, most of her stagy, distancing behaviors had disappeared. We had a new history of collaborating. Learning to use the new name would turn out to be much easier than I had once thought.

■■■

But because this was the turning point to get us to that place, gentle reader, here is where in the narrative I begin using the name Venus and she/her pronouns for her.

■■■

In the story of the Goose Girl, only a little magic from the young woman's previous life stays with her. Her talking horse, Falada, can still speak and remind her of her past and what she was destined to do. She still has the power to charm the wind and have it sweep away the unwelcome suitor's hat. She's good at tending geese. In short, she does pretty well in the natural, animal world. It's the *people* she has problems with. I can relate. Aligning my life with someone who wasn't sure who they were, who often had sudden mood swings, was difficult.

The king, whose son was supposed to marry the Goose Girl, seems to be an unusually wise person. He knows that something curious in his kingdom—a lowly girl able to make the wind do her bidding—requires further investigation. But because of her promise to not tell a living soul, she can't tell her story to him directly.

By this point, I was freed from any earlier promises to not do anything that might upset band members. So why was I still hesitant to talk about my own experience? I know at least part of the problem was that our story felt unsettled, unfinished. It seemed that every few years Venus would have some new crisis, and we'd have to make more adjustments. They weren't all gender-related. But a bigger part of the problem was mine: I had lost confidence in how people saw me.

Yet things began to get better after the release of *Venus of Mars*. The Goose Girl has to tell the truth into the dark, sooty stovepipe, a conductor of secret information with no visible listener on the other side. It's a little like telling a story to the inside of a camera. Maybe Emily Goldberg, as she started filming the story of a transgender punk rocker, decided to investigate something curious, something she hadn't expected to see in the story: that Venus and I were partners in nearly everything we did, people who deeply loved each other.

I think the film acted as a kind of stovepipe for us, telling anyone willing to watch and listen that we loved each other and that we were indeed a couple. It began to free us from some of the assumptions we'd faced for years: that Venus was willing to sleep with anyone, that our marriage was loveless, that we'd break up soon. It's even more interesting that Emily saw something between us that *we* didn't completely see ourselves. We were too close to our own lives to see the larger pattern, too absorbed by daily distractions and struggles, too often discouraged by setbacks. Maybe we'd even subconsciously mirrored those negative assumptions and forgotten the things that brought us together in the first place.

As *Venus of Mars* began to appear at film festivals around the country, it seemed that more and more people recognized and honored our relationship. Obviously, there were many who wouldn't see the film; we still ran into people who tried to interfere in some way when they saw us together. But no one would denigrate us for kissing or holding hands after watching that film. The acceptance we felt when we were together after a screening, maybe after having done a Q&A session, helped stabilize any continuing wobbles.

In November, just five months after the screening at Silverdocs, the film had its Twin Cities premiere at the Oak Street Cinema, a small, classic-revival house near the University of Minnesota. The movie had gotten a lot of local media attention—more than what usually happened for All the Pretty Horses—and the theater was packed. A warm cheer of applause rose at the end of the film. It felt good. It didn't feel as if the people in the audience were cheering just for the film. It felt as if they were cheering for our relationship.

34

■ ★ ▲ ★ ✳ ■ ▲ ● ■

2006, Phoenix and Bisbee, Arizona

About a year later, one sunny autumn day, Venus answered a call from an unfamiliar number. Someone unknown to us, a man named Scott Pierce, wanted to invite us to his gallery in Phoenix, Arizona, for a showing of *Venus of Mars*. He explained that the gallery, Soul Invictus, was a collective of alternative and queer artists, and that he wanted to exhibit Venus's eight-by-twelve-foot paintings as well as host a few performances. The gallery would pay our airfare, shipping costs, and the screening fee for the film, which went to Emily Goldberg. We could stay with Paul Tibbles, Scott's partner and another member of the collective. We debated putting ourselves in the hands of a stranger, especially at such a distance in a town where we had no other connections. Still, we'd become friends with a few people who were initially internet acquaintances, and none had turned out to be ax murderers. Venus asked a few more questions, and a conversation began.

I wondered what kind of name Soul Invictus was. I looked the phrase up online (the gallery itself didn't have a web page yet). Duh! It was a reference to William Ernest Henley's 1875 poem "Invictus" that ends, "I am the master of my fate: / I am

Brunch with Paul Tibbles and Venus, Phoenix, 2006

the captain of my soul." I had heard the lines often enough, but the poem isn't part of the academic canon. Now I read the lines more carefully. They were about struggling against the odds: "Out of the night that covers me, / Black as the pit from pole to pole, / I thank whatever gods may be / For my unconquerable soul." I liked that.

After the initial phone call, emails floated back and forth between Venus and Scott, and the plan was eventually set. Vénus would fly out there a week ahead of me to put up the art and teach a band in Phoenix enough songs to back her for a show Friday night, sometime after the film screening. We would also do a post-film Q&A, then I'd read some poems. The following night Venus would do a solo set at a nearby coffeehouse, and we'd break it up and extend it between poetry and music. Then we'd have the rest of spring break to hang out in Phoenix's warm weather.

Things still weren't perfect between us, but our balance seemed better. The band was doing a lot of regional touring, most of which I wasn't able to join, and I still missed Venus when she was gone. But there wasn't anyone in the band she seemed smitten with anymore. In fact, when she said anything about the other band members, it was often a complaint. She couldn't get into any kind of groove with them to write new songs, and it bothered her. Also, the new bass player had booked several gigs at smaller places for less pay than they used to get. Word of this got around, and the band couldn't get a guarantee as large as what they used to get. It was the beginning of the end for that line-up.

■■■

By the time Venus got the phone call offering us the chance to travel to Phoenix, we'd already experienced traveling together happily without the band. We visited Iona, a tiny one-by-three-mile island in the Scottish Hebrides, with a large group of people from my church. We attended a commitment ceremony on Martha's Vineyard between Tamsan, one of my college roommates, and her intended, Rock and Roll Rick, whose band played. And we returned to New York for an anniversary, enjoying an opera in Central Park and standing in awe as we watched fireflies mysteriously gliding from one place to another in Madison Square Park. We had arguments—including a brief yelling match on Iona, when Venus walked too fast and lost me on a walk through a hilly network of paths through high bushes—but we recovered from them quickly.

Also, while we learned earlier that music collaboration wasn't very satisfying for either of us, performing together seemed to work if we did a back-and-forth arrangement we called the tag team. It started when I was reading as part of a line-up in a bar, gallery, or someone's warehouse space. Often the performers included musicians playing a song or two. Everyone I knew in the poetry world welcomed Venus playing a song or two, sometimes even a half-hour solo set if time allowed.

But the real breakthrough came when some friends started a reading series at a short-lived bookstore and coffee shop called Marysburg Books, just around the corner from Venus's Colonial Warehouse studio in the Warehouse District. The place was mostly a coffee shop, with a long wooden counter and high windows that looked out onto Washington Avenue. JoAnne and Susan wanted to feature us as a reader and a musician for their series. It was clear Venus could hold an audience with music, but how could I avoid coming across as the dull one? I was especially concerned that my reading would seem too long. We decided to do quick mini sets back and forth, performing about ten minutes at a stretch. It was fun, not just for us but also for the audience as we bantered back and forth in mock competition. We felt like a normal couple working together on something.

The Soul Invictus trip initially worked according to the plan. Venus called when she arrived in Phoenix and assured me that Scotty and Paul were wonderful people. I would love them. I would also love the weather, which was about forty degrees warmer, a far cry from Minnesota's late February climate of ice and snowdrifts.

I arrived a few hours before the art opening and performance with just enough time to drop my suitcase at Paul's. His house wasn't what I expected at all. I had imagined a place in Phoenix would be dry and sunny, a spread-out ranch-style home, mostly patio, but this was a tiny bungalow, part of a four-house community on a shady street lined with towering palms and lush, green lawns. Not far from the front door stood a huge orange tree, maybe thirty feet tall. It was covered with oranges. Venus saw me gazing at it.

"The oranges are ripe," she said with a smile.

Paul showed me the tool they used to get the fruit off the tree—a long pole with a basket at the end of it. He stuck it into the branches, jostled a few oranges loose, and offered one. I took it and sniffed its pungent aroma in amazement. Then we went inside where Paul cut up the oranges.

This particular night was the First Fridays gallery crawl in Phoenix, so many people came and went. I kicked it off with my poems, introductory, funny, and all related to our relationship. The film rolled, wild applause went up at the finish, and we spent about half an hour answering the questions that followed the film. Then it was time for rock and roll.

Venus worried she'd lose her voice before the show ended due to a very sore throat. But her voice lasted through the performance and also the many conversations her new fans struck up with her. When it was finally time to close down the gallery, we were happy but tired and ready for sleep.

The next morning I awoke to the sound of birds unlike anything in Minnesota. Phoenix felt like a completely different world, someplace tropical. Occasionally I heard the high-pitched "Help! Help!" sound I thought might be a peacock.

"Yeah," Paul confirmed as we sat on the patio sipping coffee and nibbling fresh-picked oranges, "there's a neighbor who has some a block over. They're really irritating."

"No!" I protested. "It must be amazing having them around. They're so beautiful!" Paul shook his head.

"Yeah, but you don't want them in your neighborhood," he explained. "They just walk down the street like they own it. They block traffic. There must be about seven of them now."

An hour or two later, Venus's sore throat was still uncomfortable, and she had a fever. By midafternoon, the diagnosis came back: strep. We picked up some antibiotics, but they wouldn't heal her immediately. She couldn't do a show that night.

"Can you do it?" Scotty asked anxiously, turning to me. "I think we could get Namoli to do some music. She's down in Bisbee with my friend Wendy. They could maybe come up here." I wondered who Namoli and Wendy were, but I'd heard of Bisbee. It was a funny-sounding name to me: BIZ-bee.

"Yes, absolutely." I was lying. I worried about the reaction of a crowd of people expecting to see Venus perform and getting me reading poetry instead. But I didn't want to let them down. I wouldn't have the tag-team style to change it up and keep things interesting. But I'd figure out how to make it work.

That evening the four of us went to the coffeehouse. Venus would make the announcement that she was too ill to perform, then she would stay long enough to hear my set. Paul would drive her home so she could go back to bed, and Paul would come back to hear the rest of Namoli's set. As I stood on the stage looking down at Venus, all fuzzy and feverish, I worried about her. I'd planned to read the funnier and edgier poems to keep it interesting, but that seemed wrong now. I decided instead to read love poems and silently prayed that the meds were really going to heal her. The audience seemed to like the love poems. I gave them little stories about the background of the pieces, and they laughed at my jokes. Then Paul drove Venus home, and I went back to the table to sit with Scotty and watch Namoli's set.

The next morning, everyone was back for a Sunday brunch on the back patio slab. New people were there, a trans woman and her wife, and also Namoli and Wendy, who was helping Namoli with tour dates. Paul made mouthwatering French toast with thick slabs of brioche, and everyone got mildly hammered on mimosas made with fresh-squeezed oranges from the tree. Venus was still spongy but feeling remarkably better.

"You guys have to all come down to Bisbee!" Wendy said.

She was a short, high-energy woman with butch-short brown hair and lots of tan.

"Bisbee?" I asked. That name again. A poet/grad student I'd dated briefly in my earlier Duluth years had mentioned a friend of his was involved in an artist community in the weirdly named town of Bisbee, Arizona.

"You guys should all drive down there," Wendy said, issuing the challenge. I looked at Venus. She shrugged.

"Well, maybe . . ." I wanted to go, but I worried about Venus's health.

"Sure," she said. I decided to talk with her privately to make sure she was really feeling that much better. It seemed too much of a miracle that the antibiotics had kicked in that fast.

"Have another piece of French toast," Paul said. Then we all started planning the trip to Bisbee.

Bisbee was four hours south of Phoenix, so this wouldn't be a day trip. Wendy had a microscopic house there and couldn't accommodate guests. Bisbee had been a mining town, and many of the homes in the old part of town reflected the mining lifestyle of subsistence housing at the turn of the century. Paul went on his computer and found a hotel where we could stay, he and Scotty in one room, Venus and I in another. Another important detail: they would drive us there.

A few days later we drove south from Phoenix, past Tucson (the halfway point), and eventually turned off the interstate to head toward Tombstone, peering at the Boot Hill and O.K. Corral advertisements as we drove through. Finally, after what seemed like eons and a slow, imperceptible ascent up the hills, we were moving downhill, and the road tapered. The car slowed and nosed its way into the narrow, curving streets of the town.

Small, rectangular houses stacked like shoeboxes lined the canyon roads on the hillside opposite us. We drove past a 1930s-style, copper-colored statue of a tall, well-muscled man. He casually held a hammer in his hand.

The hotel was on an uphill swing away from the narrow downtown junction by a few blocks. The buildings and streets clung to the sides of various steep inclines, sometimes with narrow sets of stairs between them to connect a sort of winding, terraced arrangement for pedestrians. I've always liked mazy streets and the mysterious, nearly secret passageways between them. I loved that about Venice and the meandering, scrub-brush paths of Iona. It's what I experience every time I go into the woods and encounter a network of paths: the joy of finding how things are connected.

Wendy wanted us to come with her to meet Gretchen Baer, a painter with a funky gallery nearby. We went down a long, narrow set of stairs across from the hotel, around a few turns past some old, large buildings that may have once had a more industrial use but now seemed to be bars and restaurants. We found ourselves on Brewery Avenue in front of a storefront with generous front windows that had the name of Gretchen's El-Change-O! Gallery painted in grand, almost cartoonish strokes across the top of the façade. The art inside—Gretchen's paintings on the walls—was similarly energetic, in bright colors that displayed a serious irreverence for the standard way of seeing things. It reminded me of how I'd felt when I first walked into the Carlton Arms in New York, a sense that this was where I belonged.

Gretchen radiated the same kind of vital energy that her art conveyed. She was involved in several projects in town beyond the gallery and seemed to be on a mission to save the world through art in a manner that seemed genuine and not at all ego-driven. She had grown up on Martha's Vineyard and started making art there, being part of the year-round population. Then she found her way to Bisbee: on the surface a radically different place, but in some strange manner also similar. Maybe it's the artsy, kooky, small-town vibe. Maybe it's the island mentality, a small enclave in the middle of a lovely vastness.

I started to tell her about our recent visit to Tamsan's place

El-Change-O!, Bisbee, 2006

on Martha's Vineyard. "Her partner's name is Rick," I continued. "A lot of people know him as Rock and Roll Rick."

Gretchen's mouth gaped open. "Rick?!?" she said in disbe-
lief. "He's one of my best friends! And I know Tamsan, too!"

All three of us started laughing at the karmic craziness of
that, to find a slender East Coast connection traversing the
continent to a tiny town near the Mexican border, something
a quantum physics nerd would call spooky action at a distance.

We made return trips to both Phoenix and Bisbee, and
Gretchen began to book Venus for gigs there. The joyful creative
energy of this community helped us heal some of the broken
things in our relationship. At one point, she set up a show for us
doing a tag-team poetry reading and musical performance that

morphed into performance art, thanks to Gretchen: she put a divan on the stage with a throw, a lamp, and a rug. She called it "Venus's Boudoir." Dozens of sock monkeys, custom-sewn with various punk and drag costumes, lined the front of the stage. There may have even been a Venus de Mars sock monkey. Venus, wearing the full performance costume of corset, fishnets, and thigh-high stilettos, leaned back on the couch looking drowsy while I stood at the mic to read a few poems. I don't remember what I wore, probably some type of black and shiny clubwear, platform boots, and high, anime-style pigtails. I finished my segment, looked over to Venus, and nodded, "Your turn, honey." She got up, still a little sleepy, stretched a bit, and walked over to the guitar. I flopped onto the divan with pretty much the same blasé attitude. "Okay, go ahead," I prompted, hand motioning to go forward. "I'm waiting."

"Okay, I'm getting to it," Venus responded, and then played a couple of songs. She stopped after the second one and turned back to me. "Can I play another?"

"No! It's my turn to read again! Give me a chance at the mic!" The crowd laughed.

"Oh, *all right*," she teased.

It went back and forth like that a few more rounds. It was fun. Or maybe I should say it was better than fun: it was exhilarating. We hadn't planned it at all. We just fell into it, certainly inspired at least in part by Gretchen's set. It felt wonderful to collaborate.

When I began to find my poetry community a few years earlier, I discovered that the conversational timing of jazz I'd understood as a teenager stayed with me. Perhaps that's why I enjoyed creating conversations by interviewing writers for KFAI. I sat with friends in a bar writing exquisite corpse poems or sestina variations and then we unfurled them for a summary performance. I delighted in reading poems simultaneously with other people, exchanging lines, anything to mess up the normal expectation of a reading. But I didn't want to turn it into noise. I kept calibrating toward something where the melody of words could still be heard, could still be followed and understood. It seems that collaboration essentially *is* my art form.

■■■

In our most frustrating arguments, whenever Venus asked "What can I *do*?" in that impassioned tone, the tone that told me she was really trying but completely missing the mark, I also missed the mark and couldn't express what was wrong in our relationship. Venus was asking for a list of items she could check off. I wanted a life collaborator, someone who could respond to the weird little nodes of my experience and take the conversation further. Perhaps that's why her journey in gender expression, though hard for me to follow, was not as distressing as simply being unheard.

In Arizona, I began to feel the kind of collaborative interplay I had sensed we had in the early years of our relationship, before things began to go off track with categories and compartmentalization. I began to feel free.

35

■×▲✦✳■ʌ●×

2006, Tui, Spain

Shortly before we went to Arizona, Venus decided the band should go on hiatus. She thought it would be easier and less confrontational than just firing the people she didn't want to work with. She sent out an email announcing the band's hiatus. I had misgivings about putting it that way—every other local band announcing a hiatus never started up again. It would be better to get new musicians and keep the name going. But I couldn't persuade her. She embarked on a series of farewell shows with the current line-up.

A documentary film festival in northwestern Spain wanted to feature the film and fly the core band members there to perform, so that would be the last official Horses gig. The festival also flew Emily Goldberg and me there, and Emily's boyfriend, Chris, joined us. Angel Sanchez, one of the two principal organizers, whisked Emily, Venus, and me from the airport to the main festival venue for an on-the-spot television interview. The other principal organizer, Sara Garcia Villanueva, translated for us. Then they ferried us all to dinner at a nearby winery, where we sat at a long, rustic table cocooned by stone walls and talked late into the night with other filmmakers, people from all over the world.

Tui, in the Galicia district of Spain, is on the Camino de San-

Sara Garcia Villanueva, Lynette, Venus, and Emily Goldberg being interviewed in Tui, Spain, 2006

tiago pilgrimage route. Statues and other signs mark the path for travelers with scallop shells. I also learned that Tui was infused with Celtic culture. Who knew the Celts had made it to Spain? Being there felt like I was in an English or Irish medieval town, but with palm trees. The town wound around a central hill, with stone buildings, cobblestone streets, and alleys that connected everything. A large church reminiscent of a cathedral stood at the crown. The town center vibrated with small restaurants and shops, but just a few blocks away, the countryside began. From our third-floor hotel window, I could see a horse in a pasture just across the creek.

While I was falling hard in love with the festival and town, Venus's emotions were more mixed. Jendeen and Tempest (the bass player who replaced Eden) weren't happy about the hiatus idea. On the New Zealand trip, they'd become a couple; they represented a unified force, and Venus couldn't figure out how to work with this. In Tui, they didn't hang around us. I'm not

Venus in a greenroom on tour

even sure they attended the film screening. Venus seemed apprehensive about how they would interact with her during the last performance.

Emily Goldberg had told us they made a version of *Venus of Mars* with Spanish subtitles, so as we sat in the dark theater watching the film, we checked the translations. In one scene Venus rolls on the living room floor, hugs one of our cats, and says, "Eliza kitty." The translation was "*Eliza gatito*"—*gato* for cat and the "*ito*" the logical diminutive. That was sweet. But in another scene, Venus sings the word "Slice" in a shot of the band playing "God Dog," and the word "Vagina" popped onto the screen. We both shot a look at Emily, who was shoving her fist in her mouth to control her laughter. It wasn't what the lyrics meant!

Yet it wasn't hard to understand why that mistranslation happened, and possibly, in a strange way, the translator had the right idea. Many of Venus's songs have had direct or oblique references to slicing, cutting, going cold, or feeling numb, all circling around the idea of suicide, all part of her struggle of being transgender. Many years later, she would decide that she wanted to have a vagina, but at the time, when the word popped up on the screen, it felt like a wildly unexpected punch line. It felt good to look down the row and laugh. But it might have been nervous laughter. No one wants their genitalia referred to as a slice.

The next day, the day of the performance, Venus was noticeably tenser. She turned on the energy for social gatherings over lunch or dinner, but when there weren't a lot of people around, she would get quiet and sad. Jendeen and Tempest had spent most of the time in their hotel room. Though Venus didn't talk about it being their last show, I'm sure she felt the gloomy weight of it.

Her concerns deepened in the afternoon when we entered the large nightclub where they were headlining. The poster outside was big and splashy: a provocative shot of Venus, her hair tightened in high blond pigtails, glaring at the camera in her fishnets, the shiny thigh-highs, corset, black vinyl bra, and metal-studded thong. This filled up most of the left half of the poster. Written information shouted next to it, "All the Pretty Horses, Minneapolis, *acompañan ao documental* 'Venus of Mars'" in big block letters. Inside, the room was similarly huge, easily big enough for a thousand people or more. As we

Venus in front of concert posters, Tui, Spain, 2006

pushed the equipment toward the stage, Venus couldn't imagine they would get a crowd large enough to make the room feel full.

The doors opened at 10:00 P.M., and it was still very empty. Venus's concerns grew. We were at the tech booth with Calpurnio Pisón, who was getting his live veejay projections ready. He was a well-known cartoonist in Spain, famous for the character "Cutlass."

"No, no, it's okay," Calpur said. "It's a late-night crowd.

They'll all come later." It was hard to imagine this. The town itself wasn't large.

As Calpur predicted, the club *did* fill, probably about half an hour after the local deejays began. Then the band members came onstage, Jendeen first, adjusting her drums to great applause, followed by Venus, then Tempest. Venus looked back at Jendeen, who clicked her sticks to set the tempo, Tempest thrummed the first bass notes, and they launched in full bore. The crowd loved it from start to end and swarmed them afterward for autographs, wanting to talk to band members about their own individual stories. I was relieved that it had come to a happy ending, and Venus seemed delighted, too.

When the last fans left, it was time to go somewhere else to celebrate. Emily and Chris wanted to go to a late-night dance club, so we did that for a while, lining up along a stainless steel bar and sharing things we'd observed in the evening. Eventually Emily and Chris moved on to another nightclub while Venus and I remained, watching the dancers spinning on the floor, occasionally remarking on what we liked or didn't like about someone's style.

But now, even though the show had been a success, Venus began to grow restless again and couldn't articulate why. She'd been smiling and energized when the fans came to the stage eager to talk or have her sign parts of their bodies—that happened sometimes. One woman in England had her sign "Venus" across her breasts.

As usual, I'd hoped to go back to the hotel and have some private time with Venus, but she wanted to stay out and distract herself with other people. She wouldn't look me in the eyes or listen when I spoke to her. Instead, she craned her neck around to look at everyone else in the room. The dynamic was all too familiar—and maddening. I said I could go back by myself, leaving her to do whatever she wanted, but she didn't want that, either. She felt responsible for me. She reluctantly decided to leave with me.

Back at the hotel, we kept quarreling, but it didn't have the drama of some of our previous fights. For some reason, this time I knew we probably wouldn't break up over it. I still didn't know where I stood with her, but I was too tired of drama to participate. I just wanted to take care of myself and sleep. Venus grumpily crawled into bed after me.

An hour or two later, someone knocked at the door. It was Emily. She and Chris had experienced pretty much the same difference of opinion, but they hadn't argued. Instead, they mutually agreed to do two different things. Emily had gone back to the hotel, while Chris stayed out to party with others from the film festival. But it had been hours since he'd left, and Chris still wasn't back. Emily was worried and wanted to know if we'd help find him.

■ ■ ■

There's a short story by the Argentinian writer Jorge Luis Borges called "The Garden of Forking Paths." At the nexus of the tale we learn that a strange, incomprehensible novel and a labyrinth the novelist was trying to create are in fact the same thing. The novel within the story is described as difficult to understand because it is not written like a normal book, where characters make choices and can't go back to unmake those choices. In this imaginary novel, the characters still make choices, travelers encounter forking paths, but instead of just going left or right, the travelers take both paths, which then lead to a myriad of other branches. It's a little like what I experienced wandering the narrow pathways of Iona, where I'd gotten lost, where I might have also eventually crossed paths with Venus if I had kept going. It's a little like moving back and forth between parallel universes, where the other possibilities still exist.

I'd started admiring Borges sometime while I was in college striving to learn everything I could to be a poet and thinker. I don't know how I heard of him before he came to campus—his work wasn't taught in any of my courses. I'm not even sure who brought him to campus, though it might have been the Spanish professor Patrick Dust. "Señor Dust" had previously organized a vanload of us to ride up to Minneapolis from Northfield to see the famous post-structuralist Jacques Derrida lecture at the University of Minnesota. The odd thing about my memory of Derrida is I only remember what he looked like, gesturing from a podium in Coffman Union, his raffish white-gray hair catching the light, but not what he said. A friend of mine later pointed out that since this was in 1979, Derrida didn't know English well enough to lecture in it, so someone else would have translated as he spoke.

My admiration of Borges might have had something to do with the *New York Review of Books* that I picked up from the campus bookstore every week, with its distinctive line drawings. I didn't know who any of the writers listed in bold headlines on the cover were, but I liked the ring of their names: V. S. Naipaul, Czesław Miłosz, Elizabeth Hardwick. That same year, 1981, I would drive with a poet friend to see Miłosz speak at nearby Gustavus Adolphus College. But I liked Borges better because his writing was so mysterious, an intellectual Möbius strip filled with images and lyricism.

■■■

Now, in Tui, I was struck by how similar our situations were to Borges's forking paths. Emily and Chris essentially had the same disagreement Venus and I did, but they hadn't argued about it. Instead, they'd agreed to follow their own separate impulses. At the time, it seemed the better decision. In contrast, when Venus and I approached that forking path, we argued and went back to the hotel fuming. It seemed like a worse decision at the time. A few hours later, though, we were together and felt relatively secure, whereas Emily had become very worried. Perhaps we'd ended up with the better outcome after all.

Venus on the Ponte Rodo-Ferroviária de Valença, designed by Gustave Eiffel, crossing the Miño River between Spain and Portugal, 2006

Venus immediately agreed to help Emily find Chris, but I was exhausted and still depressed about the argument we'd just finished.

"You guys can go without me," I mumbled. "I just can't. Maybe come back if you need me to help." I felt guilty saying the words, but I was too tired to be generous. I needed more time to breathe through my own oxygen mask.

Venus came back an hour later. They found Chris and he was fine, still dancing and talking with friends from the festival, having completely lost track of the time. Venus crawled into bed, happy to be back. She'd forgotten about our own argument. It wasn't as easy for me to let it go, but my gut told me it would be better to live in the peace of the moment. I could honor my own emotions without being swept away by hers.

On our last day in Spain, the four of us decided to walk across a bridge that went over the Miño River. Portugal was on the other side, according to the festival staff, so essentially we could walk there for an afternoon, two countries for the price of one. Our interest rose when we learned the bridge was designed by Gustave Eiffel, architect of the Eiffel Tower. It took about a half hour to walk from the hotel to the bridge itself, and on the other side we found what appeared to be tiered mounds of land from an old fortress. A wide, graveled path led toward it, with signs none of us could read. They didn't seem to forbid entry, so we continued. The path wound in switchbacks up the

Venus, Emily Goldberg, and Chris Kleman in the Portuguese town of Valença, 2006

tiered mounds, maybe three of them. Every once in a while I would look back at what we were climbing away from: a river. Of course. This had been a strategic defense position to protect the area from invaders, perhaps Vikings. There must have been archers, swordsmen, and who knows who else scanning the river for attackers, maybe battling for their lives on these grassy slopes. It was humbling to walk through the shadows of other people's lives.

As we crested the last mound, we found an opening in the stone wall and stepped into a different world. It was a village with streets, cafés, shops that sold knickknacks for tourists, and a little wine bar where we sat at an outdoor table, marveling at what we discovered.

If I'd been thinking about Borges, I might have reflected on how our temporarily diverging paths had eventually led the four of us to this same place where we now sat on a small patio and looked at the surrounding cobblestones, shops, and people. It was a blissful closure to our trip, a reminder of how much Venus and I liked to share adventures.

36

■★▲✦✱■ᴧ●■

2008, Wellington, New Zealand

Venus wanted to tour New Zealand again. She'd been interviewed by the New Zealand version of *20/20* on the previous
trip and had a new solo album, *Trashed and Broken-Hearted*, to
promote. Matthew and Eddy were living in Wellington now,
Eddy originally being a Kiwi. Matthew said he could find musicians to back Venus for a tour with four to six gigs up and down
the north island. Venus wondered if I'd like to go. Of course I
would. I was on sabbatical and taking online classes, so I could
travel.

Eddy and Matthew gave us a rock-and-roll welcome at the
airport, tackling us from behind and loading everything into
their small car. Their house perched on the side of a steep hill
with three small terraced yards that stepped down the ravine
below. This was typical for Wellington—houses secured to
their foundations with pilings, tin roofs the norm to accommodate the abundance of rain.

Initially, it was fun—Venus played a show and Matthew ac-
companied her on bass at a small, packed bar one of our first
nights there. Eddy and the owner tended the copper-sheathed
bar together, cheerfully ringing up customer drink orders
and topping off our own drinks. Another Wellington show
was scheduled five days later, then we'd begin to tour north,

getting as far as Auckland before heading back to Wellington. The tour north was what I longed for, the chance to feel like a hobbit journeying through the *Lord of the Rings* landscape.

I hadn't anticipated how much time Venus would spend getting the new band ready. It wasn't just the evening rehearsals. She was in 24/7 band mode again, unable to compartmentalize enough to take two or three hours away to explore or even walk around the neighborhood.

I became a solo tourist. It was late winter/early spring, a consistently gray and gusty time of year for Wellington. I wandered through the downtown streets in a cold, windy drizzle, stumbled on the houses of parliament, and discovered a literary walk around the harbor. I stopped in old churches and a cathedral. I checked to see if there was anything new to post for my online classes. I was lonely but sure the trip would be better after the Friday show. I'd studied the guidebooks, thinking that since we'd come so far I wanted to see something I wouldn't be able to find in another country. It looked as if the band tour would take us close enough to visit some famous glowworm caves near the western side of the north island.

On the day of the Friday show, I arrived with the rest of the band to help with load in and watch the sound check. Then we waited for people to show up. Finally the bartender gave the nod for the warm-up band—some of Matthew's friends—to begin. That livened things up a bit. Then Venus's band came out.

She started them off with a couple of quick guitar chords, and then they were in, playing a set that was part typical Pretty Horses songs and part songs off the new CD. The audience cheered, and a few of them bought CDs before toddling off into the night. But Venus's smiles masked a deeper tension. The gig turned out to be a financial loss for Matthew and Eddy, with fewer people attending than expected.

The postmortem discussion began before the band even played their first chord: was the cover charge too high? Was some other show in town drawing away their audience? Was

the bar a venue their friends didn't like? The discussion between Eddy and Matthew continued behind their bedroom
door once we got back to the house. We didn't realize Matthew
had spent their household money publicizing the shows, renting equipment, and more. We woke up early the next morning,
expecting to pack to tour the rest of the country, when Matthew knocked on our door. He had canceled the tour. He was
worried about how much he would spend renting a large van
and paying for the fuel to drive up north.

We were stuck in Wellington in a household with a married couple having a big argument. We needed to get out of the
house. After a day or so of local touring, some friends in Auckland invited us to fly up and stay with them. So we changed
our return tickets and spent our last three days in the country
being more like real tourists. We couldn't extend the trip itself because Venus was slated to tour the southwest with a new
band she'd created, the House of Flowers.

Strangely, the debacle drew us closer together.

Venus was genuinely apologetic. She was disappointed, too,
but that was more about the missed opportunity to play and
move her career forward. She recognized how much it upset
me to spend thousands of dollars on plane fare for the chance
to see nothing. She wanted to make it up to me. At one point
when we were still in Wellington she casually mentioned to
Eddy that I'd wanted to see the glowworms.

"Oh, there are some of those on a path at the bottom of this
park near my parents' house. At least they were there when
I was a child," he mused. "I suppose they might not be there
now." He thought a little more. "No, they're probably still
there. You'll want to take the tram up the hill, then go to the
left for several streets. . . ."

We had to look for them at night because they stop gleaming when light falls on them. It was odd wandering through
the streets of a strange residential area, and one or two people
out walking their dogs gave us suspicious looks as we passed,

recognizing us as strangers. Eddy's directions had also been a bit sketchy—he hadn't remembered all the street names. But when we saw the darkened park in front of us, we knew we were in the right place.

The moon wasn't out yet, but the stars were bright. Venus touched my arm in amazement and pointed to the sky.

"I don't recognize *any* of these stars," she said, a little concerned. I had to smile.

"Sweetie, that's because we're in the southern hemisphere. The constellations are completely different."

"Oh," she said, and let it sink in. Then she smiled at me, with that brilliant smile that said, yes, this is all so amazing, and I'm so happy to be here sharing it with you.

I'd been content *knowing* the stars would look different, but I hadn't bothered to look up at the night sky. Venus got me to lift my eyes and really *see* that unfamiliar sky.

In the park, it was hard to make out where our feet landed on the dirt path that led down the hill. One of us had a cell phone with enough light on its screen to show some of the bumpy path. Then we reached the bottom and turned left to follow another path into the woods. The glowworms were supposed to be in the soil that clung to some of the exposed tree roots on the steep hillside. As we entered the woods, we lost some of the ambient light the stars overhead had provided, but we didn't want to accidentally shine the light of the cell phone on the glowworms and have them disappear in the darkness.

By now, I was pessimistic. We'd done exactly what Eddy said, and there was no sign of them.

"Let's just go on a few more minutes," Venus said.

"Okay," I replied, resigned to another failure. Then she put her hand on my arm, signaling me to stop.

"Look. There," she said. It was difficult to see at first, and then I caught sight of something gleaming. Yes. It was a glowworm, maybe an inch and a half long, turning and undulating slightly in the wet soil of an overhanging thatch of tree roots.

And then I could see another, and another, and another. It was a whole colony of them, spread out in the muddy darkness. They looked nothing like what I'd read about in the travel articles—they didn't change color or anything like that—but then these were at the foot of a hill in a small city park, not hanging from the ceiling of a darkened cave in northwestern New Zealand. They struck me as delicate, each body moving in slow motion like the arm of a starfish, their quiet light glimmering in unexpected places.

"Oh," I said, "look at them!" Venus was pulling me farther down the path, showing me new, tiny colonies of the bluish-white creatures gently curling and elongating in the muddy bank just below eye level.

"We found them," she said, keeping her voice low, as if the sound might frighten them and make them hide.

"Yes, we found them," I said, guiding her toward me. I kissed her. "Thank you for this."

37

■⋆▲♣✦■♠•■

2008, Minneapolis

Even when I was a child, I had a problem with the Goose Girl story: when she's recognized for who she truly is and marries the prince, she doesn't use her position or magical powers to rescue Falada, the horse who believed in her all along. Falada helped her claim what was really hers, and then she forgot about him. I treasured the idea of a talking horse, and I found it appalling she wouldn't even *try* to restore him to life, or, failing that, go back to the gate and talk with him. Her story seemed incomplete, a major thread still missing.

Venus and I had invested a lot of money getting to New Zealand, only to have the tour canceled. On top of that, Venus had put thousands of dollars into creating a CD she never had the chance to sell there, and I was making less money due to the sabbatical. The household couldn't handle it financially.

I told Venus we had to get a housemate if we were going to make ends meet. I couldn't keep paying for everything all by myself. Any band income went to paying for the studio rent, and I paid all our other expenses. We'd had housemates before, and they'd gradually drifted away. When we didn't find new ones, it seemed we'd finally graduated to a level where we could have some privacy. Venus didn't want another person living with us. As someone who was trans, she felt uncomfortable inviting someone else in. I understood that, but I was adamant. We'd already refinanced the house four times to pay off at least a hundred thousand dollars in credit card debt.

With Venus on tour with House of Flowers, I resumed the patterns I'd developed as a band widow. I went out to poetry readings at night, sometimes reading with the line-up, sometimes enjoying it as an audience member. I was now a regular with the Bosso Poetry Company for once-a-month shows at Dusty's in Northeast Minneapolis. I'd developed a habit of standing near the bar, right foot propped up against the lower rung of a tall stool, and setting my wine glass next to my folder of poems to sketch an invisible perimeter around my spot near the center. One night, I was talking to fellow poet Scott Vetsch. I'd been reading with him since the open-mic days at Kieran's in downtown Minneapolis. In previous conversations, we discovered we'd just missed meeting each other at Carleton, where he'd dated someone on campus, and at the U, where he'd gone to some of the poetry events I organized.

"New Zealand was amazing," I said, "but the tour got canceled one day in." I shook my head. No one would want to hear details of our financial woes. "We lost a lot of money," I mused. "I think we're going to need to get a housemate to get back on track." Scott was sympathetic. He knew about money problems.

"Hey," he said. "I've got an idea. Winona's got this friend who needs a place to live. He's really cool. I think you'd like him." Winona was Scott's teenage daughter, still in high school, rebellious as hell, but a good kid with a loving and creative heart. "It's a friend of Winona's from South High who's in the class ahead of her. He just graduated, and he came out to his mom as gay. They had a huge argument, and now he's living with various friends. No one for very long." He'd stayed with Scott and Winona a few nights and was currently with another friend, but that friend's mother was getting tired of it and wanted him out.

"I already told you about him—remember, last winter when

you wanted Winona and her high school friends to read poetry on *Write On! Radio*, and she suggested someone else? That was Anthony." I remembered. I had been dubious of the substitution at that time, so I'd asked Scott about him.

"Oh, I think you'd like him," Scott had said. "He's a cool kid."

"What's cool about him?"

"Well, he doesn't dress the way the other kids do. He's all in black. I guess you'd call it goth." Scott had thought a little more. "I've seen him walking to school, and he has an interesting way of walking, really deliberate."

So I'd called Anthony. He was flattered to be invited to read his poetry on a radio show but felt nervous. I didn't realize at the time how shy he was, and he ended up declining the invitation.

Now I needed a housemate. But an eighteen-year-old? I appreciated his problem. Several of my students, not to mention friends, had done unpleasant stints of couch-surfing. If Venus was concerned about having a housemate insensitive to her trans identity, maybe a young, gay man would allay those fears.

"Hmm," I said, reluctant to commit.

"You'll meet him at my party," Scott offered.

Scott often had big parties in the fall, usually near his October birthday, just when the weather was right for bonfires. Although his house was on a regular city lot, being there felt almost like being back in the country—the lot went deep, and he had a broad backyard, a vegetable and berry garden, and a large fire pit. And plenty of beer. I raised the formality level slightly every time I brought over a box of cheap wine.

So Scott made the introduction, maybe a week later, as each of us nervously sipped our Leinenkugels on the low deck off Scott's kitchen. As predicted, Anthony was impossibly thin and dressed entirely in black. He wore some makeup and had enameled his long fingernails with dark polish. He was a first-generation descendent of the Mille Lacs Band of Ojibwe from his mother's side and Latinx from his father's side. His full, black hair fell several inches below his shoulders.

I don't remember what we talked about. I think I asked him where he worked and was relieved to find he had a job at a pizza place. Good. I could depend on him for rent. I told him what the room was like—we were in the midst of repairing water damage to the ceiling, so there were some squares of unfinished drywall that still had to be mudded and painted. Oh, not a problem, he beamed. He'd be happy with it just as it was. I wasn't surprised to hear this. I remembered my summer in New York, feeling like an intruder.

I told Anthony a little about Venus and me. I had to be serious on one point. "Because Venus never wants to be arrested and locked up in a men's holding cell, we can't have anything illegal going on under our roof. That includes underage drinking"—I nodded to our bottles of Leinie—"and smoking pot."

Anthony completely agreed. He was gracious and honest— it felt right. I told him he could move in whenever he wanted, which turned out to be two days later.

The morning after the party, I called Venus. They'd already played in Bisbee and were starting on their way back north. I told her we had a new housemate.

"What?!"

"I told you, we need a housemate. You haven't been able to bring in any money. We need the money to pay our bills."

"But don't I get a say in this? Don't I get to talk to him?"

I knew she would be upset, and her anger was justified. But I had felt so sorry for Anthony.

"I know I should have waited before saying yes. And I *would* have waited, but he really needs a place right now." I heard a long exhale on the other end of the line.

"Okay," she said. "I don't feel good about this, but we'll see."

I was sure Venus would like him. When Venus arrived home a few days later, she found she did.

In the meantime, I'd driven Anthony to the fourplex about two miles away where his mother lived. Someone had to supervise him while he moved—I'm not even sure if his mother was there—so I waited in the car as he went back and forth, bringing out plastic bags of clothing, books, and CDs. He had never owned a suitcase. His father had died when he was just a baby, and his mother raised him alone; he'd grown up in poverty. He had an ancient PC with a bulky drive unit and separate monitor that a sympathetic high school teacher had given him. Anthony was worried that because it was so old, moving it would make it impossible for him to transfer the files to something else. His writing was important to him even then.

When we got back to our house on Portland Avenue, we both breathed a sigh of relief. The computer worked. I had a spare bed, dresser, and bookcase for him. I found a kitchen cupboard where he could store food, though most of what he ate at that point was what he got working at the pizza place. I couldn't give him much else. I was fascinated to find that in addition to writing and drawing, he was taking singing lessons from a semiretired music teacher who didn't charge for the lessons. More important, Anthony had a high school friend he talked with often—Sasha, a one-time girlfriend turned lifelong friend who had been the first person he came out to. She was already attending a community college in downtown Minneapolis. In another year, he would summon the courage to follow in her footsteps. Eventually she would earn her doctorate in American studies, encouraging Anthony to also continue in graduate school.

■■■

Perhaps something from my childhood primed me to embrace the idea of intentional families. When I was in my early teens, my mother invited John Matthews, a stout, elderly man from church, to have Christmas dinner with us. He brimmed with gossipy stories about Duluth's elite families in the 1920s and 1930s and peppered his banter with expressions like "Drop-kick me, Jesus, through the goalposts of life." My mother cringed at every tale he told, but the holidays when Mr. Matthews held forth at the table burst with a new energy. He revived my dream of what family holiday dinners *could* be, something we lost when my older siblings moved away. Some of my friends met Mr. Matthews, and by the time I was in college a few of them drove him to Northfield for a rowdy student banquet in his honor. They persuaded Carleton to let him stay in a room reserved for special visitors, saying he was a potential donor. He was penniless but loved a good joke and basked in the attention.

Or maybe I was ready for the intentional-family concept because that was how LGBTQ+ folks created families in the days before gay marriage and adoption by people in that community were legal. Whatever the reason, I was amazed at how fast Anthony's presence in our house began to make us feel like a family.

I had wanted for so many years to have children. We'd nearly gotten divorced over Venus's mostly hostile attitude toward it. When insemination didn't work and all the other avenues were blocked or too expensive, I reluctantly gave up. I channeled the emotional drive to parent into an interest in other people's children. I tried to help them, particularly the teenagers, but I always stood at an enormous distance from them.

■■■

Anthony needed that kind of young-adult nurturing. His mother, despite her own problems, did a great job in tremendously difficult circumstances raising him to be a kind and thoughtful person. She deeply loved him. But together they had experienced too much instability. Speaking euphemistically of his childhood, Anthony described it as chaotic. When he told her he was gay, at first she seemed to accept it. Later, as she drank, they argued, and she threw him out in a rage.

He needed a chance to discover who he was away from that turmoil. It may sound strange to say that Venus and I could be steady, reliable presences, but we were, especially when someone else needed us to be that way. Venus cheerfully helped Anthony troubleshoot his computer problems and talked to him about art. When Anthony got mugged waiting for a bus, Venus took charge and drove him to the emergency room. I saw all that familiar generosity and compassion in her that had gone absent in the hyperdriven band years return.

Eventually Anthony's relationship with his mother improved, but not enough for him to live with her again. His mother had essentially shoved him out of the nest, and it was what he needed to begin discovering who he was and who he could become. He finished college and earned a graduate degree in poetry.

I did what I could to let him reconcile his past with his dreams for the future. One day he came home with an old, black toaster, presenting it like a prize he had won. He'd bought a new toaster for his mother—maybe it was a Christmas present—and then asked cautiously if he could have the old one. He was thrilled that she said yes. As we set it up on the kitchen counter, he explained that he was sentimental about this black, scratched-up toaster full of permanently baked-in crumbs, an appliance older than he was, because it reminded him of his grandmother. She had passed away when he was a small child. He remembered her as the family stabilizer, a loving force who disappeared from his life too soon, someone whose strength he wanted to remember.

The next year, when I started planning the annual Christmas card, I thought of Anthony. For several years we'd made our own cards, often with little illustrations of the cats and horses. As the technology changed, we graduated to photo cards. Did Anthony want to be in the Christmas card this year? He did. We took several photos posing with the snowy front porch in the background, each of us holding a cat, all of us equally concerned about getting the look just right. Venus saved it by Photoshopping the best images together. From that point on, we all knew we were some kind of family.

Anthony with his mother at his graduation from Hamline University, 2015

The three of us introduced each other to new worlds. We went to the music recitals that Anthony sang in, and I read rough drafts of his early poems. We shared book recommendations, and he sometimes helped out at band events. I taught him how to ride a horse. It wasn't his favorite activity (too many mosquitos and other insects), but he got good enough so that when he fell off, which he did, he was able to get back on. I wanted him to learn that he didn't have to be afraid of things.

We helped him move his mother from the fourplex to a new apartment—a symbol of starting over for her because she had stopped drinking. As she and I sat next to each other in a row of plastic folding chairs set on a sunny lawn at Hamline for his college commencement, I'm sure she remembered his growth from the time he was a baby while I reflected on how much he'd bloomed in the last six years. But both of us had similar reactions when he walked across the stage in that distinctive, loping walk to receive the diploma for his BFA in creative writing. I felt a familiar knot of strong emotion welling in my throat and broke into tears. I looked at Anthony's mom next to me, and she was doing the same thing. We hugged and held to each other, speechless at our sudden welter of sobs, then laughed, then cried some more. I wasn't his mother. Maybe Venus and I were his supportive aunties.

38

■ ⋆ ▲ ✦ ✳ ■ ♠ • ■

2008–2009, Minneapolis

Somewhere along the line, the House of Flowers band quietly faded, having never developed its own signature, and All the Pretty Horses restarted, performing a Halloween show at the 331 in Minneapolis. I don't know if it was because I had more time to enjoy music during my sabbatical, or that Venus was less chaotic about band business than previously, but the restart of the Horses felt like a comfortable existence. Maybe with Anthony around, Venus was aware of the need to be a kind of role model. She seemed more grounded.

I was also more grounded in my creative life. I'd been selected as a mentee for a Writer to Writer series and met with friends in a writing group. We made short pilgrimages together, at one point trekking north to Collegeville to hear Donald Hall read at a local college. My friend Jules Nyquist suggested visiting the graves of famous writers, and we took to lying on the ground beside their headstones, cuddling up to the dead poets. The scent of cut grass and damp soil tugged at me, telling me to hurry up and do more.

The most famous local poet whose grave we visited was John Berryman, who leapt to his death off the Washington Avenue Bridge between the University of Minnesota's East and West Bank campuses. He was buried in a cemetery on the outskirts of

St. Paul next to his mother, with an obscure flat headstone that sank below the turf line. I asked one of my graduate school professors what Berryman had been like. Marty Roth didn't have to think long before responding, "Berryman was an alcoholic. All alcoholics are assholes." I had hoped for something more, but it was hard to argue with him. Around a self-destructive person, there was always collateral damage.

Venus's and my relationship had weathered a lot of that kind of damage, and it seemed we'd made it through to the other side. Venus was happy to be playing with Trever Hawley, a new drummer who was a quick learner and instinctively knew what kind of sound the music needed. Even better, he was a genuinely nice man.

Chi Chi Valenti, creator of the nightclub Mother we'd visited so many years earlier, invited the Horses to play for a new installment of Click and Drag in Lower Manhattan. Venus was able to make it work with just herself and Trever. Mother had closed by then, and Chi Chi now spent her time promoting themed extravaganzas like Night of 1000 Stevies around New York and beyond. Trever brought a boyfriend, and the four of us walked the city, looking at the lights in Times Square and taking in New York's preholiday glow. Click and Drag was a carnival of elaborate costumes and booming music, with a ghostly gothic ambience lit by hundreds of little tealights. Venus and Trever as a two-person version of the Horses killed it.

In February of 2009, Venus went with me to Chicago for the Association of Writers and Writing Programs conference, an enormous writers' convention, attending several events; we talked about writing and our plans for the day, separated to explore our own curiosities, then orbited back to each other later.

A month later we flew to Phoenix, rented a car, and drove to Bisbee for the Venus's Boudoir gig, where the collaboration felt effortless, even joyful. With Gretchen, Wendy, and a few other new friends, we climbed the mountain at the far end of Old Town Bisbee. When we got to the top, where previous climbers

Gretchen, Venus, and Lynette striking poses on Bisbee Mountain, wearing masks Gretchen brought along, 2009

had erected various shrines over the years, Gretchen handed around several animal masks she'd brought along. We donned them, striking curious poses around the boulders. Venus played the lion, the ruler of the mountain, and we roared along with her. She was usually so preoccupied with all the things that might go wrong, but now she laughed, smiled, and roared. I felt in tune with her.

Sometime during that March trip to Arizona, we were hanging out in the late morning at Paul Tibbles's house in Phoenix, the one with the orange tree. Venus came back to the living room from checking her email to say she'd just gotten a message from Mary Lucia, who was inviting the band to do another Rock for Pussy show.

"Wow, that's great!" Mary Lucia seemed to like the band, but Venus sensed there were other people involved who weren't happy with her presence. So each year we'd wondered whether she'd get the call.

"I know," she said, "but now I have to figure out what Bowie song we'll cover before someone else nabs it."

"Do 'Heroes.'" I don't know why I suggested that one. Every year I had a strong feeling that Venus should do a particular Bowie song. Sometimes she followed my suggestion, sometimes she didn't.

"I don't know . . ." came the answer. This was her standard reply to any musical suggestion. It didn't bother me. She had to think it through.

She rebutted soon after with another suggestion, a process we'd gotten used to doing. Venus was more often intrigued by the songs that hadn't been big hits. If she was going to do a cover, she wanted to make her own version of it, so that meant reimagining the song, stripping it down to its bare bones, then fitting it to her vocal range and guitar style.

Once Mary sent out the email, everyone would claim a song. Most participants were just singing, with the well-practiced house band backing them. But Venus had always chosen the long way around. It started because she hadn't felt comfortable with the usual way of participating with the backup band. Most participants played pretty much what you heard on the record, making it easy for a vocalist to learn the part without more than a final run-through before the show. But since Venus preferred making her own arrangements of the songs, partly to play to her strengths and partly because the rearrangement felt more like her own piece of art, she'd asked a few years ago if her own band could play on the piece. The organizers decided the only convenient time would be in the middle of the show, when the house band took its break. The tradition of the halftime show was born.

Coming from a performance-art background, Venus always made it more than a music event. There were costumes, dancers, bubble guns, people handing out roses to the audience, large balloons bouncing around, and more. When I watched them rock out "Fame" the previous year, dancers and extras whirled around onstage with cameras, playing traffic cops and paparazzi. I loved it, then felt an unfamiliar ache: I wanted to be included. I tried to reject the sensation of feeling left out because it made no sense. It wasn't as if I'd asked to join them and been rejected. I could have been a go-go dancer any time I wanted, yet I didn't feel confident enough about my body to be onstage like that. I felt conflicted about how people would see me versus how I wanted to be seen. It also just wasn't a way I wanted to express myself.

I wanted to be part of the creative process on some level— the sounds, the words—but I had never wanted to be in the band. It seemed Venus's approach and mine were too different to make it fun. The collaborative approach that I learned playing jazz was my gold standard, and realistically, I could never give up large chunks of time for rehearsals and touring. I had other things I wanted to do, as well as the things I *had* to do to keep a roof over our heads and the lights on. Every year at Rock for Pussy, the band knocked it out of the ballpark. Now, I began to fantasize about being a part of it in some way.

Shortly after we got home, Venus confided, almost as an aside, that she'd volunteered to do "Heroes."

"Great! That feels like the perfect song for right now."

"Yeah, but there's a complication."

"What?"

The problem was that the band was scheduled to do a residency the same month at First Avenue's side bar, the Seventh Street Entry. She couldn't reschedule this close to the event.

"Oh no! Does this mean . . .?"

"It's okay, sort of. Our residency nights are Thursdays, and Rock for Pussy is a Friday."

"God, that's lucky."

"Yeah, but it's going to be crazy for me. I already have to rehearse a different line-up for each week at the Entry." I nodded, remembering. The residency concept had been brilliant: four nights of songs from the first four professionally produced All the Pretty Horses albums, with guest spots from musicians who had been in the band for those albums. They were people who hadn't performed with Venus in years. The early plan had been for each line-up to re-create the whole album the musicians had been a part of. That plan soon got scaled back. Former band members didn't want to relearn a whole set. There wasn't enough rehearsal time. "And then there's learning the new song for Rock for Pussy," Venus continued. "You know, I think I'd like you to play violin on it."

"Are you . . . are you sure?" I wanted to make sure she wasn't following a sudden impulse she would later regret. The tag-team approach with music and poetry worked, but this was different. I was a pretty mediocre violin player. I knew what notes to play, but my fingers didn't move fast. I prayed we could come up with a line that wasn't literally too much of a stretch for my hand.

"Yes, I think this will work," she smiled. "The song really calls for it."

I was giddy with the prospect of once again being on the inside of a musical collaboration with her.

Sometime in the next month Venus pointed out that Pandora would be playing for one of the nights of the residency at the Entry. Of course Venus had been aware of this all along, but she waited to tell me only after Pandora agreed. I felt some phantom bully shove a heavy object against my stomach. It was irrational, but something levitated from my body memory and shot me back to a manacled time where I cowered in the shadow of a grocery store on the corner of Twenty-Fifth and Third, longing for shelter and kindness, wondering what to do next.

I'd seen Pandora only once since she left the band, at a memorial for her ex-boyfriend, Stefan Olson. As we walked slowly along the receiving line after the service, I could see that she felt genuine distress at Stefan's death. I'd imagined the strain, the anguish of losing someone you were estranged from but had loved, perhaps still loved, and her sorrow shot through me. Without thinking, I reached out to hug her. This time, she didn't go stiff. She didn't exactly hug me back, but her arms tilted forward toward my sides. I didn't sense the same hardness in her. I mumbled something about condolences. It'd lasted only a moment, all I could handle, and perhaps all she could handle. Now Venus was explaining that Pandora would play with the band again. My stomach churned as I imagined the rehearsals. Telling Venus how I felt about that period of our lives had never worked. I decided to power through it. I detached, and some kind of automaton version of me sat in the kitchen and agreed that there was no threat. That moment at Stefan's memorial had done nothing to relieve my anxiety over what I still perceived as her strange power over my marriage. My skin and bones could hold and contain me, but inside a seething mass kept writhing.

Another worry developed a few weeks later. We didn't have any rehearsals scheduled for the cameo, and no rehearsals meant no arrangement, nothing I could practice on. The residency rehearsals didn't start until sometime in late April due to everyone's availability and Venus's calendar of other gigs. I was happy to let the other musicians negotiate their own issues with time, but I needed something to start working with, something that gave me a chance to think about what might work.

"So when are you going to have an outline for how 'Heroes' works?"

"I just got back from the Duluth show. Soon. There's plenty of time."

A few days later: "Have you thought much about the arrangement for 'Heroes' yet? I was just wondering what I should plan for."

"We just got back from the Winona show. It'll be soon. I'll have something."

A week later: "So, any progress on the arrangement for 'Heroes'? I'm worried because I need some time to get up to speed."

"Right. I'm just bringing Bill in for the first album in the Seventh Street Entry line-up. I do miss playing with him."

"Yeah, you guys always blended together so well. Even the vocals."

"But he isn't drumming anymore. He's still on top of everything, but he doesn't want to be in bands anymore. Hey, I need to tell you what's going on with him . . ."

Another week passed. While Venus was downtown at a rehearsal for the second-album group, *Queens and Angels*, I pulled out my violin, punched up the "Heroes" track in the dining room, and started messing around with ideas as I listened to it. Venus might change the key and would definitely alter the arrangement, but at least I had an idea of what might work. When she got home from rehearsal with the *Queens and Angels* group, I mentioned what I'd done.

"Okay, fine, but it's all going to change anyway."

"I know, I know, but I just want to get a sense of what the possibilities are. I don't play violin every day. I'm just starting to get the callouses on my fingers back. If you want me to sound decent and not mess up, I need more time to practice."

"Oh. Okay." She gave a sigh of resignation and bent down to rummage through some papers in the beat-up olive drab pack she carried, found the lyric sheet, then walked over to pick up her guitar case from where it rested against the dining room wall. She hauled it to the couch, unbuckled the latches, and carried the guitar to the opposite couch and sat down, experimenting with a few notes. Relieved, I went upstairs to work on the content for an upcoming class.

Pandora was scheduled to play a few songs Thursday, the night before Rock for Pussy, with the line-up for *Ruin*. She'd been able to make only two rehearsals and wasn't playing the whole set. I repeatedly ran up and down the stairs between the Entry's basement dressing room and the main level, getting various items Venus requested. I dreaded seeing Pandora.

I ran down the stairs for the third or fourth time, and finally she was there, holding her bass, sitting next to her boyfriend, a guy who reminded me of her first husband. She looked great, as usual. Chaotic fears buzzed like a hive of hornets inside me. But she also seemed uncomfortable. We looked at each other hesitantly, and one or both of us said hello and gave a quick smile. Then I turned to face Venus and made myself chatter about something I was helping with. I was determined to demonstrate to Pandora and the universe that I had never been a drag on the band, that I had in fact been doing everything I fucking could to help it succeed. Then I gave another quick nod of acknowledgment to her and escaped up the stairs.

■ ■ ■

I wish I could say this was the moment I finally realized she had no power over me and that I could forgive her. It wasn't.

That wouldn't happen for another ten years. My life with Venus
would develop a pleasant rhythm: I would publish a couple of
poetry books, and Venus would continue with music and performance art projects. Everyone would know her as Venus de
Mars and use she/her pronouns for her. I would continue to use
the name Venus when talking about her with other people, but
thinking of her as Venus still swept me back to a painful past.

And then, in 2018, Venus announced to me that she was
going to have gender confirmation surgery and legally change
her name to Venus de Mars.

Her decision was definitely an announcement. We had no
discussion leading up to it, no easing into the topic, and there
had been no asking what my feelings were. She expected me to
argue and reject her.

Of course I didn't, but we needed to figure out what brought
us back to places like this. Venus's manner in communicating,
almost defiant, made me question everything I thought I could
rely on. If she could spend decades saying she *didn't* want the
surgery and that I could call her by her former name, what else
might she change her mind about? Would she suddenly decide
she didn't love me anymore?

She got a court date for the legal name and gender change
within months of her telling me. I felt guilt-ridden that I
couldn't attend because she'd scheduled it on a critical teaching day. I was also bitter because it seemed she hadn't *wanted*
to share it with me. It felt like the worst days of my experiences
with the band all over again, but it wasn't the band anymore,
it was something else that I couldn't name. At least she col-
laborated with me on scheduling the surgery when it became
clear that I would need to take time off work to be with her
at the Mayo Clinic in Rochester and also to take care of her
post-surgery.

We needed months of hard conversations to recover my trust
in our relationship and forge a path forward. For once, our conversations were mediated by a therapist who didn't need us to

explain the transgender experience. The world had changed, and our therapist had worked with many trans clients, enough so that she could tell that Venus's being trans wasn't our central issue. The process we went through with her was *not* equivalent to ripping off a bandage to let an open wound bleed a little. It was more like taking the broken bone of our relationship that had somehow healed crooked and shattering it all over again to set it right. I didn't think Venus was going to stick with the sessions, but she did.

We realized that the problem so many years ago was not so much Pandora, or even the band. Venus had put Pandora and others into the role they were in to distract herself from her real feelings. Growing up at a time when it wasn't acceptable to be transgender, and feeling there was something inherently wrong with her, imprinted her with self-hatred. Even after coming out and being accepted by many people, she experienced powerful surges of feeling unlovable and sought validation from the stage and fans. I certainly understood that part of it. But when she wasn't absorbing a rush of love and acceptance from the stage, she sometimes projected her feelings of self-loathing onto me. In that logic, even when I said I loved her and stayed with her, she feared I would probably eventually leave her. Therefore, the argument ran, she should get ready for me to reject her by rejecting me first. That was what she steeled herself for and half expected when she announced her plans for surgery and everything that went along with it.

■■■

It must have felt very strange for Pandora at the Seventh Street Entry, entering into this charged past. I wonder if in the year and a half that she remained in the band after our blowout she sensed a slippage from the pedestal Venus had put her on. The night she walked out, she had been angry that Venus made negative assumptions about her. It was the same kind of thing

Venus sometimes projected onto me. But neither Pandora nor I had anything to do with this. It was something Venus would have to work on: finding an *internal* basis for self-esteem.

Pandora left immediately after the Entry performance. There was no lingering after the show to reminisce with fans and other band members. At the time, that was as much closure as I could expect. My fever of anxiety calmed. Venus and I had no arguments, and, more important, I hadn't felt cast aside. We were going to be okay. Maybe.

"When is sound check?" I asked the next morning, ready to get on with what I considered the big show, the one *I* would perform in. Mainstage, First Avenue.

"Oh, I don't know if we'll get a sound check," Venus responded.

"What?!?"

"Well, you know the house band, they kind of have their own concerns."

"Yeah, but you've got all these musicians, you've got all this equipment you've got to position onstage. They need that worked out ahead of time, right?"

"Yeah, but . . . I don't know. I don't think they like us." I realize now that perhaps she was rejecting them before they had the chance to reject her. At the time, what she said struck me as unreasonable. I decided to plan for sound check and get there early.

We did get a sound check in the late afternoon, and the engineer was efficient and kind about making sure I knew to position my violin just below the mic. I was ready. I knew the notes and, back home for a last-minute change of clothes, discovered a patent leather motorcycle jacket Venus hardly ever wore in one of our closets. I could wear it for the show. It was roomy enough to bow in and had a relaxed, cool-glam vibe. Venus meanwhile was gathering items for her costume, including some bare branches from the bushes in front of our house that she'd put in her hair for a previous show. Holding them over a slab of cardboard in the basement, she'd methodically misted them silver with spray paint. When tucked into her hair, already up in punky pigtails, the twigs seemed like antlers.

Anthony was also pacing back and forth, coming downstairs to ask for advice on some kind of wardrobe question, then running back upstairs to try something different. Shy as he was, Anthony had volunteered to be one of the dancers onstage and was trying for a suitable goth-glam look. He eventually settled on a black skirt, fishnets, and heels borrowed from Venus, with black lipstick and a thick, black, cock-feather boa that gleamed in the light.

As I sat in the kitchen waiting for the three of us to get in the van and head downtown, I ran over my part in my head. The piece itself, while anthemic, is pretty much the same verse and chorus over and over. Venus's method for keeping it interesting was to start slow and quiet, then build. She'd be solo most of the first verse and chorus, with me adding slow, high-pitched, wispy violin harmonics near the end of the first chorus. Then the other musicians would begin to come onstage, building more volume and power. Several dancers, including Anthony, would come out just past the midway point and start whirling handheld beacons, whipping up the energy to the triumphant end.

At halftime, the large movie screen came down. We waited next to the stairs for the previous performers to come off the stage. When we were cleared to go, we shot up the stairs to our places, instruments and stage props in hand. Within a minute, it seemed, the stage lighting dimmed and the screen began to roll up. A spotlight focused on Venus, the rest of the stage still dark, and the audience quieted. She played a verse with just the guitar for the intro, then started singing the first line. I could hear a few cheers from the audience as they began to recognize the song. More cheers rose from the audience as Venus sang the next few lines, lines about two people who could overcome the odds together. I tucked my violin under my chin and began to silently find my first note, pressing my finger to the string and listening for its tiny reverberation, using the ambient light bouncing off Venus to see. Then I began the off-kilter harmonics.

I later learned that the lyrics were inspired by watching two lovers kiss next to the Berlin Wall. It felt like we'd been through that kind of oppression, with people trying to build a wall between us. Venus must have felt the same way, because when she got to the end of the first verse, she gave me a quick look to see if I got it. I did.

She launched into the second verse and continued to glance over to me, now singing about the kinds of arguments couples have, the arguments that lovers have. So many crappy—and, to my mind, unnecessary—arguments persisted between us, and here that same dynamic was being described in a song. But maybe the arguments happened because we continued to love each other fiercely. It was how two independent people had to work things out.

Raymond on lead guitar joined us with a distortion line, emulating the familiar hook. I kept on with my unsettling harmonics a while longer. It felt right. And the rest of the band started slowly coming in, a slow ramping up of sound. As the volume mounted toward the chorus, Venus kept looking back at me and probably couldn't see my nod, curled as I was over the violin. *Yes, we can do this!* my brain shouted.

By now, the dancers were coming out of the background, waving their searchlights, some handing out roses to the audience. I could see Anthony at the other end of the stage, black boa feathers shining in the lights. He was syncing with the other dancers, following Dawn McCool's prompts about handing out the roses. *What a great kid*, I thought. I had moved into long, low bow strokes with occasional harmonics and low, punctuated rhythm. I couldn't hear myself anymore, a phenomenon Venus had often described to me, so I watched my fingers to

Lynette on violin with Raymond Breed, 2009. Photo by Joe Szurszewski

make sure the right note was sounding somewhere out there in massive stage speakers.

We hit the final flourish and then the song was over, its echoes melding into the shouts and applause of the crowd. Then we all hopped off the stage even faster than we'd come onto it, giddy with adrenaline, making room for the house band. Back in the dressing room, I smiled at Anthony and Venus. We'd done it. Anthony didn't want to go out into the audience, feeling self-conscious, and chose to hang in back with the other dancers. That was fine. We both gave him long, sweaty hugs, then Venus and I clasped each other's hand and headed out into the audience to watch the second half of the night from the floor. It was time for us to enjoy it together.

Acknowledgments

This book could not have been written without the generous support of a community of writers. Abundant thanks go to the people in various writing groups who gave me feedback and encouragement, among them Kara Garbe Balcerzak, Kris Bigalk (who started it all by repeatedly urging me to write this story!), Josh Cook, Amy Fladeboe, Jonathan Heide, Melody Heide, Bronson Lerner, Samantha Ten Eyck, and Richard Terrill. I am also grateful for my Bosso Poetry Company family who listened to parts of the narrative in draft form and reassured me that they wanted to hear more. Special thanks also go to Patricia Weaver Francisco, who mentored me through many of the hard, early stages of this book, Jaime Karpovich, who gave me kind and invaluable editing feedback, and Anthony Ceballos, who graciously helped with fact-checking and word-smithing. I am also grateful for the talent and support of my fabulous editors at Minnesota Historical Society Press: Ann Regan, Em Poupart, Shannon Pennefeather, and freelancer Jill Twist. Special thanks are also due to the Minnesota State Arts Board for an Artist Initiative Grant that helped me move from early stages of this book to a complete draft, and the Writers House (Kirjailijatalo) in Jyväskylä, Finland, which provided a place to write without distractions.

Finally, I want to thank Venus de Mars, whose unflinching support for my writing kept me going. Excavating a buried past was a hard process for both of us. Thank you so much, Venus, for your willingness to look back on this with me to get the story right. You truly are the love of my life.

Wild Things has been set in Sirba, a typeface designed by
Nicolien van der Keur and published by Type Together.

Book design by Wendy Holdman